Bowling Psychology

Dean Hinitz

Human Kinetics

Library of Congress Cataloging-in-Publication Data

Names: Hinitz, Dean R., author.
Title: Bowling psychology / Dean Hinitz, PhD.
Other titles: Focused for bowling.
Description: Champaign, IL : Human Kinetics, [2016] | Includes
  bibliographical references and index.
Identifiers: LCCN 2015049770 | ISBN 9781492504085 (print)
Subjects: LCSH: Bowling--Psychological aspects.
Classification: LCC GV903 .H56 2016 | DDC 794.6--dc23 LC record available at https://lccn.loc.
gov/2015049770

This book is a revised edition of *Focused for Bowling*, published in 2003 by Dean Hinitz.

The web addresses cited in this text were current as of January 2016, unless otherwise noted.

Acquisitions Editor: Tom Heine; **Senior Managing Editor:** Amy Stahl; **Copyeditor:** John Wentworth; **Indexer:** Dan Connolly; **Permissions Manager:** Martha Gullo; **Graphic Designer:** Kathleen Boudreau-Fuoss; **Cover Designer:** Keith Blomberg; **Photograph (cover):** Justin Horrocks/iStock.com; **Photo Asset Manager:** Laura Fitch; **Photo Production Manager:** Jason Allen; **Art Manager:** Kelly Hendren; **Illustrations:** © Human Kinetics; **Printer:** Versa Press

Printed in the United States of America   10 9 8 7 6 5 4 3 2 1

The paper in this book is certified under a sustainable forestry program.

Human Kinetics
Website: www.HumanKinetics.com

United States: Human Kinetics
P.O. Box 5076
Champaign, IL 61825-5076
800-747-4457
e-mail: info@hkusa.com

Canada: Human Kinetics
475 Devonshire Road Unit 100
Windsor, ON N8Y 2L5
800-465-7301 (in Canada only)
e-mail: info@hkcanada.com

Europe: Human Kinetics
107 Bradford Road
Stanningley
Leeds LS28 6AT, United Kingdom
+44 (0) 113 255 5665
e-mail: hk@hkeurope.com

Australia: Human Kinetics
57A Price Avenue
Lower Mitcham, South Australia 5062
08 8372 0999
e-mail: info@hkaustralia.com

New Zealand: Human Kinetics
P.O. Box 80
Mitcham Shopping Centre, South Australia 5062
0800 222 062
e-mail: info@hknewzealand.com

E6412

To those who enter and walk on the path of mastery,
it is no easy trek.
The trolls are often disguised, and the guides and teachers
are commonly in hidden form as well.
The journey is challenging.
But beyond the periodic pain and discouragement
is a payoff that has been lauded throughout the ages.
The journey really is the destination.
This book is dedicated to all of you who take it on.
You are in special company.

Contents

Foreword by Jason Belmonte vi

Acknowledgments x

Introduction: The Road to Championship Play xi

Chapter 1   Goal Setting and Self-Assessment 1

Learn the essentials of goal setting and the ingredients to craft
a clear vision for your game.

Chapter 2   Thinking Like a Champion 20

Explore the secrets of a champion mindset. Learn to develop
the traits, personality characteristics, and thinking modes of
championship players.

Chapter 3   Establishing Your Preshot Routine....................... 37

Learn to design and implement a powerful, effective preshot
routine.

Chapter 4   The Shot Cycle: One Shot for the Money 49

Dial in the essential elements for delivering your best shot
under any circumstance. Learn the keys to managing
excitement and mastering the competition to create your
customized shot cycle.

Chapter 5   Toughness to Overcome Adversity 70

Develop mental toughness, and take an inventory to see where
you stand. Learn to autograph your shot in the heat of
competition.

Chapter 6   Mental Secrets to Making Spares......................94

Learn to be a great spare shooter. Absorb detailed tips, strategies, and systems to make spare shooting work for you.

Chapter 7   Raising Peaks and Filling Valleys 116

Bust your slumps by fighting your way through tough times. Discover ways to come out on top of any challenging situation.

Chapter 8   Team Building 151

Learn what makes a world-class team, how to train like world-class teams, and the best strategies for improved teamwork and communication.

Chapter 9   Coaching and Raising a Champion 171

Read the cardinal features of successful coaching and effective parenting for athletes.

Chapter 10   Putting It All Together to Play Boldly 194

Combine all you've learned to play boldly at will. Overcome the seven deadly sins of bowling on your way to becoming a bomb-proof bowler.

Bibliography 224

Index..226

About the Author 232

Foreword

Welcome to *Bowling Psychology*. You're about to join me on a journey with Dr. Dean Hinitz. Each of you reading this is on your own championship path. And much like me, you'll have to carve out the individual footsteps toward your goals.

Your mental game is as individual as your fingerprints. Clarifying, enhancing, and honing it is a significant part of the ticket to championship play. I have known Dr. Dean since I came to the United States to play on the PBA Tour. As much as I have enjoyed our discourses over the years, I know that you're going value your time with him in this book as well.

A champion's story is written on the pages of your practices, your challenges, your resilience, and your resolve. In this book, Dr. Dean will help you to author the outcomes you intend to have. This book is an invitation to join me in exploring how one transforms into a champion.

People are often curious about the origins of my two-handed delivery, and the path of my championship journey. In truth, a journey that has been extraordinary has pretty ordinary roots.

My bowling story started very simply. My parents built a bowling center when I was barely six weeks old. They were not bowlers. In fact, neither had ever rolled a bowling ball. Rather, they built the center as a business opportunity. There I was, an 18-month-old, with nothing better to do than to try to roll a bowling ball. Of course, I was not strong enough to hoist the ball in a conventional fashion. So I intuitively did the only thing that remained to me. I learned to roll and control the ball with two hands.

I did not know right from left or one hand from two at that age. And no one told me that I could not play that way. And no one told me that I was doing anything wrong. That would come later. I was 19 years old before I learned that there was another two-handed player out there (PBA and World Ranking Masters champion Osku Palermaa).

I did have success early. By the time I was four years old I was playing competitively with older kids. That is when my mum and dad started to receive pressure to have me bowl conventionally. Thank goodness, what mattered most to them was that I was having fun, and that I was out of their hair in the bowling center. No one had a plan for me to be a tour player. They just made sure that I was having a good time.

Everything changed shortly thereafter. From the time I was five years old, up into my teens, I heard every day that I was throwing the ball wrong and that I would never be any good unless I changed. There are those who certainly tried to coach me out of my style of play. In fact, I tried to bowl one handed a couple of times, but the ball just went dead straight, and it wasn't fun for me.

Although there was pressure to change, there was no logical reason for me to do so other than to look like everyone else, and to be normal. Fortunately, I am stubborn. I'm not going to listen to anyone if I'm not clear that what he or she has to offer might help me. If someone tells me to do something different just because the way I do it isn't normal, I resist that. I think that great champions, leaders, and winners of anything have a similar quality. Being effective is more important than garnering the approval of everyone around you.

In the early part of my career, I had no aspirations to be the best bowler in the world. I was having fun and enjoying myself. But things sort of took off. I won my first doubles tournament at age 4. When I was 12 or 13, I was giving adults a run for their money. At age 14, I started playing for the adult Orange city team. We played other towns within a few hours' drive of Orange, and I was beating people 20 years or more older than me.

As far as I knew, I was the only one in the world playing the way I did. Certainly no one locally bowled with two hands. And not even anyone in Australia. Then I started to play internationally. At a youth tournament in Thailand I saw Osku Palermaa. By then, I was always the guy who hooked the ball the most, and who threw the most powerful messenger pins. I was shocked out of that reality. Simply put, Osku did everything more and better than I did. If not for Osku, I might not have progressed as I have.

I had to ask myself what I had to do to compete with him. We did become friends, and we developed a friendly rivalry. My bowling IQ went up. I no longer wanted to be the best two-hander in the world. I wanted to be the best bowler in the world.

There's an entire chapter in this book on goal setting. I have always set goals, and the goal to be the best in the world drove my work ethic. The question became "Whom do I have to beat, and what do I have to learn to beat him?" I believe that it is important to have goals. Mine was to be the best in the world. What's higher than that? Once I became player of the year, the goal advanced to retaining that. I have won three United States Bowling Congress (USBC) Masters titles in a row, yet I know that I have to learn more, and to not be satisfied with the place that I am in.

Dr. Hinitz teaches about mental toughness, and there have certainly been dark parts of my journey. I do something that used to be really unusual and different, and it still is. It was only when I had international and PBA success that more and more people tried bowling with two hands. Very early on, I had the support of my friends. But with success came resentment. People said that I was cheating. I had to sit down with the rule book and read it cover to cover to make sure I wasn't doing anything wrong.

Other issues came up. People suggested that my father put out an easy shot for me at our bowling center. I even had to check with my dad to make sure it was not true. Ironically, we had such an old simple lane-oiling machine that he couldn't have put a special shot out for anyone. When I won in other bowling centers, they had to find other reasons that I was winning. At 17 years old, I started running people over in national tournaments. But it was when I started to have success on the national level that I really felt resentment expressed toward me.

I have learned something about achieving goals and succeeding. When you come in last, people don't care about you. When you win some of the time, they notice you. When you win more, they start to care. If you really start to do well, the negativity then becomes intense and challenging.

I have had to hear derogatory quips and comments throughout my career. It didn't matter whatever I did sometimes. People couldn't make sense of how well I was doing. They didn't look at the immense amount of hard work I was putting in, or the effort I was putting into improving my mental game. It didn't seem to matter what I did—some would always assume I was doing something wrong.

At a deep level, it was difficult to be viewed in that manner. It hurt my soul. But if I could give anything away to up and coming players, it would be for an athlete to play to his or her own heart. You have to keep your focus on the game. I attended to the support I received among a special group that included my wife, my kids, my friends, and my fans. I had to let go of trying to impress or influence anyone else. And I certainly had to hold on to my sense of humor.

When I came onto the PBA Tour I was surprised in the beginning. I had thought that the lifestyle would be an easy transition from the European Tour. I was leaving a place where I had a lot of friends. Osku had already broken the ice in terms of two-handed play. I was given feedback that I would be a flash in the pan. I was told that after two or three events I would likely go and stay home, or that I would be a gimmick used only to generate publicity.

Well, I am no gimmick, and I didn't stay home. Far and away the most difficult thing for me has been to be apart from my family in Australia. But after that, it's not the nerves, it's not the financial pressure, it's the negativity that the worldcan deliver if you let it, that can be so challenging.

In *Bowling Psychology*, the essentials of thinking like a champion are seeded throughout the book. Here's one of the most important elements that one has to learn. There comes a point when you know yourself. There's a point when no matter what anyone says or does, you still bring the best version of the player you really are. I know how hard you have to work to make it out here. That is what you have to trust and to fall back on.

I strongly endorse setting goals. I have won the last three Masters Tournaments and the last two Tournaments of Champions. I won consecutive Player of the Year honors. Being the best player in the world is a lot to handle mentally sometimes. Now where is the bar? I'm the first person under that bar, so it is up to me to push it upward. There is no coasting. I have to make sure that if someone is going to beat me, they have to earn it.

This book guides you in becoming a champion. You have to understand that there is a part of the mental game that becomes part of your character. My story embodies it.

- You must be willing to go where you're going to go without any evidence that it can be done. This takes a profound belief in yourself.
- You have to reach for the stars even if no one agrees that you can do it.
- You have to persevere with or without the approval of others.
- The only authority you need in order to go forward is your own.

You can do what I have done. The arenas, the titles, the leagues, and so on might be different, but the path is the same. In this book you'll find tools and strategies as well as suggestions from great champions on how to achieve your goals. Whether the sun shines on you, or you have blood and tears on your face, never give up. I will be the first one there to congratulate you when you cross the finish line.

Jason Belmonte
Winner of 12 PBA titles, including six major tournaments, three-time PBA Player of the Year, two-time winner of the ESPY for Best Bowler

Acknowledgments

I wish to thank the hundreds of coaches, players, friends, and loved ones who contributed to *Bowling Psychology*. This book was written *through* me much more than *by* me. Rather than a formal focused effort, much of the material for *Bowling Psychology* was generated near ball returns, in between competition blocks, and in excited conversations about what does and does not work in competition.

I want to give special thanks to Fred Borden and Jeri Edwards for giving me a chance and a start with Team USA and to Rod Ross and Kim Kearney for our continued alliance with the national team. I am extremely appreciative of the sharing and friendship I have had over the years with coaches Gordon Vadakin, Mark Lewis, Dale Lehman, Del Warren, Randy Stoughton, Susie Minshew, Ron Hoppe, Sharon Brummell, Ken Yokobosky, Brian O'Keefe, Lou Marquez, Richard Shockley, Brent Sims, Kenny McPartlin, and Ron Bruner.

There are more players, league mates, coaches, and friends in the bowling universe than I could reasonably thank here. Many of you gave direct quotes and interviews in this book. I sincerely hope all of you recognize yourselves in these pages.

The staff at Human Kinetics instructed, guided, and prompted the completion of this work. Special thanks to Tom Heine and Amy Stahl.

My mom annoyed me my entire life with her insistence on proper grammar, proper speech, and overall etiquette. Now, of course, I am profoundly grateful to her. Her grace and wisdom have become like compass points for me. The memory of my father, David, is still the North Star with respect to integrity issues. My sisters Jill and Connie are like safety nets in the stormy seas of daily life.

Steve Graybar and Gary Atkinson should bill me for all of the consultation, sharing, and friendship I have exacted from them. Anne Archer has been perhaps my greatest teacher, helping me to relearn who I am and to see beyond "the matrix" in order to live authentically.

Introduction: The Road to Championship Play

**Perhaps we'll never know how far the path can go,
how much a human being can truly achieve,
until we realize that the ultimate reward
is not a gold medal but the path itself.**

George Leonard, *Mastery: The Keys to Success and Long-Term Fulfillment*

Welcome to championship bowling! Since the publication of *Focused for Bowling* in 2003, I've had the opportunity to work with thousands of players in a variety of contexts. The past decade has been a research and development process in which the principles and suggestions from the first book could be road tested for practicality and validity.

The results have been remarkable. Using tools from *Focused for Bowling*, I've been invited to be part of numerous national collegiate champion teams, to work with many professional tour players, and to see several of those players inducted into the USBC Hall of Fame. I've had the honor of being the sport psychologist for Team USA. During those years, the United States bowling team has set records for medals and scoring at virtually every international competition in which they've been engaged.

More than anything, however, I've had the privilege of working with many of you reading this book at clinics and conferences from the East Coast to the West Coast and throughout middle America. *Bowling Psychology* is dedicated as much to the everyday man and woman as it is to the elite world-class player. The book will take you as a player to the top of whatever competitive mountain you wish to climb. The same mental game strategies that the most esteemed bowling stars use are available to you here.

The universal rules for success are house rules. What works for the superstars works for everyone. Fortunately, we have access to a lot of proven champions. In *Bowling Psychology* you'll find interviews, tips, and quips from many of the greatest players ever to shoe up.

These elite players are not physically different from you. Bowling is unique in that there's no ideal body type. We have Norm Duke, small in stature but among the most prolific titlists of all time, and Wes Malott, a giant by comparison. Both have been players of the year. We have the slightly-built tensile strength of Carolyn Dorin-Ballard alongside athletic Kelly Kulick. Chris Barnes could have excelled in any sport (and did as a youth). Kim Kearney declared she was going to the Olympics in *something*. She did it as a bowler. There are many potentially successful body types. But there's not a lot of variation in championship consciousness. Winners tend to think, practice, and compete in similar ways.

What makes the greats great is an overriding intention to achieve to the maximum of their potential. Do you have that? This is not a question of who wants it most. If wanting were the key, everyone would have titles. Wanting is not in short supply. What *is* in short supply are the consistency, dedication, and intention that carry you past the stumbling blocks.

You must get past fatigue and past the periodic disappointments of attempting to master this game. It's easy to train when the bowling gods smile on you. It's quite another thing when you haven't won in a while, or *ever*, or when you've been hurt, or when it seems as if you can never get your competition nerves under control.

I'm often asked how much of bowling is mental. The answer, for starters, is that the game is 100 percent physical. Bowling involves a ball, a body, lanes, oil, and pins. These things move in relation to each other. There's no game without them. In this sense, bowling is physical.

Concurrently, bowling is 100 percent mental. Every time you attempt to learn a new skill or to tune up an established skill, you are focusing on an aspect of your game. The key here is that you are *focusing*, an essential mental game skill. When you choose a ball to use on a particular lane's oil pattern, when you pick a line to play, or when you make sure that you are set before you push the ball away, you are *choosing* and committing. These are vital mental game qualities. When you tense up, it is mental, as it is when you relax.

Nothing happens in bowling if you don't show up with your brain, your mind, and your heart. The psychology of bowling is the psychology of life. The house rules are identical. What works in bowling works everywhere. What works in any other aspect of life works in bowling. If you discover some discrepancy in this, recheck your figures. You'll find that the principles involved in intention, commitment, focus, and freedom apply not only to bowling but to success in general.

The challenges involved in the evolving game of bowling, and advances in some of the technology of sports psychology, have demanded a continuous update of the way bowling is played from a mental point of view. *Bowling Psychology* provides significant updates, accents, and new chapters from

Focused for Bowling. Interviews with top players illustrate the application of many of the main points and skills.

You do not need to read this book sequentially chapter by chapter. Reading it in sequence will certainly provide you with the terms and concepts used in later chapters, but the design of the book is to allow you to quickly tune in to any particular area of interest or concern.

Chapter 1 is Goal Setting and Self-Assessment. It's said that it is hard to hit a target with your eyes closed. In this chapter you will clarify where you're going with your game. Goals are important. Living, or bowling, without goals is like boarding an airplane randomly. You know you're going somewhere, but you don't know where. You can only hope it's somewhere rewarding. If you don't pick your destination, and how you'll get there, you leave too much to chance. You can do better. The in-depth interview with Hall of Famer Kim Kearney will highlight this process.

Chapter 2, Thinking Like a Champion, brings you into the mind of a champion. This all-new section lists the traits, personality characteristics, and thinking modes of championship players. You can self-identify where you stand with respect to your own championship qualities. Are champions born or made? Make no mistake, you would never have mastered walking and turning door knobs if you didn't have it in you to keep striving. We just get discouraged along the way. In this chapter you'll get a glimpse into the thought processes of three-time Three-time PBA Player of the Year and Master's champion Jason Belmonte.

Chapter 3 is a visit with a vital old friend, the preshot routine. The preshot routine is your home away from home. Adding to this revised chapter from *Focused for Bowling* is Carolyn Dorin-Ballard, Hall of Famer, International Gold Medalist, and two-time PWBA Player of the Year, as she shares her preparatory shot routines. You will, of course, design your own.

Chapter 4, The Shot Cycle, is a revision of the original work from *Focused for Bowling.* I have learned that a key step that's essential for learning, emotion management, and improvement must be added to the execution of a shot, a frame, and a tournament block. USBC Queens and World Ranking Masters champion Diandra Asbaty is one of the great international amateur bowlers of all time. She shares how the application of the shot cycle formula carried her through a phenomenal career that has seen her win championships at virtually every level.

Are you tough enough? Some would say mental toughness is the *sine qua non* of the championship player. In chapter 5, Toughness to Overcome Adversity, you get to conceptualize toughness and see how you stack up. The annals of bowling are rife with players who had to battle adversity and injury to reclaim their place among the hall of champions. See if you have what it takes. Hear from tour players themselves about how they wrestled with their particular demons. Rick Steelsmith discusses his journey from masters' champion, to injury, to return to the professional tour and induction into the USBC Hall of Fame.

Over time, no one can strike enough to make up for missed spares. Spare shooting is the single most-cited reason for made and missed tournament advancement cuts, as well as championships, at both the individual and (especially) team level. Chapter 6, Mental Secrets to Making Spares, is a combination of mental game strategies, such as focus and concentration, and formulas, such as pure intention for shot making. PBA and Team USA star Bill O'Neill shares his insights about his rock-solid spare game. In addition, U.S. Gold coach Susie Minshew details her spare-shooting systems to provide you with an extremely user-friendly mechanism to confidently make great spare shots. The professionals must make spares for a living, and as PBA champion Patrick Healy Jr. once said, "I can't afford to spot 11 pins to anyone out here."

Anyone who plays the game for any length of time experiences highs and lows. Sometimes those lows are pretty hard to work through. In chapter 7, Raising Peaks and Filling Valleys, I address the issue of burnout and discuss how to work through and out of slumps. Mike Fagan is one player who had an early promise of success, followed by significant gaps in winning. Ultimately, Mike prevailed to win both the USBC Masters and the PBA World Championship. In this chapter Mike shares part of his journey with us.

Chapter 8 is a new section on team building, an understudied aspect of our game. Team play occurs at every level of bowling. The highlight of bowling league for most players is the team that they play with. Women's bowling is one of the fastest-growing sports in college athletics. Collegiate bowling, both NCAA and club, is one of the most exciting venues for team competition, rivaling international play. Even at the professional level, teams have been assembled to provide an interesting alternative to traditional individual play.

Doubles play is a popular tournament format as well. Virtually all the constructs from larger team play will apply for you as you enter yourself as a double.

In working with Team USA and many collegiate champion teams, some of the dos and don'ts of bowling effectively with fellow players have emerged. You will have the opportunity to translate the ingredients of top team play to your league, high school, college, or national team. Gordon Vadakin, head coach at Wichita State University, has won more collegiate titles than anyone in history. In this chapter he shares insights about his road to success.

Another addition to the original book is chapter 9, Coaching and Raising a Champion. Most coaching instruction focuses on skill development. By contrast, in this chapter we explore ways that coaches and parents help and hinder the development and performance of athletes, both children and adults. This is accomplished from a relational skill, as opposed to a physical skill, perspective.

At tournaments and clinics, some of the best-attended and energized presentations I've done have been in this area. Many who are in leadership positions have shown a commitment to the latest technology concerning effective coaching and parenting of athletes. Jeri Edwards, former head coach of Team USA and current head coach of the Puerto Rican national team, shares a special section for coaches: Making Parents Your Allies.

Chapter 10 is probably the chapter to reprint and put in your bowling bag. Putting It All Together to Play Boldly is every bowler's intention, and this chapter shows you how. You'll learn how to embrace competition, orient your thinking, and use the mental strategies that pros use to achieve success. This chapter includes a summary of the book's central points, and promotes putting together everything you've learned in the previous chapters. We'll hear from Hall of Famers like Jason Couch and Amleto Monicelli about mental game tips that helped to build their careers. The chapter includes 10 mental game recommendations from some of the greatest players and coaches in the game.

Make this book your roadmap to championship play. In any journey there are easy and pleasurable portions, and there are steep hills. There is sunny weather mixed with squalls. Sometimes we stumble. The incredible feeling of mastering new skills, and reaping successes, reminds us of the value of working our way through the tough parts of the adventure. The beauty of this enterprise is that it's a perfect mirror. You get out of it almost exactly what you put in.

You have made it this far. Lace up your shoes, check your gear, put your intention into drive, and let's walk the road to championship play together.

Not I, nor anyone else can travel that road for you.
You must travel it by yourself. It is not far. It is within reach.
Perhaps you have been on it since you were born, and did not know.
Perhaps it is everywhere—on water and land.

Walt Whitman, author, *Leaves of Grass*

CHAPTER 1

Goal Setting and Self-Assessment

**The game has its ups and downs,
but you can never lose focus of your individual goals,
and you can't let yourself be beat because of lack of effort.**

Michael Jordan, six-time NBA champion

Tell me what you want. Then let me follow you around for three days, and I will tell you whether or not you are likely to get it. In fact, I will invite you into the bleacher seats with me to watch yourself in action. And we can reflect together on what works, and what does not. Your words, your habits, and your commitments will provide all the clues we need.

It has been said that knowledge is power. But if knowledge were enough, we would all be physically fit and financially rich, and we would all bowl with amazing skill and proficiency. The truth is, knowledge is *not* enough. Nearly everyone knows that to lose weight you must eat more lettuce and fewer candy bars. Very few people who make New Year's resolutions to get in shape are confused about exercise and nutrition. We all know that you must exercise, at least a little, to get fit. That you must study to get a decent education is also well accepted.

Yet candy bar sales remain through the roof. Most New Year's resolutions end up in the trash can. Video games are a gravitational pull away from studying. And the idea of really doing what it takes to be a champion remains a fantasy for many talented athletes. Bowlers around the world express distress that they are not getting better, competing better, or scoring better.

The question is, with all of the education and tools available to us, why are we not all thin, happy, rich, and making all of our spares? We know the success of self-improvement programs of any kind generally hover around 2 to 5 percent. And in actuality, those 2 to 5 percent of people who lose weight, get fit, improve their grades, and rigorously practice their bowling are those who are going to get better at things anyway. They are just smart and motivated enough to find a vehicle for success that makes it easier on them.

By reading this book you have chosen to educate yourself and be among the small percentage of those who succeed. But education, of course, is seldom enough to become great at anything. In this chapter we are going to look at what greatness takes . . . greatness in *anything*. If you want to have success in life, to achieve your goals, you must do what successful people do. Let's now look at what they do, and how they do it.

NINE SECRETS
OF GOAL ATTAINMENT

It's what you learn after you know it all that counts.

John Wooden, head basketball coach, UCLA (1948–1975)

Read through the nine principles that follow and decide which ones you can plug into. If you've already heard some of these secrets, bear with us. These pearls of wisdom deserve the repetition they receive. Learning, or reviewing, these nine secrets will put you in perfect position to set your own goals.

1. **You must do more than you think.** One of the problems with bowling is that once you understand the fundamentals of the game, you can bowl pretty well—maybe even very well—without practicing much. It's no secret that forgiving oil patterns can make players look great, as can just the right ball matched with soft lane patterns.

The truth is that if you examine the habits of most bowlers, they are doing far less than they could to excel. Very few attend to the diet, stretching, and exercise patterns that most athletes acknowledge are necessary to reach their full potential. The good news and the bad news for bowlers is that our sport can be performed, sometimes at a very high level, without being athletically fit.

Sure, arguments can be made about the many champions who clearly don't maintain ideal fitness levels, or even have good practice habits. Yet, the counterargument is two-fold. First, we'll never know what these players might have accomplished if they had had the discipline to trim themselves into top form. Second, though a few bowlers might claim they practice and receive coaching the way that champions should, most would not claim they are doing *all* they need to do to be the bowler they want to be. The truth is that what you do *every day* determines whether are not you are a champion far better than the number of titles you have. *Being* a champion is just that—*a way of being*!

2. **Simply rolling balls does not make you better, or even get you in bowling condition.** Some bowlers believe that the more they bowl, the better they will get. This might sound reasonable, but sometimes the opposite is true. Try this: Ask a bowler to roll five of her very best shots while you shoot video. Then, without telling her, also video five shots from the middle of her standard practice. When you watch these videos, you'll nearly always see a clear distinction in physical form and apparent concentration.

This has several implications. Most bowlers are at least a little lazy. They might not put maximum effort into every approach, such as the knee bend on the slide. Thus the bowler is not working the muscles involved in bowling to the utmost effect.

Similarly, the mental game associated with focus, concentration, risk, and effort is being exercised at less than 100 percent. The result? The bowler ends up being less the bowler than she could be. Because she has not practiced properly, the level of intensity and focus of pressure during a competition might feel unfamiliar to her. If she had engaged in *deep practice*—which we will soon discuss—the competition would seem routine, and her confidence would be brimming.

3. **You do have time to read, train, and practice.** Yes, you have time to practice. You have time to do anything you want to do. You check e-mails, watch more TV than you would believe, explore the Internet, and shop for clothes. You can see exactly what people are committed to by simply watching what they do. When you are dating, you might neglect sleep, skip TV, even miss meals if it means being with the person you want to be with. If you want a good grade in a course, you will lose sleep to study for finals. If getting better at bowling is a priority for you, you will show this in your reading, practice habits, and coachability.

4. **Overtraining your "A" game will not lead you to mastery in bowling.** Many players are like fighters who have a favorite punch. Their jab wins them a lot of fights. So, they practice the jab, have fun sparring with the jab, and fight with the jab. And if they do in fact have a good jab, they will sometimes win with the jab . . . until the jab doesn't work on a particular opponent.

It is a really great feeling to execute your favorite shot on your favorite line, with your favorite ball. In fact, it can feel so good that you can become a one-trick pony who can really score when the lanes are just right. But true mastery goes far beyond this. Mastery is the physical, mental, and emotional ability to adapt, adjust, and score in a wide variety of circumstances and conditions. The bowling masters are those who become the true legends of the game.

5. **Practice in equals performance out? Not always.** If you take proper care in painting a wall, you might be surprised how well you accomplish the task. But if you have painted the wrong wall, it doesn't matter how well you stroked the brush.

Practice in and of itself means nothing. You can work on your release, your step cadence, your swing plane, or your thought patterns, but if you think you're doing the right thing, while you're really doing something wrong, you'll only get really good at bad bowling. Periodic positive results do not mean that you are practicing properly. As they say in school, have someone check your work—for example, a coach.

6. **In hard conditions, the lanes are *not* working against you.** Sport conditions, "burned" conditions, and designer patterns are not out to get you. They are simply life asking whether you can execute the informal Marine motto: Improvise, adapt, and overcome.

Bowling is an IQ test. The lanes ask, "Can you solve me? Do you get it?" There is no agenda to make you fail. There is nothing less personal than a lane condition. Look at it like the best of you is being called forth, not plotted against. Don't sweat a thing—just do your best. Make it your mission to be able to play on anything.

7. **Your bowling environment is working for you.** If you watch a basketball game at any level, you'll see opposing fans yelling and waving signs and balloons during free throws. Oddly enough, players become very proficient at seeing their way through the tunnel of noise and movement to focus on their shots. The truth is, if you really want to disrupt a player's shot, you should try for absolute silence. The silence highlights the strangeness of the situation, signaling the brain that something is "off."

We see the same thing in bowling. You throw a string of strikes in a row, and suddenly things get quieter. Often some part of you becomes aware that everyone is treating you differently. That highlights that things really *are* different. Something inside tightens, and *shazam*—it changes.

The noise, the movement, the rudeness, the laughs, the distractions all work in your favor! Anything that creates any kind of noise provides a tunnel for your vision. Then, you should expect it to get quiet as you play better. The more normal that all aspects of your environment seem, the better you'll be able to focus and concentrate. Make it your mission to feel you can handle virtually anything that occurs while you're bowling.

8. **Maybe you don't need to rev it up, or hook the ball more.** Everyone says that "straighter is greater." But do you really believe it? The problem is that straighter never makes anyone gasp. No one ever remarks (admiringly) about how straight someone can roll the ball. No one ever asks how few boards someone crossed on the way to striking.

At a clinic in Dallas where I worked with PBA star Norm Duke, Norm shot a 10-pin spare by rolling the ball right up the 1-board, bringing his hand up the back of his strike ball. Norm also showed all kinds of mastery of hand positions, ball speeds, and ability to strike at all angles. Yet at the end of the workshop, when students asked questions and gave feedback, they remarked most about that one particular feat of crawling the ball up the 1-board—for these students this was the most impressive demonstration of all the skills this great champion demonstrated.

The truth is that you might not need to get more action on the ball. From the vast array of physical and mental elements to choose from, you must decide what is most needed in your game. It is entirely possible that more revolutions is not a magic key to wringing the most out of your body, your game, or your results. You must ask and sincerely answer what is needed in your game.

You might not need to get more on the ball—but you might still need to add leverage, power, and consistency. You might need simply to be more accurate. You get to decide which elements to put on your list of goals.

9. **This is not a training diet—this is your life.** We've already recognized the lack of effectiveness of diets. The same is true for bowling tips, secrets, and the latest advice. Do the suggestions really work? Yes, almost without question. And just about anyone can incorporate them.

But here's the rub. Most athletes do what feels good. Only true champions do what works. So you can behave like one of those amazing 2 to 5 percent of top-tier athletes . . . or choose not to.

The truth is we're discussing a way to approach not only bowling, but everything else as well. If you hang out with any bowler through three practices, and maybe one competition, you can pretty much learn all you need to know about his personality, commitment to the game, and potential for improvement. This approach is not a diet. It is an approach for virtually everything you do.

Set some training commitments, improvement goals, and competition outcome marks. Then track what you actually follow through on. Likely, your adherence to your resolutions will resemble the way you have treated school, business, and even relationship commitments. Give your word on what you will do. Keep your word. See how things turn out. I think you'll be happy with the results.

SETTING A CLEAR VISION

**Outstanding people have one thing in common:
an absolute sense of mission.**

Zig Ziglar, inspirational speaker

In the early 1960s President Kennedy informed the world that the United States was going to put a man on the moon. At the time, those involved in the space program lacked the know-how to get the job done. NASA was only a few years old.

What President Kennedy presented to the citizens of the United States was a compelling vision of where he intended to lead the nation. He offered an energizing invitation to the entire country to come with him, and, powerfully, he mobilized the resources required to get the job done. On July 16, 1969, President Kennedy's vision was realized. Apollo 11 blasted off for the moon. Four days later, Neil Armstrong took the first lunar stroll.

President Kennedy had demonstrated a platinum model in vision, commitment, and ultimate achievement.

In this chapter I'll help you establish a vision of the bowler you want to be. You'll set your goals accordingly and then decide what kind of push you're going to put into play to become that bowler. This is your own mission to the bowling moon. To succeed you'll have to make an honest assessment of what is working and what is breaking down for you.

First, sit back and really think about where you're going with your bowling. No kidding, no pie-in-the-sky craziness, no taking it easy by lowering the high-jump bar to something you can already reach. Without a clear vision of where you intend to go with your bowling, you are in serious danger of not going anywhere. You go where your eyes are looking!

Here are the three essential ingredients for success in establishing your vision:

1. A clear definition of what you want to do
2. Self-credibility
3. An action plan to make your vision a reality

Wishing is never enough. Let's consider these three ingredients in order. Reading books about the sport, playing on a league team, doing tournaments, and practicing at lunch might all help your game, but progress can often be sluggish or nonexistent.

Most people practice when they feel like it, and skip practice when they don't. They credit fortune if they have a high-scoring outing. If you ask typical B-plus to A-minus competitive bowlers what they intend to be averaging, what skills they intend to improve, and even what they intend to do in tournaments, most have no real plan. However, talk to high-level bowlers (or elite athletes in any sport), and they can describe to you their vision and their plan to achieve it.

Vision and Mission

Before we continue, you should understand the difference between hope and real vision. A wise man once said that those who dine on hope soon starve to death. Hope is leaving it up to the bowling gods to make you strong and coordinated, to make sure the lanes are oiled right, and to have a messenger pin take out the 10-pin. Hope relies heavily on chance, luck, and fate.

Successful businesses have vision and mission statements that declare what the business stands for and provide stockholders with plans for how to achieve high financial goals. Successful athletes have their own versions of vision and mission statements. Vast amounts of research suggest that this is a good idea.

Vision is a portrait painted with words that state what you intend to accomplish. The mission part is a simple, brief description of what you are going to do to get there. The two kinds of visions are personal performance goals

■ Championship Goal Setting With Kim Kearney

**I'm going to do this right. I'm going to do this right.
I'm going to do this right.
And then when it's over I like my chances.**

Kim Kearney, USBC Hall of Fame, USBC Silver coach,
two-time U.S. Women's Open champion, 10-time professional champion

In 2004, Kim Kearney (then Kim Terrell) squared up to bowl the biggest tournament of her life, the Women's U.S. Open. At that time, this tournament paid the largest prize in women's bowling as well, $50,000. When it was over, and Kim had won, she had two reflections on the experience. First, in that moment she just wanted to keep bowling, and second, it was the first time that she had played a tournament from start to finish completely in the present moment.

As you would guess, this result didn't just happen out of nowhere. It started early, very early. Kim has been setting and keeping goals since she was a kid: "My first goals were probably academic, somewhere around third grade."

Goal setting is actually a way of being, not just a trick or a skill that an individual picks up. Hence, goal setting does not stop once one has hit the mark. When you're a goal setter, you simply cue up the next one.

Kim was inducted into the USBC Hall of Fame in 2012. I asked her why she still competes. Her answer is classic for a champion: "I still compete to see what I have in me. I love setting goals, developing a plan to reach somewhere higher. I've learned so much since I stopped competing regularly. I have all this knowledge that I want to put to use." She knows that a lifetime of setting, training for, and attaining goals has been a transformative process.

Courtesy of Storm Products, Inc.

Kim has coached both college and for the U.S. team, and she now wants to integrate her athlete self with her coaching self. "I'm curious and anxious to see who that bowler is. I'm so different from what I was. I have this unbelievable test ahead of me, and I want to see where I land. Why do we compete? We want to see where we fall when we give our best. Where does it stack up?"

Even if you haven't previously lived this way, it can all change for you in an instant. You can follow a similar path, and cultivate a similar attitude. There was a necessary shift in self-determination for Kim, as far as bowling goes: "I was an average player until college. The family bowled. I was content with league. When I got into college I realized I could be better if I attacked bowling in a logical way. I made a plan. 'These are team practice days. This is my own practice time.' I always had a plan of attack. I wanted our program to be successful." Kim drove herself by observing how great players, and great teams, were training, and pushing herself past her own comfort zone. "When I wanted to go home early, I remember saying to myself, 'What are others doing? What are they doing in Wichita?' And then I demanded more of myself."

(continued)

Kim Kearney *(continued)*

The process of deciding what you're going to do, clarifying your vision, and then charting a course to your desired outcome is ongoing. Bowling was designated as a demonstration sport at the Seoul Olympics in 1988. Kim determined that she would be an Olympian. "As soon as Olympic bowling was an option, there was no stopping me. I made journals. I tracked what I was eating, how I was training. I can remember leaving the Olympic training center and wanting to be seen as their [other Olympic athletes] equal. I decided that I'm going to do this differently. What are the things that are going to make me a winner? I addressed all of those pieces, the mental game, the physical—anything that was going to make me a winner. That was the way I thought that was supposed to work."

After college, and after the Olympics, the next step was the women's professional tour. Always in mind was the possibility of graduating someday to the pinnacle of career achievement. "I remember going to the Hall of Fame the first time and thinking that this is the coolest place in the world. I took pictures. I knew that in my career, if that's where I want to be, then I have to reach these goals. In the tougher years when I was on tour I asked some of the players who won how they did it. My goals had to be specified and attainable."

Goal setting and goal attainment became part of Kim's way of being. You can choose this for yourself. "The way my brain works, there is always a cause and effect in the world. If I do *this*, than *that* would happen. I wasn't sacrificing anything. It felt like this was the only way to do it. I honestly don't know any other way to do life. That's what I learned from [Dr. Dean Hinitz]. It's about bringing everything I have, and then I'm cool with wherever it puts me."

Kim learned and practiced what we should all learn and practice. As Muhammad Ali said years ago, "The fight is won or lost far away from witnesses, long before I dance under those lights."

and competition outcome goals. You have a great deal of control over the achievement of personal performance goals. Competition outcome goals feed the ego, but are more difficult to predict. They tend to involve beating opponents and winning tournaments or championships. Fortunately, personal performance goals tend to lead to positive competition outcomes without you even having to tweak your game.

Personal performance goals focus on all the things you can do to improve your game independently of how anyone else bowls—goals such as raising your average, improving your percentage of solid pocket hits, improving spare-shooting, strengthening your mental game, and so forth.

There are other personal performance goals that I like even better. These involve only the elements that you control within yourself. They include physical improvements such as release timing, solidity at the line, and elbow position. They might also include lane play sophistication such as learning the most effective modes of attacking different oil patterns, ball speed, and tilt/roll options. Perhaps most impressively, they might include learning to play freely without fear, concern, or overthinking.

Establishing a Personal Yardstick

There is a significant difference between personal performance goals and competition outcome goals. You can achieve a personal performance goal (PG) of throwing 12 pocket shots in a game, but still not have a perfect game. Likewise, you can bowl a great game with a solid base, good balance, great timing, and powerful delivery (all personal PGs); score a robust 260; and still get beat by someone else's 270 game.

If you choose to focus on personal performance goals, you can have a positive and satisfying experience even if you leave a ringing 10-pin (i.e., the 10-pin stands even though a pin rings around it) or if someone else bowls a better game. Performance goals focus on skill sets, such as maintaining balance at the line, having a free arm swing, using proper thumb-release timing, and hitting the mark a certain percentage of the time.

Perhaps the easiest, and ultimately most satisfying, performance goal to achieve is to bowl freely and whole-heartedly. To throw 6, 8, 12, or more shots a game with total commitment, heart, and effort will wring the maximum effect out of any physical game development you'll ever have.

There are two important reasons for making personal performance goals your highest priority. First, you can measure self-improvement without relying on lane conditions, other bowlers, or pin fall. Second, a focus on personal performance goals gives you your best chance at winning and improving.

Working on personal performance goals sets up higher scores, increases your chances of earning cash, and improves your probabilities of winning. Focusing on competition outcome goals might serve as motivation, and can positively drive practice habits, but far too much is out of your control. In fact, wanting to win too much can cramp your competition mental game. The point is to become a great bowler, especially under pressure. All you have control over is what you bring. Focus on that, and when it is your day to win, you will be ready to meet it.

Pointing at the Prize

Deciding on competition goals is like setting a point on a compass. You point your finger and say, "I am going *there*—no kidding!" Jason Belmonte (winner of three consecutive USBC Masters Championships) has spoken about his vision and clarity around becoming the best bowler in the world. He has said that a person needs to be able to see the result they wish to have.

Having a direction helps you set up a training and competition program. Your competition outcome goals also let your coach know how hard to push you. In addition, you can see which training behaviors are in line with where you have declared you are going.

If you decide competition outcome goals (scores, titles, money, etc.) are the most important thing to you, you invite two major risks. First, your happiness and sense of satisfaction are tied to pin fall and pin carry, other bowlers' abilities and performances, and having your "A" game with you all the time. Second, you risk creating increased pressure and concern as you bowl.

Ironically, you can actually bowl worse as you raise the importance (in your mind) of having to put up a certain number, or even as you become aware that you are close to achieving your goals. Pressure can increase even more if you have not won for a while, or if you have come close to a championship without winning it.

Competition goals are fine for offering a compass point or direction, but living in them as a constant priority is not likely to advance your game or bring success.

The Ultimate Confidence Builder: Your Word

Before we get into the how-to, I have some questions for you. Are you a person of your word? Are you credible? Do you do what you say you are going to do? Do you trust yourself? What has your success rate been on keeping resolutions? How have you been at keeping promises to yourself?

Vision and goal setting without action is mere fantasy. You might say what you're going to do, what you intend to win or score, and how you'll train, but if you're like the typical promise or resolution maker, you might well trip up in your follow-through.

Here's an example. Let's say you make a New Year's resolution to run one mile on Mondays, Wednesdays, and Saturdays. For the first week, you execute perfectly. The weather is great. You feel strong and motivated. During the second week, things start to change. Your enthusiasm for the new program starts to wane. Your muscles complain a little bit. Then on Saturday the weather shifts. It is overcast, damp, and cool. You say to yourself, "I'm tired; the weather's no good. I think I'll wait until tomorrow."

When you change your plans without writing an escape clause into your personal resolution ahead of time, you have broken your word to yourself. If you are creative and inventive in justifying breaking your commitments, then envisioning and goal setting will have much less personal effectiveness. The solution is to hold yourself completely accountable for success or failure and for keeping your agreements. Pure and simple, the more you give your word to yourself, and keep it, the more confidence you'll develop.

Write It Down

Get out a piece of paper and a pen. Better yet, start a bowling notebook. A notebook is great for recording goals, insights, quotes, league and tournament results, and trends, and also for archiving league and tournament memorabilia. A well-kept notebook will become your own ready-access coach when your game breaks down and you need to review your bowling checkpoints.

Self-check right now: Will you actually begin keeping a notebook? You can get a good look at your willingness to take action, and to be coached out of your comfort zone, simply by examining whether you're open to performing this one task.

Take a moment to write down your thoughts, feelings, and goals. What do you like best about bowling? Why are you so invested in the sport? Note your vision, dreams, and expectations for what you intend to accomplish. Do you love the challenge? Are you an athlete who has found a sport for your 30s, 40s, and beyond? Do you think you can run with the big dogs? Do you want to learn to hook the ball a ton? Do you want to hit what you're looking at every time? Do you want to average 220 in league play?

Don't set your sights too low. Low expectations leave you bored with your goals and unsatisfied when you achieve them. Set lofty but not crazy goals. Better to shoot for the moon and end up on a mountaintop than to shoot for a minor hill that's too easy to reach. That said, make sure your goals are within your range, or else you risk becoming discouraged and giving up. Setting excessively high goals is an easy excuse for not reaching them.

Be specific. Establish goals you can measure and evaluate in terms of successful bowling. Although performance goals should be your main focus, include competition outcome goals, too. Remember that as you meet performance goals, competition outcomes such as winning, cashing, and raising your average will improve as well.

Short-Term Goals

Goals can be short term or long term. Short-term goals are more immediate and time limited, such as maintaining a strong, balanced finishing position on every shot; achieving consistently correct thumb exit timing; employing a reliable spare system; hitting the pocket on 90 percent of your first shots; or bringing complete focus and attention to every shot. Once you have integrated your short-term goals into your game, they continue to serve you. They become basic parts of your repertoire to maintain, build on, and improve.

Long-Term Goals

Long-term performance goals often take months or even years to achieve. Examples include raising your average 20 or more points, making 95 percent of your nonsplit spares, mastering multiple hand positions, starting for a college team, earning a pro card, or even winning a major title.

In addition to offering performance enhancement, long-term goals also often contain competition results, including titles, cash, making tournament cuts, and even hall of fame selections. As previously mentioned, these kinds of goals will steer training, coaching, and analysis of competition results. Use your notebook to record short-term and long-term goals. Your experience and skill level should determine where you set your goals.

Evaluate Results

After a short period of time, you need to evaluate your goals and progress. It is important to accurately map out where you performed in terms of your stated goals. Skipping this step is a big mistake—like rolling balls without watching how the pins fall.

THE TRUTH KEEPS YOU
ON YOUR PATH

Checking results equals poking your nose into the truth. If you can't handle negative feedback, you're in for a much longer, more painful road to improvement. To make the most of your short- and long-term goal evaluation, distinguish between taking stock of your improvement and taking stock of yourself. Bowling feedback is not about you personally. It is only about your bowling.

True feedback is difficult for many people. Think of the first time you heard your voice on audiotape (most of us think there's something wrong with the recorder) or saw yourself on video ("Whoa, that's what I look like from behind!?"). It can be startling to view yourself from a neutral, objective standpoint.

Many athletes focus on the negatives of falling short of perfect goal attainment. This is a mistake. You must be willing to accept accurate feedback about movement and goal achievement, while learning to remain positive, encouraged, and excited about your progress. Without the willingness to examine the truth about your form and your results, your progress will be much slower.

You can use any written form to record what you will do. Just make sure you have a way to keep yourself honest about following through. Post your goals where you can see them. Develop a user-friendly, reliable system for recording and tracking personal performance and competition outcome goals. Figure 1.1 shows a sample bowling achievement log; figure 1.2 shows a sample bowling performance evaluation. These are examples only. Use a system that works for you.

Whether you share your goals with others is a personal question. Some people fizzle out after making their commitments known to others. Others respond well to having a witness. An important move for you, if you want to be accountable to someone, is to have a coach, teammate, or friend witness your goals. Making a public declaration inspires many athletes to keep commitments. Telling someone what you plan to accomplish puts you and your word on the line.

There's no limit to the physical and mental game skills you could record in logs such as those shown in figures 1.1 and 1.2. Seeing the evidence of changes in your game gives you satisfaction as you master the game. Increased skill development is linked to increased self-confidence as well.

It is not enough to clarify specific goals. You must also have an action plan for getting there (Murphy 1996). Like everything else in goal setting,

Name: _____ Date: _____

Skill or activity	Strong	Average	Needs improvement	Specific goal	Target date
Spare shooting			X	Learn reliable spare system; make 80% of nonsplit spares	Nov. 11
Balance at the line		X		Show strong, stable finishing position on every shot	Oct. 15
Pocket hits		X		Learn to hit my mark and hit pocket on 90% of first shots	Dec. 1

Figure 1.1 Sample bowling achievement log.

Name: _____ Date: _____

Skill or activity	Available statistics or personal/ coach rating (1 to 100%)	Comments
Spare shooting	Made 16 of 20 nonsplit spares (80%)	Pulled head up early on missed spares
Balance at the line	Solid, no wobble on 30 of 36 shots (approximately 85%)	All six wobbles were on corner pin spares
Pocket hits	Hit the pocket on 22 of 33 first shots (66%)	Need to follow through after release

Figure 1.2 Sample bowling performance evaluation log.

the action plan must be specific and measurable, which simply means that goals and changes are spelled out in such a way that you can assess for sure whether you have followed through. This is vital because compliance with your action plan will tell you what's working and what's not working in your training program.

How well you follow through on the action plan demonstrates your degree of commitment, dedication, and stick-to-it-iveness. And, as mentioned, the bonus pin for compliance is that every time you do what you said you would do, you increase confidence in yourself. As a side note, most people notice they have similar levels of commitment and keeping to their word in other parts of their lives. This is one aspect of sport that allows you to build character as well as skill. How you address your bowling commitments will likely mirror how you address other life commitments.

YOUR ACTION PLAN

Your action plan is the "how much by when" part of the process. In the action plan, you lay out what it takes to achieve the results you say are important to you. You list the number of practice sessions, daily repetitions of single-pin spares, number of coaching contacts, and so on, that will take place. If you skip this step, you leave a bit more in the realm of luck than in the realm of "I did what I said I would do."

The three rules of action plans are to keep them simple, specific, and measurable. When the day, week, or tournament is over, you have to be able to look at your action plan and know, yes or no, whether you followed it. This step is vital because whether or not you follow through on your action plan tells you about your own level of commitment, as well as whether you have set up a good program. If the plan needs to be changed or adjusted, that's fine, but changes are based on data and feedback, not on how you feel on a particular day.

Pick out a skill or activity. Lay out how to go about mastering it, follow your plan, and then take a look at what you have accomplished. Figure 1.3 illustrates a sample action plan. As you can see, the action plan is really another way of declaring yourself. This is not about playing it safe. It is about putting yourself in gear and participating fully. Playing it safe is for people who watch bowlers only on TV. By committing to action, you are pledging to participate.

Review the completion of your action plan commitments. Remember these basics:

- Keep the action plan manageable. Don't overwhelm yourself with requirements.
- Keep the action plan consistent with your own level of interest. Practice skills that match your level of play as well as your hopes and dreams concerning where your game is going.
- Look at your accomplishments and struggles with a critical eye. Not achieving the desired result in terms of skills and scores is different from not keeping your word about training commitments. If you break your training schedule, consider the possibility that you set up something too hard or too boring to complete. Bowling doesn't just build

Skill or activity	Action plan	Accomplishment record
Making 10-pin spares (90%)	Will practice 3 times a week for 3 weeks; shoot 20 10-pins per practice	Made 7 of my 9 commitments
Pocket hits	Will practice 3 times a week for 3 weeks (part of other practice sessions); count how many times out of 20 I hit my pocket-shot mark	Made 7 of my 9 commitments

Figure 1.3   Sample action plan.

character, it also reflects character. Do you break or keep your word elsewhere? The answer is probably the same.

Figure 1.4 shows a sample journal page that you can copy and use to record your own personal vision for success.

Potholes and Pitfalls

Let's look at some of the most common pitfalls in setting and completing goals. Watch out for these. Like hitting a pothole in the road, you can encounter one of these problems before you know it and significantly damage your plans to become a better bowler. For the best results in your vision, mission, and action plans, watch out for the following:

• **Goal blizzard.** This is the result of setting so many goals that you lose focus, can't adequately monitor how you're doing on each of your goals, and perhaps end up getting bored or overwhelmed by record keeping. Maybe later, when you get good at the goal setting and action-plan process, you can increase the number of goals in your personal plan. For starters, keep the number of short-term goals at around three. Rank them in order of importance.

• **Goal mush.** This means setting goals that look good but are too general to measure. For example, improving the first shot, getting better at spares, and improving your mental game are fine targets, but you must have a measurable way of knowing you are improving. To clean up these goals, you could modify them to improving first-shot pocket hits from the current average of 7 per game to 10, increasing your spare making from 75 to 85 percent, or practicing any of the mental game tools in this book for a declared percentage of shots per game.

• **Goal fit.** The goals you set must have some juice for you. If you're going after something just to satisfy a coach, or because you think you're supposed to do it but don't really want to, you are setting yourself up for failure in complying with your program. If your action plan is either too easy or too demanding, you'll probably wash out. Set goals that fit your style, personality, and life.

• **Goal lock.** Goal lock happens when you fail to change and modify goals based on performance. Throughout practices and competitions, you'll see which goals are too far-reaching, or too simple, at any given time. If you fail to reset your sights, you'll sabotage your goal-setting program. If you're not achieving your goals, simply readjust desired improvements into smaller bites. This is not failure—it's being smart about your growth as an athlete.

• **Competition outcome goals tunnel vision.** Remember that competition outcome goals (scores, victories, money, and so on) depend on external factors such as pin fall and the performances of competitors. Tying your sense of success solely to winning, particularly in any one tournament, is a blueprint for frustration, low self-esteem, and quitting. Performance goals that involve

Name: _____ Date: _____

Short-Term Bowling Goals

    1. _____

    2. _____

    3. _____

Long-Term Bowling Goals

    1. _____

    2. _____

    3. _____

Specific skill or activity	Self-rating (1 to 10)	Specific goals	Target date

Performance Evaluation

Specific event and date:

Skill or activity	Personal record (how I did : 1 to 100%)	Comments
Goal 1		
Goal 2		
Goal 3		
Action plan		

Skill or activity	Action plan (what I will do by when)	Accomplishment review
Goal 1		
Goal 2		
Goal 3		

Figure 1.4 Bowling goal achievement journal.

From D. Hinitz, 2016, *Bowling psychology*. (Champaign, IL: Human Kinetics).

personal improvement in skill areas and execution will leave you feeling satisfied, believing in your bowling, and eager to set new challenging goals. Again, you're also more likely to improve your competition results.

Breakdown

The final aspect of your personal vision for success is knowing how to deal with your goals and action plans—both when you fall short of your goals, and when you achieve them. The Japanese have a process called *kaizan*, which means continual improvement and a search for excellence. Look at what you achieved, where you are succeeding in the overall game of improvement, as well as where you have stumbled. Follow this essential process early and often.

FIVE STEPS TO EXCELLENCE

When assessing the effectiveness of your goal setting, consider these five steps—they've been the staples of champions through the ages.

1. **Tell the truth. Look at and acknowledge the goals you met and didn't meet and plans you followed and didn't follow.** This can be challenging at first. Some people have a hard time recognizing what they haven't done well, particularly if they've made declarations to others. At the same time, most of us don't like to look at our own shortcomings. But you must be honest. You might or might not like what you see, but you'll know what to do next.

2. **Immediately review the parts of the plan that assisted you in success.** This will get your feedback and examination off on the right foot. You also want to make sure when recalibrating new goals that you don't throw the baby out with the bathwater. Start by simply asking yourself what worked. No matter what happened, if you clear your head, you can always find positive aspects of your bowling.

3. **If you didn't achieve a goal, figure out why.** Don't jump on your own case. Avoid judging yourself. If you have a shame attack, you're going about this wrong. Look at your motivation, some of the pitfalls and potholes discussed earlier, and other unforeseen problems.

4. **Consider what you have to modify to meet your training and competition goals.** You can clarify your action plan, hire a coach, mark out training time in your calendar, or whatever else is necessary to make changes. List your answers.

5. **Modify your commitments, goals, action plans, and then go forth.** Be bold. Just make sure you spell your action plans out in ways that you can examine and measure later.

Go through the goal-setting process early and often. As time passes, it will become second nature, and you'll complete the five steps more rapidly. Once you start holding yourself accountable for what you achieve, or don't achieve, you give up blaming and feeling helpless and get to experience the power of goal setting, commitment, and success that true champions experience.

**If you limit your choices only to what seems possible or reasonable,
you disconnect yourself from what you truly want,
and all that is left is a compromise.**

Robert Fritz, organizational consultant

Much is made of goal setting, not only in sports, but in business as well. The truth is that it takes guts to set challenging goals. Don't feel you have to go it alone. Sharing your goals with a trusted friend or a coach helps you stay focused. If uncertain, ask for feedback.

It is critical that the goals you set be both worthy and attainable. At the end of the day, you really must believe that what you intend to do is possible. You can't be blowing smoke at yourself, selling yourself a used car, or merely be cheerleading. You have to believe—all the way down to your bone marrow—that you can and will achieve your goals.

No one wins all the time. But I can assure you that people who win repeatedly plan on winning repeatedly. For example, Norm Duke has acknowledged that he's human when it comes to nerves, injuries, and slumps. But in his storied career— 38 titles—he plans to win every time.

SUMMING IT UP

Transforming yourself into a champion is a constant process. Becoming a champion and maintaining championship form, mentally and physically, is rarely a result of a spectacular insight or event. Much more often it's a process of attending to the long-term efforts involved in training and competing.

You must be willing to see your target. No, not the target on the lanes—your target in terms of achievements and accomplishments. Both short term and long term, know what you're going after, whether it's your league average or specific tournament results.

**What you get by achieving your goals is not as important
as what you become by achieving your goals.**

Henry David Thoreau, American author

Rehearse and practice. Use the tracking systems we've described in this chapter. Or make up your own. But keep track. You can be formal, recording your percentage of "playing to win" shots, or simply report to your playing partner, coach, or yourself. Check yourself on your first and second shots. Rate yourself. Be realistic but tough.

You either make a plan and stay true to it, or you let life's bumps get in the way. Those who persevere find something heroic in themselves. They know the truth of the champion who lives within them.

CHAPTER 2

Thinking Like a Champion

**The danger for most of us
is not that our aim is too high and we miss it,
but that it is too low and we reach it.**

Michelangelo

Back in August 2008, at the USBC U.S. Women's Open, Kim Kearney did something really remarkable—she won this major title for the second time. As any serious bowler knows, it is a phenomenal accomplishment to make the telecast at any tournament. Carrying it further, most bowlers never win a professional title, much less a major.

Kim has 10 titles and a USBC Hall of Fame induction. She has done it before. She did it again. And if she had the chance, she would probably bet on herself anytime she went head-to-head with anyone in the world.

There are several notable features about her victory. Kim is older than a good deal of the field. At the time of her victory, she was coaching at Delaware State University. Now, she is the assistant head coach for the U.S. team. And although she practices, she no longer defines herself as both an athlete and a bowler. She is a teacher now.

The mettle that Kim brings to her goal setting (see goal setting in chapter 1) is the mettle that she brings to competition.

**I knew I couldn't make mistakes against Carolyn. . . .
It took me a minute to regain my composure after that. . . .
I was just hoping for an opportunity in the 10th frame, and it happened.
It's been a great week, and it's really satisfying
to reach my goal of 10 career titles.**

Kim Kearney, winner, 2008 USBC Women's Open

Kim made many mistakes on her way to the final, notably a missed spare against Carolyn Dorin-Ballard in the semifinal. Instead of becoming flustered, she waited for an opportunity to get back in the match. That chance did appear, and Kim exploited a mistake by her opponent by striking in the 10th frame to advance to face Trisha Reid in the final.

There is a distinct difference in the attitudes and messages in the quotes from these two finalists. Trisha Reid is a very talented and trained athlete. Based on her statements and her results, she appears to have had her sights, goals, and expectations in a very different place than Kim, the eventual champion.

> **It feels great, just awesome, and I'm still overwhelmed . . .**
> **even though I finished second, I still feel like I won.**
> **I really came here to make the top 12 for the Women's Series,**
> **and everything after that was icing on the cake.**
>
> Trisha Reid, runner-up, 2008 USBC Women's Open

This chapter is about becoming, maintaining, and recovering your championship self. The way things shake down in competition is that bowlers' results over time are almost always in line with how they see themselves, the goals they set, and the realism with which they expect great achievements.

The point of view adopted here is that if you're talented enough to get to the finals, you can win. Even if the oil pattern seems to substantially favor your opponent's game, you can have the mental game advantage (it's just that some games end a few frames too soon, that's all). It seems intuitively obvious that given two bowlers of nearly equal ability, the one with the championship mindset will win most of the time. Every bowler ultimately makes choices that determine his or her championship future.

CHAMPIONS THINK DIFFERENTLY

> **The number one problem that keeps people from winning**
> **in the United States today is lack of belief in themselves.**
>
> Arthur L. Williams, founder of A.L. Williams Insurance Company

Two fundamental thought processes distinguish consistent champions from the rest of the pack. In identifying the first of these two modes of thinking, we must remember a fundamental principle of winning: a person's results in anything, over time, will tend to be consistent with what he or she thinks they will be.

Take this example. Let's say you're in school and you're interested in dating someone. You do not know who yet—you just want to date. When you walk into a classroom you will likely do an instant assessment of where you fit in the dating pool.

By whatever standards you set, you likely will not ask someone out who is below your assessed attractiveness level. Similarly, if you decide to ask someone out who you rank above yourself on your rating scale, you will probably fail to give the date your best shot, or you'll anxiously mess things up in short order.

The same is true in competition. Champions look at the field, and in their heart of hearts, they feel they deserve to win, and will win. But if you're attempting to achieve higher than your true self-belief, you will often choke because you're flying too high. In order to win you must adjust your scale of worthiness. You won't win, if in your heart of hearts you do not think you are worthy of that result.

The second distinction of champions is that they interpret signals different from the way that common athletes do. For instance, a normal person riding a bicycle uphill stops when her legs burn. A champion notices the signal of burning muscles, but it does not change her training. She might even take the burn as a good sign.

Any normal athlete can have slumps, bad games, and fatigue. When she does, she might quit, or perhaps lower her intensity. When a champion has such experiences, she re-doubles the effort to persevere. Her response is deeper commitment, not withdrawing or easing up.

CHAMPIONS: BORN OR MADE?

Champions aren't made in gyms. Champions are made from something they have deep inside them: a desire, a dream, a vision. They have to have late-minute stamina, they have to be a little faster, they have to have the skill and the will. But the will must be stronger than the skill.

Muhammad Ali, professional boxer

Champions are born. Almost all children observe the skills, capabilities, and privileges of adults, and think to themselves, "That looks great; I'm going to learn to do that!" Everything from walking, to turning doorknobs, to riding a bike, falls into this category.

Kids have an inherent belief in trial and error, falling down, getting up, and ultimately mastering whatever they choose to try. We must watch over children because they tend to be overconfident in their abilities to succeed in the world. They will climb too high, jump from the furthest step, and wrestle with the dog. All the while they are clear that they can do whatever they set out to do. This is a form of championship mindset. It is the belief that you can perform and achieve anything that you set your mind to do.

Champions are also unmade. Children are sometimes ridiculed for trying things, teased for failing, told they are stupid, or redirected to activities that others want them to be involved in. Generally, you have to be instructed to think less of yourself and your abilities. You have to be shamed for failing. Or you have to have a lack of celebration of *you*, and your achievements, to learn that you are not a champion.

You have a champion in you. The question is whether you have learned some things in life that would have you believe, at least subconsciously, that you are not a champion.

You can know there are negative tapes playing in your head if you consciously doubt that you can learn, achieve, and win. If you get excessively nervous when you compete, you might have a personal history of self-doubt running you. If you're afraid to set big goals, you have another clue about your own negative learning.

SELF-ASSESSMENT

**The most fundamental aggression to ourselves,
the most fundamental harm we can do to ourselves,
is to remain ignorant by not having the courage
and the respect to look at ourselves honestly and gently.**

Pema Chödrön, author and Tibetan Buddhist

If you hear negative tapes playing and replaying in your head, there are three things you can do. First, you must tell yourself the truth. Ask yourself these questions:

- Do I get overly nervous?
- Do I have self-doubt?
- Do I resist shooting for the moon in my goals?
- Have I lost the edge in my belief in myself?
- Do I get to the finals but never seem to advance or win?
- Do I choke off my corner pin, or other spare shots?

From the truth comes the solution. From self-deception comes more pressure, fatigue, and failure.

Second, you must get realistic feedback about where your game stands. Virtually no one can have a completely realistic view of how they show up in any aspect of life. The closer you get to knowing how your body moves in space, the closer you are to athletic genius. In all aspects of your game, pick those who are not afraid to tell you the truth—and then ask them to tell you the truth. Relatedly, you must find out what you need to do to compete. Cheerleading won't do it. Find players or coaches you trust, and get the real skinny on your game.

Last, you must convert to a positive, but realistic mindset. Once you are competing, you must have a fundamental belief in the physical game you have developed. If you can get to the pocket and then make your spares, you can generally advance. If you can get to the finals, you can win. So many variables are involved in this game—if you don't fully believe in yourself, you'll almost always come up short.

■ Looking Inside the Mind of Jason Belmonte

**Being a fighter is not something to turn on and off—
it is something that you are.**

Jason Belmonte, winner of 12 PBA titles, including 6 major tournaments,
and three-time PBA Player of the Year

In 2015, Rhino Page had demonstrated a remarkable recovery from wrist surgery and a forced layoff from competing on the professional tour. He had culminated this courageous return by qualifying first for the television step-ladder finals of the PBA Tournament of Champions. The road would end there for him, however. Rhino would meet the previous year's titleist, Jason Belmonte, for the title. As valiant as Rhino was, the final score (232–214) did not fully reflect Jason's dominance in the match and in the tournament.

Jason Belmonte

Look at the self-statements of the two players. Rhino reported on the pressure he felt throughout the tournament: "All week long, everybody was like, 'Well, it must be nice to lead the tournament all the way through.'" "And I go, 'It's such hard work when you know that guy's right behind you, striking that much.' You're just as mentally exhausted as you would be if you weren't striking that much" (David Woods, david.woods@indystar.com. February 15, 2015).

Jason came from a very different mental set, particularly heading into the final: "You have to hand it to Rhino. He had battled back from a lot to get to this position. But, for Rhino, it may have been the worst-case scenario when I made the finals. I had won the previous majors. I had just won the Masters for the third straight time. I was going to strike every frame. I was going to win this."

There's a distinct difference between champions and the rest of the field. That difference is not always in the result. No one wins all the time. And one can have championship mettle and still not come home with a title. The difference is that champions *know* what they are, no matter what's happening in any given circumstance. Others believe that they have to *prove* what they are.

It's as if by winning players think they'll transform themselves. In reality, most often it's when athletes have an unshakeable belief in their worthiness as champions that they can play freely, without the burden of proving anything to anyone.

Jason Belmonte has had a twisting, turning path to making himself into a champion's champion (see the foreword to this book). In some ways, his journey has been unique, and in other ways he has trod a classic hero's road, studded with success, marked by stiff adversity, before emerging onto the victory stand.

Jason still gets nervous and excited. And despite his many achievements, he still has to bring himself to the moment when he trains and competes. Through his triumphs and temporary setbacks, Jason has settled on some keys that travel with him across continents and to tournament play around the world.

Jason has learned something very important after facing the best players in the world, some of them among the best of all time: It simply doesn't matter whom Jason plays. "Other players might think that they're playing against me, and that could affect their thinking." It's different in Jason's mind. "In a sense, I am always playing against the same opponent, no matter who it is. I have really worked hard to not let personal feelings affect my bowling. I cannot allow myself to bowl worse against friends, or against anyone else I have history with. Because of that, my record against noted adversaries is good. If you want to beat a particular individual too badly, that can work against you; you make more errors."

Jason has a continuous improvement plan, as well. "I don't care who I play. I simply don't like to lose, in general. My personal feelings take a backseat. If I don't win, I leave the lanes disappointed. Then I figure out why I lost, and make myself better."

A lot of bowlers think they must have ice water in their veins to compete at the highest level. Jason sees this entirely differently. It's about what you do with the energy of excitement that matters, not whether you feel it. "I still get nervous to compete. Particularly if we've had some time off, the first game back can still be a little shaky. I have worked hard at dealing with the jitters. Now, I like that I get nervous. It means that I am alive, and that I still want it. It gives me another challenge to overcome."

Jason is not immune from distracting, even negative, thoughts or feelings. When that happens, his strategies are simple and effective: "Sometimes I will know it's a critical shot, the target seems smaller, and the legs get unsteady. I just do a reality check with myself. The truth is that the target is big, and that my legs are powerful. I allow myself to know that things are not as hard as I was making them. Once I do that, I believe that no matter what I am going to execute the best shot I can."

Once the competition starts, Jason's routine is as ordered as an airline pilot. "On television I know that I have already done the hard work. I don't let my mind go anywhere but the field of play. I stay right on the lanes. My focus is directed to the right location."

"I know that I am lucky to do what I get to do. Before the match I look around at what I am privileged to experience. I do not want to block all of that out. I see the kids and the signs. But once I start, my attention is all on my routine. I know what I need to do."

Jason does not engage a lot of technical thoughts when he plays. He trusts his training and his game. "I'm not thinking about much, specifically. I've bowled enough frames to let my body just do it. My subconscious pretty much says, 'Hey leave this to me I can do it.'"

Jason has figured out that when you truly enjoy the way you play the game, that great execution itself can bring you into sync. "It's about targeting, and feeling the ball come off my fingers. It's a relaxing feeling to do it well." There's not much mental interference here at all. "I do what I can to just bowl the way I know how to. Once I get off of my chair, I'm on autopilot."

After the shot is rolled, Jason lets go of the competitive moment and clears his mind. "I let go of the ball, and then look around. I typically smile a little bit. I look

(continued)

Jason Belmonte *(continued)*

at good things, the fans, and the kids. It relaxes me. You are in a great situation. Enjoy it."

There is no thinking ahead about honors and awards. Jason has experienced that in his career, and that's exactly when he cracked his shins on his championship trajectory. "I would catch myself thinking that I'd have to do better in order to achieve something, or how I might have to do in the next 20 events. That was a mistake. It is much more simple than that. Every time I step up on the lanes, I have to try to be the best. Bowling is frame-by-frame, event-by-event, not year-by-year. I had to remind myself that I won player of the year by bowling frame-by-frame. I have one shot to throw. That's my only responsibility."

Jason has a main beam that supports the whole structure of his championship mind set. It's the commitment to being a champion as a part of his soul. "I would say of all the mental game attributes I have, there's one that I'm most proud of. I never stop, no matter what. I'm always fighting until the end. Even if it's mathematically over, I never give up. Even if it's a fill frame, I bring it all. Being a fighter is not something to turn on and off— it's something that you are."

Imagine that every positive or negative self-belief rolls around in your head like it's hitting an echo chamber. Subconsciously, you are always hearing either faint cheering or faint booing. Think of the difference for you if a real audience were responding with boos or cheers. "Yes, I can" or "No, I can't" are always subtly running. Listen, identify your attitude, and if necessary get busy reprogramming your computer. The voice inside that you listen to is the one that determines the quality of your shots.

It helps immensely if you have people around you who have a realistic and honest belief in you, your capabilities, and your right to succeed. It often takes a clear, sweet, positive bell to overcome the negative buzzing that might be directing your bowling. Make sure you are accessing, and listening to, the right people. Once you find them, keep them near you—at least in your head.

The plan is to build a champion. Here is a way of assessing your own shots and efforts in any competition, from league night to tournament play. Use this scale:

- **Playing to win—3 points.** This is the only category for true champions. When you are playing to win, you are centered and focused; you have a plan and let it all go freely. You play and practice as if you have $100 on every shot, and you enjoy how good it feels to play this way.

- **Playing not to lose—2 points.** This is when you are careful, cautious, overcontrolling, and often pointing shots. This is fear-based play. When you do well from this perspective, you generally feel relieved, not joyous.

- **Just playing—1 point.** When "just playing," you are simply going through the motions. You might roll shot after shot in practice with no true intention. In competition, you just try to get to the end of the game. There's no real heart in the game here. It's boring to play this way, and no fun to watch, either.
- **Not really playing—0 points.** This is the quitter, the person who doesn't even do the minimum to get better, support the team, or recognize the impact of his or her behavior on those around him or her. If life is a character test, this is a failing grade.

I encourage coaches to use this scale when they assess player tryouts. You can measure each first shot, each spare shot, each game, and each block using a similar scoring system. Although the observer criteria are somewhat subjective, most bowlers and coaches really do tend to agree on what they are looking at.

More important, most bowlers can identify which of the four categories any shot they make falls into. If you're willing to stay disciplined, awake, and aware, you can train yourself into a *playing-to-win* mindset. This is the realm in which champions operate.

CHAMPIONSHIP THINKING IS A PROCESS

Transforming yourself into a champion is a consistent and constant process. Becoming a champion, and maintaining championship form, mentally and physically, is rarely a result of a single insight or event. More often it really is a *process* of attending to the "tapes" in your head, and changing the echoes, as necessary. These tapes are messages you have received about yourself throughout your lifetime.

Positive and negative comments from parents, teachers, coaches, and others can become internalized. Without knowing it, you unconsciously, or sometimes consciously, replay these messages and let them affect you. You must have the right people around you to add productive input to your internal loudspeakers.

You must be willing to see your target. Not the target on the lanes, but the target in terms of your achievements and accomplishments. Have the courage to know what you're going after, whether it's your league average or your tournament results, short term or long term.

And then rehearse and practice your efforts. Use the 4-point scoring system listed earlier. You can be formal and record your percentage of "playing to win" shots. Or you can simply report to your playing partner, your coach, or yourself. Check yourself on your first and second shots. Rate yourself. This is how you practice to be a champion. This is how you practice for whatever "show" you are striving to be on.

Are you up for the challenge? If you're willing to be a true champion, then yes you are!

CAN YOU WIN?

No matter how tough, no matter what kind of outside pressure, no matter how many bad breaks along the way, I must keep my sights on the final goal, to win, win, win—and with more love and passion than the world has ever witnessed in any performance.

Billie Jean King, former number one women's tennis player

Before the Women's 2012 U.S. Open in Reno, I had a conversation with one of the top-named competitors before the tournament started. This former champion was doing some last-minute preparation for the competition, and I asked her an important question: "Can you win this thing?" There was a pause, and some more thought, a bit more pause, and as the moments dragged on, I answered for her: *"Not right now, you can't."*

If it takes that long to consider whether you might succeed at any mission, you might have a significant problem. Change frames of reference for a moment. Let's say you're taking a trip across country. Consider asking your airline pilot any of the following questions:

- Do you think you can fly this thing?
- Do you think we can get to our destination?
- Do you think you can handle any inclement weather along the way?

If your pilot flinches, hesitates, or balks in any way, you might want to consider changing flights. If you cannot drive your vehicle with authority and assurance, your destination becomes increasingly questionable. In bowling, you yourself are the vehicle. Hence, we could ask you before a tournament:

- Can you play the game?
- Can you win?
- If things don't go your way, can you persevere, stay centered, and continue to bowl well?

Your unrehearsed, authentic answers to these questions will tell you whether you are prepared to win in any competition venue.

In this chapter we're concerned with performance in high-stakes competition. Because bowlers' abilities and aspirations are so varied, the meaning of "high stakes" is always defined by the individual bowler. There are a few special keys to understanding what it takes to excel. Once mastered, you can play anywhere, and if it is your day, you can win.

I'VE BEEN THERE BEFORE

Perhaps the single most important element in mastering the techniques and tactics of racing is experience. But once you have the fundamentals, acquiring the experience is a matter of time.

Greg LeMond, former American professional road-racing cyclist, Tour de France champion

There's a myth in sports that if you just get to the championship round often enough, you will get used to the experience. Then, supposedly, you sort of automatically figure out how to win. Examples abound in virtually all sports—football, basketball, bowling. You see a head nod when first-timers get to the final and then lose, as if people are saying, "You have to get there a few times before you can win one."

Take the 2015 USBC Masters played in Green Bay, Wisconsin. With over three hundred competitors, only a handful of familiar names would make most fan's betting board. Jason Belmonte, Pete Weber, Tommy Jones, Walter Ray Williams Jr. and Chris Barnes, and a few other all-stars were expected to quickly rise to the top. The smart money always picks the experienced warrior. In fact, the smart money did not completely predict who ended up in the final five on the telecast. Jason Belmonte and Pete Weber did make it, and in a hard fought battle, Jason bested A.J. Johnson for his third Masters title in a row (the other two players in the stepladder final were Martin Larsen and Mike DeVaney).

But, as a rule, is experience really your best ally? Some bowlers think they will somehow acquire the know-how to roll shots under pressure merely by competing and making cuts. This is the belief that mental toughness, and the ability to focus, are absorbed based on experience.

But the contrary might be true. Here's another way to look at the situation, one that tends to be a pressure builder. The more times you put yourself in play, and the more times you make the finals and do *not* win, the more likely you might be to fail again. In some cases, experience might actually hurt you.

Most bowlers who miss 10-pin spares on TV do not feel that the experience of missing spares gives them more confidence to shoot more of them in the finals. Chop the 2-4-5-8-pin bucket a couple of times in a tournament, or worse yet, in sequential tournaments, and this typically does not lead to the "been there before, ready to make this one" feeling.

And, ultimately, if you're in contention to make the show, or repeatedly in position to win, and you don't complete the victory, this can lead to an increased likelihood that you will lose or choke the next time(s) you get a winning opportunity.

What often happens with the awareness of one's perceived failures is that there are multiple negative associations with the opportunity and experience of being in position to win. Unconsciously and consciously you know what happened the last time(s). And it is worse yet if there has been public commentary about your tendencies on TV or in pressure situations.

The rule of thumb for accomplished competitors, as well as those who make mistakes in key situations, is that when the pressure heats up, they automatically revert to behavior patterns that are grooved-in the most.

If you generally make one awful shot in finals games, you'll tend to find a way to make another one on the next big day. If you sweat spares, with a mixed history of making them under pressure, you might be a phenomenal spare shooter in practice or league, and still grab the ball too tightly when the lights get too hot.

So, does practice always make perfect? No. It's much more accurate to say that practice makes permanent. If you practice in a relaxed manner, you might get better, but you won't necessarily get better at playing in pressure situations. That takes something more.

IT MUST BE REAL TO GET THE FEEL

A diamond is a chunk of coal that did well under pressure.

Henry Kissinger, former Secretary of State

You must be able to imagine with crystalline clarity what it feels like to bowl in the Masters or the U.S. Open. Top athletes in any sport do this. Be mindful here. Most bowlers can fantasize about playing in the finals; on the other hand, most bowlers almost never picture themselves shooting spares under pressure. You might want to see that in your mind as well.

When you practice, try alternating strike shots with spare shots, even if you strike on your first practice ball—just as you try to create muscle memory by repeating your best technique on shots. You have to create a subconscious competition memory by simulating pressure in as many ways as you can.

The alternative is the time-tested method of competing as much as you can in the hope you'll get accustomed to pressured play. Your acquired habits in relaxing the tension in your body, focusing, and getting involved in the process of performing when the heat is on will develop just like any other muscle memory.

STREET FIGHTING

**Some people say that I have an attitude—maybe I do.
But I think that you have to.
You have to believe in yourself when no one else does—
that makes you a winner right there.**

Venus Williams, former number one women's tennis player

Occasionally, you might find yourself up against a "big dog," someone who is so established with his or her titles, experience, and level of play that he or she seems invincible on the lanes. It might not be nice, or ladylike or gentlemanly, but there's a way to approach this problem.

As an example, before the 2012 Women's U.S. Open, one athlete I spoke with was recognizing that there were a few women playing who felt like champions, seemingly all the time. They expected to win, and wouldn't wilt if given the chance on the outdoor lanes in downtown Reno. This athlete was lamenting that she used to feel that way, but it was a long-lost feeling that seemed impossible to recapture.

I asked her a question: "Could you take any of them in a street fight?" The athlete brightened, laughed, and replied with confidence that she could at least bring a battle. More seriously, we discussed taking that attitude to the tournament. So, here's a question you can ask yourself: "If I had to do any other kind of battle with my opponent, could I win or at least put up an amazingly stiff fight?" Whether it is street fighting, a battle of wits, chess, or a baking contest, could you win, or at least bring some game? When you can locate that feeling, the one that makes you know you can bring a fight, you'll find the true champion inside of you—the one who can play anyone, anytime.

TAKING A SHOT TO THE MOUTH

All the adversity I've had in my life, all my troubles and obstacles, have strengthened me. . . . You may not realize it when it happens, but a kick in the teeth may be the best thing in the world for you.

Walt Disney

Bowling is always a test. Something unexpected, unplanned for, and unrehearsed will happen in every single match. It is lawful. The universe always delivers. It always finds the edge of your tolerance, the edge of your sense of safety, and the limit of your willingness to wipe the blood off your nose and to play anew.

Champions do not get blown off course by turbulence. They learn strategies that work. Here are great questions for your mental game. You have to become an expert at asking:

- What am I supposed to learn here?
- What am I supposed to master?
- What quality am I supposed to possess to deal with this?

You are going to take a shot to the mouth. It is guaranteed. Did you prepare? You must love to compete and to take and pass life tests. You wouldn't be here right now if this were not true. For any situation that can occur during your bowling, you can develop the strategy of looking up (or wherever you believe answers come from) and asking, "What am I to do?"

The answer is as simple as going on any journey. Can you fly this thing? Will you get to your destination? Can you handle challenging weather patterns? Bring these questions with you. Don't hesitate. Prepare for a champion's trip.

CHAMPIONS THINK AND ACT IN SPECIAL WAYS

Watch your thoughts, they become words;
watch your words, they become actions;
watch your actions, they become habits;
watch your habits, they become character;
watch your character, for it becomes your destiny.

Frank Outlaw, late president of the Bi-Lo Stores

In the 10th frame of the 2015 Mark Roth/Marshall Holman PBA Doubles Championship, PBA champion Andres Gomez needed three strikes to force his opponent to mark. The oil pattern was touchy and strikes by both doubles teams were hard to come by. He not only packed the tenth, he ended up forcing a one ball roll-off. In the roll-off Gomez threw a strike to win the match and advance. It was not just the fact that he struck at crucial times, but watching him, his self-assuredness and commitment to his shot left no doubt that he knew he was going to do it.

WHO DOES THAT?

First we might ask, "How do players *do* that?" But, more important, we should ask, "What *kind* of person can do that?" More to the point, do *you* have the right traits? And if you don't, can they be developed?

There are lots of questions right there. The most important one to you is whether or not you have what it takes. The other key question is whether you can develop these winning traits.

Winners really do come in all shapes, sizes, and personality styles. What is clear is that no one can surgically graft the right stuff onto you. However, with the right motivation, intention, and guidance, it might very well be possible for anyone who can hang in there to develop winning personality traits and success-oriented thinking.

Clutch performers are special in bowling. And in other sports there's a long list who fit that description. NFL quarterback Tom Brady, pro tennis star Roger Federer, and PGA golfer Jordan Spieth are some world class examples.

If we go past the stage that everyone can see, the performance, and we talk to the athletes themselves, much is revealed. We can also give them personality tests, and talk to significant others. When we do this, some really important information emerges.

THINKING AND PERSONALITY TRAITS OF CHAMPIONS—THE TOP EIGHT

There may be people that have more talent than you,
but there's no excuse for anyone to work harder than you do.

Derek Jeter, five-time baseball World Series champion

The following list might be considered eight of the top traits for winning personalities. If you already possess any one of them, that's great. If you're not strong in an area, decide whether you could make a desired trait part of who you are.

1. **High motivation and commitment.** In some ways we could begin and end here. Without this quality a bowler will stop training as soon as the going gets too rough. When you have true commitment, you have the world. You'll work through fatigue, injury, disappointment, momentary failure, self-doubt, or any other setback. Your intention is your four-wheel drive. If you have it, you just keep on going.

2. **Goal oriented.** It has been said that you can't hit your target with your eyes closed. Great bowlers are up to something. They have a plan, and they follow through to make sure that it happens. Reaching for the stars is wonderful. Pick a star. Now pick a strategy to get to that star—and follow through.

3. **Optimism and positive expectations.** This quality is an essential part of being able to see the upside, the learning, and the growth in every training and competition experience. Without this winning trait, there are so many pitfalls on the road to winning, and on the road to winning again, that lesser individuals cannot keep traveling.

It doesn't take much imagination to come up with all the things that can feel like setbacks in your body, in training, and in competing. Winners understand this. They act as if the bowling universe gives them exactly what they need in order to strengthen, learn, develop as a person, and become a champion. Losers tend to feel that life has ganged up on them. Are you a winner?

4. **The right kind of perfectionism.** Typically, perfectionism can be crippling, with its overemphasis on doing everything exactly right. Certain kinds of perfectionism can cause overthinking, self-punishment, and a negative emotional life.

The winning kind of perfectionists still maintain high standards. Often they like to be well organized, but not always. Most important, they don't sweat mistakes or missed shots, and they don't mentally self-punish. This kind of winner does not get overly concerned about the judgments or criticisms of others. They know their own standards, and they know that the critics don't roll the ball—they themselves roll it.

Champions use perfectionism to drive their practice plans and practice shots. They suspend perfection demands once the competition lights come on, shifting into the mode of bringing maximum effort to shots.

5. **A striking ability to focus and concentrate.** Way beyond most competitors, athletic champions can zero in on key performance elements. They are uncanny in their capacity to remain untouched by distractions.

A term for this trait might be called "quiet mind." The bowler has one point of relaxed, clear focus. Time stands still. Nothing outside the moment at hand matters. And the critical point is this—champions stay awake and aware immediately after shots. This allows them to dispassionately sense and see what has happened and to make adjustments for the next shot.

6. **The ability to handle virtually any stressor that comes up during training or competition.** Superiorly trained soldiers learn that all battle plans change once the enemy is engaged. They know that they will deal with situations as they occur and change.

Winners have a sense of confidence about their military-like capacity to adapt, improvise, and survive anything that comes their way. They keep anxiety at bay, have excellent levels of emotional control, and don't let any of the storms of bowling life overwhelm them. A winning trait is to be an athlete who's able to say, "I'm even better under pressure." With the game on the line, a champion wants the ball in her hand.

7. **A winning personality that includes mental toughness.** Mental toughness can be defined in many ways. Think of a long-distance runner, a boxer, or a veteran bowler. In any one of these cases, how would you define the athlete's toughness? Dealing with pain? Falling down and getting back up? Getting dominated by opponents and not giving in?

No matter what happens, the mentally tough *just keep coming*. They might not be the most gifted athletes in the world. But they're the ones with blood on their faces, mud in their hair, and tears streaking their cheeks . . . and still going on. Others might shake their heads in disbelief, but when the dust clears, the mentally tough are still standing.

8. **Intelligence quotient.** Sports intelligence is a newly recognized aspect of a winning personality. A person can be a genius, or simply really smart in many things. She can be smart in math, reading, music, problem solving, or other areas. Being bowling smart means you have the ability to accurately analyze your own performance, create and innovate on the lanes, and be an astute student of the game. Bowlers who have sport intelligence can learn even more readily from instruction.

FINDING THOSE PARTS OF YOU

A man is but the product of his thoughts; what he thinks, he becomes.

Mahatma Gandhi

Knowing all this about winning personalities does not necessarily leave you in one of the two camps—the winners or the losers. Consider the eight traits just listed. Does any one of them feel completely foreign to you? Probably not. Assess which traits you have the most and least of, and which you think you need the most. These traits are like vitamins—your body needs them, but some more than others. For instance, the first trait listed—high motivation and commitment—is near the top in terms of what you require to have a winning personality.

Number eight, the intelligence quotient, might not be as crucial if you have great coaching or pro shop help. If you lack trait five—the ability to focus and concentrate—you're likely to encounter significant, long-term competition problems. The good news is that trait five, like all the other winning personality traits, can be developed and improved by reading this book, listening to your coaches and sports psychologists, and learning from other mentors you locate.

There is a fundamental psychological principle that you only recognize qualities in another person that exist within your self. If you can identify with any aspect of being a champion, it means that quality exists within you, but it may be lying dormant. In your mind's eye you can use imagery to see that part of you being activated…and then act on it.

WINNING PERSONALITY RATING FORM

Can everybody be a player of the year? Well, no. But you can absolutely develop the traits that the best of the best have. To assess your current levels of the winning personality traits, use a rating form like that shown in figure 2.1. Then go to work developing your winning personality.

I wish I could throw every shot like it was the ninth frame and I just had the front seven and a spare.

Ken Yokobosky, former Team USA coach

If you're not moving through training and competition the way you wish, rescan this chapter. See if you can find your solutions here. You can find something in this chapter specifically for you nearly every day. The principles presented here will work for as long as you are committed to employ them. No one is excused. The beauty of this game is that nature does not lie, even if we want it to. Your results will tell you if you have been playing by the champion guidelines. After that, play every frame as if it's the ninth, and you just had the front seven and a spare!

10 = very strong; 5 = average; 0 = very weak

1. Motivation and commitment: _____

   Comment or plan: _____

2. Goal orientation and goal setting: _____

   Comment or plan: _____

3. Optimism and positive expectations: _____

   Comment or plan: _____

4. Positive perfect habits: _____

   Comment or plan: _____

5. Ability to focus and concentrate: _____

   Comment or plan: _____

6. Handling stressors in and out of the bowling environment: _____

   Comment or plan: _____

7. Mental toughness: _____

   Comment or plan: _____

8. Intelligence quotient: _____

   Comment or plan: _____

Scoring: Overall, as a champion, you should have a score no lower than 64. If your score is below 56, you're probably not getting champion results. Below 50, and you have some thinking to do about what you're up to. If you're below an 8 on any given measure, challenge yourself immediately to bring that score up.

Figure 2.1 Winning trait self-assessment and development plan.

From D. Hinitz, 2016, *Bowling psychology*. (Champaign, IL: Human Kinetics).

CHAPTER 3

Establishing Your Preshot Routine

The best way to predict the future is to create it.

Peter Drucker, educator and author

Welcome to the big time! Elite golfers, gymnasts, divers, and bowlers all must make their moves at critical moments, and they must do it alone; no one is allowed to touch the athlete or change the game. The performer is called on to deliver the goods in front of the entire universe. This leaves all kinds of time for mental gears to churn in preparation.

Many world-class athletes who must execute a skill without facing a defense develop pre-skill routines to help clear their minds and shake off pressure. Michael Jordan bounced and spun the basketball a precise number of times before shooting a free-throw. Jordan Spieth lines up his shot, measures his swing, and sets his feet before each swing. Baseball pitchers handle rosin bags, spit, and rub the ball before throwing a pitch. Great athletes from every sport, including professional bowlers, know to set themselves up to repeat desired action sequences. In the suggested tips for the mental game, world-class coaches and competitors make this point repeatedly (see chapter 10).

Though no one can see the silent part of a great athlete's preshot routine, this element is every bit as essential for success as going through the physical motions. The goal of the preshot routine is to firmly establish the three Cs—concentration, confidence, and control—by combining physical behaviors with mental preparation.

WHAT IS A PRESHOT ROUTINE?

Routine is liberating—it makes you feel in control.

Carol Shields, *The Republic of Love*

The preshot routine is a standard, established sequence of thoughts and motions that the bowler performs before rolling the ball in game situations. Preshot sequences serve to focus, coordinate, and relax you, increasing the probability of throwing a great shot.

The physical aspects of the preshot routine are obvious, but there are treasures to be found in the silent, mental part of a great athlete's set routine before performing a skill. Internal preshot self-direction is every bit as essential as the physical sequence. In reality, the mental and physical aspects of the preshot routine are so intertwined that it would take surgical intervention to separate them. You must attend to both to reach your maximum potential.

Top bowlers go through set sequences of behaviors before they roll their shots, regardless of the situation, tournament, or practice. The preshot routine might start as early as when the bowler rises from his chair, or he might begin his routine just before going to the line by wiping off the ball, drying his hands, and shuffling his feet.

Competition environments are twofold: the external environment and the environment inside the athlete's head. Lane conditions, noise, lights, and opponents jumping up out of turn are examples of external environment factors, whereas ball choices, questioning what happened on errant shots, and the importance of the next rolled ball are all aspects of the internal environment. Get a hundred bowlers in a room, and you'll hear a hundred different stories about the crazy, distracting thoughts that shoot through their minds in high-intensity situations.

The preshot routine is a way to create order out of chaos. It's a way to set the gears of a complex machine so they run smoothly under any circumstances. In this chapter we'll explore the psychological reasons for making sure you have a consistent, rehearsed preshot routine.

PREDICTION AND CONTROL IN HIGH-INTENSITY SETTINGS

The rules of survival never change, whether you're in a desert or in an arena.

Bear Grylls, adventurer and author

A basic psychological survival principle supports the good sense of developing a preshot routine. This principle centers on prediction and control. To suspend anxiety and maintain confidence you must be able to accurately predict what's going to happen and control your responses to the situation.

■Honing Your Preshot Routine With Carolyn Dorin-Ballard

It's pretty cool to think about when I had to do a preshot routine to get up and make a shot to win a match.

Carolyn Dorin-Ballard, USBC Hall of Famer

Carolyn Dorin-Ballard has won almost everything there is to win in amateur and professional bowling. She has won world championships as a member of Team USA, has been the player of the year two times, has 20 professional titles, including 3 major championship titles, and once rolled 21 consecutive strikes over two games to set the record for televised bowling. However, her career has not always been all glamour.

It was 1994 on a cold winter night in Tennessee, and Carolyn Dorin had never won an individual professional bowling title. Later she would be considered one of the greatest female bowlers of all time, and win a lot of them, but back then she was still unproven. Carolyn had made the finals, but the tournament was put on temporaryhold.

The power had gone out in the bowling center. Players were huddled in the bar around the fire for warmth. The TV trucks awaited a generator so they could film the telecast. She was waiting to work her way through a step-ladder of future Hall of Fame bowlers.

There was not a lot that Carolyn could pack with her to prepare her for this circumstance. She was on the road, away from most of her support system, bowling in a final that would end sometime around midnight, ultimately playing against one of the all-time best tournament performers, Aleta Sill.

Carolyn did, however, pack the three things that would propel her to that title. She had an amazingly efficient approach and delivery honed by thousands of hours of practice, trust in the game she brought, and very important, a preshot routine that allowed her to feel composed, confident, and at home with her game.

In that midnight hour, Carolyn had to fill the 10th frame with strikes to force Aleta to strike on her first ball. Carolyn did it. "I really feel that that night I was prepared, and it worked." What followed was one of the most epic careers in all of professional sports.

The game has changed a bit in terms of lane play. Carolyn's game has changed and evolved with it. In the more than 20 years since that first title, there's one thing that has not changed. Carolyn brings her preshot routine with her on every shot, every time. "The preshot routine is the same. It may just vary in time a bit depending on the situation. . . . It's kind of cool to think about how many times I've done that preshot routine."

One of the strengths of Carolyn's game is consistency—under any circumstances. At the Kegel International Training Center in Lake Wales, Florida, Carolyn is recorded as the most accurate player in the history of the testing center. She once hit the

(continued)

Carolyn Dorin-Ballard *(continued)*

same target on the lanes 30 times in a row at the exact same speed!

So what does Carolyn do? Here are some of her key preshot components:

- I don't watch my opponent.
- I always look down.
- I wipe my ball off at least three times.
- I stare at one focal point.
- I close my eyes and put myself somewhere where it's easy.
- I breathe and rarely look up before I get up on the approach. ("I know the task at hand; there's no reason to look around.")
- I just say, "Hit your target." I feel that if I hit my target I have my best chance to have my best result.

Carolyn has two key recommendations with respect to the construction and execution of a preshot routine. First, she's clear that everyone's routine is individual to themselves. "I teach everyone that they are unique. Some people start their preshot routines waiting in the chair. To say that it happens all in that one second before the approach, well, probably for most players, but not everybody."

Carolyn recognizes individual differences in competitors' needs for shot preparation. However, for herself, she does not add self-talk components. "Everybody needs to find what is going to get them into their zone before they get up on the approach. That is key. Because when you're not in your zone there has got to be something that triggers you to get back into what you do. I don't really think. I never said to myself, 'throw it good.' Going through my preshot routine is really all I thought about. I never said all the other stuff."

"It really is simple. We as bowlers make it harder than it really is. You want to manipulate everything, but you really can't. What I did to actually prepare myself to get up on the approach was so simple. That was a big part of my success."

With experience and thousands of preshot repetitions, Carolyn has grooved in her competition mentality. "I think that preshot routine is very important. It gets you into the routine of doing the same thing over and over again. You don't want to rush through it; you want to take your time. It makes you consistent. It allows you to be in the same zone each time you step on the approach.

As a competitor and as a champion, Carolyn has integrated her preshot routine into who she is as a person. "Now when I close my eyes on the approach, I think more of where my life is now. No matter what the result is, nothing that detrimental can happen."

We should all be so free.

This makes perfect sense in survival terms. Think about life before civilization. People living in the wild had to be able to notice changes in the environment rapidly, and predict the behaviors of other creatures such as wild animals and human enemies. If they could not predict what was going to happen, or take control over their fight-or-flight options, primitive men and women were likely to end up as lunch. Prediction gave them time to prepare; control gave them the chance to avoid the situation or to prevent it from escalating.

Anxiety leads to vigilance, which, in the case of primitive people, was probably a good thing. Without the ability to predict when trouble would strike, or a sense of control over some situations, primitive people would have been anxious all the time.

When anxiety becomes overwhelming, it leads to panic, which severely diminishes fine motor coordination. Cave people learned to attend to signals that something was about to happen, which helped them handle dangerous situations; they also had to learn to control their anxiety to avoid panicking.

All this has direct application to your bowling game. The "wild" atmosphere of the bowling center is your unpredictable thoughts, feelings, noises, lighting, and lane conditions that might attack you. In essence, your concentration, attention, and confidence are threatened. An internal sense of danger comes from the pressure of having to win or the fear of a bad outcome. Your task is to introduce order, control, and predictability into the competitive situation. The preshot routine allows you to establish a sense of steadiness and safety in the face of all the possible internal and external distractions you might experience.

Ultimately, you should strive to achieve the ideal performance state whenever you compete. The goal is to take the best of what you achieve in practice, when your mental and emotional state is relaxed and unpressured, and transmit it to league and tournament play. To do this, you need to groove in the preshot routine in practice, when bowling is free flowing and your mental state is unharried. Your preshot routine then becomes a natural part of your competitive bowling, signaling your unconscious mind that everything is under control. This routine also prepares you to go through the entire shot cycle, described in chapter 4.

SETTING UP AN EFFECTIVE PRESHOT ROUTINE

Whatever good things we build end up building us.

Jim Rohn, entrepreneur and motivational speaker

You create your preshot routine by establishing a chain of naturally related events. This creates a sense of order. For humans, it's natural for events that occur in sequence to cue the same sequence in the future. This chain of events can be created consciously or unconsciously.

For example, smokers who like to smoke after meals automatically have thoughts and reactions that cue them to want to smoke after they eat. People who like to snack when they read or watch TV start getting munchie urges when they pull out a book or turn on the television. In those examples, smoking is like a preshot routine for winding down after a meal. Eating is like a preshot routine for relaxed reading or TV viewing.

The natural human tendency is to automatically associate pleasant and positive events with the thoughts, feelings, and actions that precede them. By consciously designing the links in your brain before bowling, you exploit this natural tendency. Planning and organizing a preshot sequence will help you attain better performances, such as those found in practice, all the time.

The obvious place to start in creating a preshot routine is with the motions you already naturally use before you roll the ball. Most experienced bowlers have characteristic habitual patterns. Some behaviors are easily recognized, and others are not. The task is to pick three to five elements of the approach sequence that lead to shot delivery. Then use these same elements every time you prepare to roll a ball as a way of cueing attention, focus, and positive feelings.

Setting up your preshot routine is like throwing a lasso around concentration. Though you can't expect to keep all thoughts from your mind, you can learn to keep your mind from wandering so much that your concentration shifts. A personalized routine pattern steers concentration in a single direction even when other thoughts and noises intrude.

CREATING THE PRESHOT ROUTINE

The first step in preshot design is observation. As mentioned, you probably have three to five behaviors that are characteristic of your approach. Look for actions that provide a feeling of being synchronized, as in this example:

> I take a full, relaxing breath, inhale and exhale, at the ball return. I wipe off the ball. I take a good look at the lines and visualize the mark and projected ball path. I silently say the word *trust* in my mind. As I do, I feel the surge of trust in my ability and training, and the ball's design to roll properly. I set my feet. I see the mark one more time. Then I start my push-away.

Every bowler has a preferred sequence. Make sure your sequence has these four essential elements (Vernacchia et al. 1996):

1. **Notice what is important and let everything else go.** Observe the lanes and surrounding competition area. Note anything that is important to be aware of: pin configuration on spares, oil-pattern mapping, sources of noise, and so on. You have nothing else to do at this point except conduct a comprehensive scan.

   Remember prediction and control? Awareness of the playing field lends a sense of mastery to being in the bowling competition environment. You can't, of course, control everything. Lane oil is invisible, bad racks can be hard to spot, and other people behave unpredictably. Decide what's important for you to notice, and let the rest go. This gives you a sense of control over what you can do, no matter what's happening around you. In a nutshell, pay attention to anything around you that matters, and discard the rest.

2. **Get your strategy in order.** Have a strategy for where to focus attention. This is a sequence. A hundred things could distract you, including various thoughts, emotions, physical sensations, noises, and other bowlers. No matter what else is knocking on the door of your awareness, your preshot routine provides a place to focus attention.

Some common points of focus are a relaxed arm swing, a steady head, watching the mark, and being solid at the line. Some players will make sure they quiet their minds by looking at the manufacturer's logo on the ball return. Other possibilities include generating warm confidence, using positive self-talk about what you will do, and imagining putting energy into the ball. Pick a strategy that works for you and repeat it until it becomes as automatic as muscle memory.

3. **See what will happen in your mind's eye.** Visualize what the ball will do on the lane, or how you would like your body to feel at any point of your approach and delivery. Areas of intention might include roll and rotation, ball path, breakpoint, soft hands, steady rhythm, or solid foundation. Seeing and feeling behavior, as if viewing the future, can result in your mind and body making all kinds of subtle adjustments to create the visualized intention.

When visualizing, you should be mentally, physically, and emotionally in the moment of what you are about to create. If you have the bowling skills to make it happen, your unconscious mind can fulfill your visualized mission. An important note here is that great visualizers focus only on what they intend their body and ball to do. They avoid thinking about the consequences of making or missing the shot.

4. **Use a cue.** Using a cue is like pulling on one strand of a spider web and having all the other strands come together. All mental, emotional, and physical training meshes smoothly without having to think about them. The 2004 USBC Open Singles champion John Janawicz simply repeated the words, "push, posture, post" on his way to a record 858 three-game set.

Other useful cue words for bowlers are *finish* or *post,* for finishing in a balanced, bowling-trophy position, or *now*, *free*, or *yes!* Some bowlers prefer cue phrases, such as, *I am an athlete. I am strong. I am solid.* The point is to use a silent trigger that coordinates and focuses you. It's best to keep your cue brief.

The preshot routine is one of the most reliable tools in the mental game arsenal. It's an oft-cited key that champions of many sports say they rely on. The routine triggers a sequence of positive thoughts, feelings, and actions. It's also an internal resource that generates familiarity, positive feelings, and a sense of control over your own reactions under pressure.

THE ANSWER*

Hey . . . I'm about to bowl one game for $20,000!

Kari Schwager, Mini-Eliminator finalist

I did it!

Kari Schwager, 2007 Mini-Eliminator champion,
First woman to win an amateur megabucks tournament

---

*Adapted from D. Hinitz, 2007 (Apr.), "The answer," *Bowling This Month* 14(4).

In the moments before you execute a shot, your brain is a busy place. We are verbal creatures by nature, and therein can lie both our problems and our solutions. As part of your preshot routine you can learn to harness your subvocal self-talk to bring yourself into the present moment. You can then direct your athletic efforts in the most productive way.

On February 9, 2007, Kari Schwager did something that no woman had done in the history of Las Vegas Megabucks tournaments—she won. Initially, Kari was not the odds-on favorite to pull off this feat. The field at the Mini-Eliminator was studded with world famous competitors. Her closest opponent, U.S. team member and PBA champion Rhino Page, had nearly won the National Amateur Championship a month earlier.

Many questioned whether Kari had what it took to win the Mini. She answered them all. Curiously, she brought something to her mental game that most athletes would never think of—she brought questions. Her answers to those questions took her to victory.

Two Questions

Bowlers often talk of playing a *feel* game. Your preshot routine is designed to get you into the kind of zone that lets your feel for the game predominate. *Feel, flow,* and *being in the zone* all mean pretty much the same thing.

No matter how you describe that feeling of being *on*, two qualities are essential to the experience. First, you are completely present in the moment. Second, you know exactly what you intend to do.

The problem is that many athletes wait for *the zone* or *feel* to visit them. They don't know how to trigger the flow that will allow their best bowling to emerge. This of course leads to unpredictability and inconsistency in performance. When will you feel enough flow to bowl your best? Good news is just around the corner. You don't have to leave yourself open to the blessings of the gods of competition. You simply have to craft your preshot routine to serve you.

Interestingly, your mind can't resist answering questions. Just read the following:

- What is your mother's maiden name?
- What was the name of your first pet?
- What is the color of your favorite bowling ball?

Amazing, right? Once a question enters your mind, your mind automatically provides an answer.

What does this have to do with your preshot routine? Simple—you have to know what to ask up front. Two questions can zoom you into peak performance mode.

Question 1: *Am I present?* Yes, you actually ask yourself this question, quietly in your mind. *Am I here?* Develop the discipline to ask this question before each and every shot. The benefits are many. Once you ask the question, you automatically know the truth of your answer. It's hard to lie to yourself. If your mind is elsewhere, focused on past shots, future consequences, fears, or frustrations, you'll know it, and you can adjust.

How do you adjust? This part is easy. Demand of yourself—*be here.* Yes, that's right. You simply say to yourself, *Be here now.* When you consciously command yourself to be present, it's like a cold glass of water in your face. It snaps you to attention, and it shakes you free of past frames and future consequences.

You must show up for your frames, and for your life. Ask the question. *Am I here?* Insist that you be here now. No need to keep the receipt. You own the results. If this simple command to yourself does not snap you to focused attention, try a second question.

"What do I need to know?"
Kari Schwager's silent question before each shot on the final day of the Mini-Eliminator

Question 2: *What is called for here? Or, What am I doing? What do I need to know?* These are orienting questions. They bring you into the moment and make you whole.

Your answer can be internal or external. It can be mental, emotional, physical, or spiritual. You might be aware that you need to remember a key element or movement in your physical game. You might be aware of needing to attend to some aspect of lane play or ball roll. You might remember to stay positive with your self-talk, to visualize, to breathe, or simply to play with an open heart. Ask yourself, *What am I doing? What is called for here?* You might be amazed at what is revealed to you.

Another striking thing is how difficult it can be to maintain the discipline required to ask yourself these simple questions before every shot. Most of us experience periods of mental and physical laziness. Bowling has a high frequency of roll, reload, roll, reload, and so on, which wears down your mental muscle tone. But a big part of establishing your mental game is to remember to ask the two questions.

How do I want to play this shot?
Jack Nicklaus's favorite self-talk question

The Wrong Street

Now there are a number of questions that bowlers privately ask themselves that send them into a tizzy:

- What if I choke?
- What if I miss this spare?
- It's only a five-pin, who could miss this?
- What if I make a fool of myself?

- What if I don't make the cut?
- What if I don't shoot the number?
- What if I don't carry?
- What if I grab one?
- What if I don't get my exemption?
- What if I lose to this guy?
- What if I just wasted my entry or bracket money?

Such questions are common among competitors. But any time you ask these questions you are heading down the wrong street. Your subconscious mind says, *Well you asked, let me show you.* Anything you say to yourself triggers a visualization in the conscious and unconscious mind. When you entertain these kinds of doubts, you're preparing for failure.

Preparing to Win

Every battle is won before it's ever fought.

Sun Tzu

There is one question to ask when you're practicing, when you're beginning a tournament, or when you're entering any critical game or frame. *What do I need to do to win?* Bowling is a sensitive game. Small changes in mood, muscular and emotional tension, confidence, and swing plane can result in significant differences in pin fall and carry.

What do I need to do to win? With proper training, this question will trigger a series of progressive questions or statements from which you can choose to focus your attention. For example, one of these questions is, *What is my target?* If you ask this question before every shot, you'll clear your mind from overthinking your swing mechanics. This question directs you to the present moment and orients you to the process of what you are doing, with no stress about outcomes. Remember that it's common to laze into playing shots without formally re-declaring what you are doing when you bowl. Asking this question steers your mind in the right direction.

I have recommended several questions to ask yourself as part of your pre-shot routine. These questions let your natural game emerge, but you need not use all of them. Pick one or two and see how they work for you over time. If you're not happy with the results, change your question. The important thing is to train yourself to ask the right sort of question before *every* shot so that the same response—confidence and control—is triggered every time.

The Fork in the Road

When you arrive at a fork in the road, take it.

Yogi Berra

The road of self-generated questions splits. Pick your route. One fork presents you with open-ended, negative, fear-based questions such as *Why me?* and *What if?* Questions like these can lurk in the subconscious (and conscious) mind and trigger visualizations of choking and losing.

Let's return to the questions that should become your training tapes for process-oriented excellence. Take your pick:

- Am I here and present?
- What is called for here?
- What is my target?
- How am I going to play this shot?
- What is being asked of me?
- What qualities of a champion do I need to call forth?
- What do I need to do to win this frame (game, match, tournament)?

These are powerful forwarding questions, self-talk visualization tools for success. Do what the champions do—prepare your mind to win.

THE THREE Cs

Championship bowlers demonstrate the three Cs of champions: consistency, confidence, and control. The preshot routine is an effective setup for all three. Given that a bowler rolls hundreds of shots during a tournament, the ability to repeat good shots is essential. Knowing that you have a means of focusing coordination and attention boosts your sense of confidence. Owning and practicing your preshot routine effectively can lead to a wonderful sense of overall control of your game.

To have the benefits of consistency, confidence, and control, you must practice your preshot routine consistently in training. Don't ever roll a throwaway shot—not during training, not during league play, not during tournaments. Every shot is an opportunity to redefine, regroove, and rehearse the preshot routine. Even when you're horsing around, blowing through a few frames, or just warming up, do not skip this step. Lock it in. This will build trust in yourself so you won't have to be concerned about distractions and changes in the competition environment.

All bowlers seek a sense of prediction and control over shots, games, attention, and confidence. The preshot routine is an internal message system that tells the brain, "Ground control to competition brain, now starting the system sequence to liftoff."

You can use the steps in this chapter in any order. Add, subtract, mix, or match them in the way that works best for you. Don't worry about taking the extra few seconds you might need to own an effective internal rhythm.

Every bowler must get to the ball, view the lanes, breathe, and deliver the ball anyway. When your preshot routine fits your hand like a glove, you give yourself the best chance to say, "Hey I did it!"

CHAPTER 4

The Shot Cycle: One Shot for the Money

**To win takes a complete commitment of mind and body.
When you can't make that commitment,
they don't call you a champion anymore.**

Rocky Marciano, undefeated heavyweight boxing champion

In December 2015 at the Rolltech PBA World Championship, Gary Faulkner Jr. made his first professional television show. He had to work through a grueling stepladder of champion players, Scott Norton, Ryan Ciminelli, and E.J. Tackett. In so doing he became the PBA's second African American titlist, and he won a major championship title to boot.

This former collegiate star rolled six strikes on his first eight attempts in the title match. Overall, in his three matches, he probably only threw two shots that he would have wanted back. Once he got going, Gary's demeanor was regal. He carried himself like a seasoned self-assured champion, "The first shot I was nervous, but after that I didn't think about anything. My mind was free. I didn't watch the other guys. I don't show a lot of emotions. My goal is always to win; I didn't come here to lose." (Vint 2015)

Frame to frame, Gary's behavior was like an imaged copy of the last one. He would go through his preparatory sequence, set himself, execute, watch his shot, calmly reset for the next shot, or rest. Even after the commercial break, there was no visible change in either his physical sequence, or his impressively calm demeanor. Without being able to peek directly into Gary's brain, the viewer was treated to an exhibition of phenomenal bowling, and a visible demonstration of the shot cycle.

What if you made the PBA TV telecast for the very first time? What if you were given one shot at making it? A host of mental game tactics could pave your way to victory, including one special strategy that you can use anytime, anywhere on your mission to hit your peak in competition.

There is a way of approaching every strike, every spare, and every game that will ensure you play your best game under any conditions. The other advantage to this approach, for anyone seeking to improve, is that it keeps you on a continuous process improvement path. In this chapter we're going to look at what to do with your one shot—which is all you really have at any given time, anyway!

In 2001, in *Focused for Bowling*, I wrote about staying in sync throughout the shot cycle. Over the years there has been refinement of the principles involved in the delivery of your best shot—both in bowling and elsewhere in life. In this chapter, I'll update the steps for a successful plan for any shot, or for virtually any activity in which you're involved.

One of the frustrations of bowlers at every skill level, from beginner to touring professional, is the change in tension levels, feel for the ball, and timing when entering a competitive situation. Bowlers who deliver the ball wonderfully in practice, even shadow practice, right before the competition, sometimes lose their coordination and steadiness when the lights come on.

Many great bowlers exhibit deliveries and shot cycles that are beautifully synchronized, or in sync. To be in sync means to be in the right frame of mind and physically coordinated from the time the ball is picked up, through the delivery and release, and into the recovery and preparation phase for the next shot (see description of Gary Faulkner Jr. at the top of this chapter). All great players have marvelously synchronized shot cycles.

It would be poor etiquette to identify professionals who have fragmented or unbalanced shot cycles. Most of us can recognize when an athlete appears to be overly mechanical when the pressure is on, or overcome with anger or frustration when things are going badly. Bowlers who don't regroup after an errant shot, or a clutch shot by an opponent, show up for ensuing shots looking rushed or frazzled. This often causes a decline in performance for the remainder of the game.

There are many ways to regulate the competition engine so that shots can be executed as cleanly and confidently as in practice. One of the best ways is to take control of the accelerator and brakes in the internal nervous system. When people talk about someone getting nervous, it simply means that action hormones like adrenaline are sending messages throughout the body. The energy conductors, the nerves in the body, become over-activated. In this chapter you'll learn to set up and manage your thoughts and feelings from beginning to end for superior shots and games—under any circumstances.

If your only exposure to competitive bowling is watching pro bowlers on TV, you might believe that top athletes rarely get tense, anxious, or worried about performance. Many of the top pros seem calm and cool as they deliver shot after shot. During the finals of the 2015 Rolltech PBA World Championships, a statistic flashed on the screen about Scott Norton. In more than 60 games of qualifying that week he had made 106 out of 106 single-pin spares. On non-split spares Scott is essentially automatic It is not that Scott is completely dispassionate, with ice water running through his veins. He is as passionate a player as you will watch compete. It is just that no one does this without having a process that is so grooved in that it is unshakeable.

Many bowlers, even elite professional bowlers, can worry about doing well and overactivate their nervous systems, causing sweaty hands and jerky coordination. Overthinking takes on a life of its own. Other bowlers manage to remain in sync despite feelings of excitement and nervous tension. They have learned to tame anxiety and bring out their best in high-stakes situations.

Staying in sync is about working effectively under any circumstances to call forth great performances under pressure. There's nothing wrong with emotional activation—it's normal when participating in an important event. In fact, the body doesn't make a distinction in the adrenaline surges created by fear, anxiety, excitement, or anticipation. It's up to you to harness your body's reactions productively.

RECOGNITION

Self-awareness is value free. It isn't scary.
It doesn't imply that you will subject yourself to needless pain.

Deepak Chopra, author and public speaker

The first step in learning to stay in sync is to know when your emotional levels are interfering with your bowling. This can be difficult in the macho world of competitive athletics. Acknowledging basic human reactions to the excitement, concerns, hurts, and hopes of high-stakes league and tournament play can be embarrassing. Athletes sometimes pretend they don't experience the distracting, even disturbing, feelings that everyone feels at times.

Any kind of game situation—from league play to high-roller, big cash prize tournaments to trying to make the cut on the professional tour—can stimulate a range of feelings, from fun and excitement to being over-amped. Tension tends to escalate during certain moments in a game, such as when you have to make a key spare, when you're finishing a game or series that's going very well (or very poorly), or when you're performing for an audience.

Ups and downs in performance reflect your skill and training. Bowling significantly or consistently worse in competition than you do in practice is a sure sign that your mental and emotional states are changing the way you deliver the ball.

A reminder is in order: excitement and arousal are not emotional villains. A certain amount of excitement is helpful in getting us motivated. Having the juices flowing can also motivate increased focus and contribute to the enjoyment that should be part of any competition.

Every bowler has an optimal level of excitement at which he or she feels sufficiently motivated but not overwhelmed. When the emotional energy to compete is lacking, then flatness, loss of focus, and boredom can result. When the excitement level is too high, choking can occur. Freedom of movement and flow can falter, coordination can get mechanical, and concerns and worries might increase.

Young or inexperienced bowlers might not recognize what's happening to their emotions and energy. They might feel something happening in terms of excitement, tension, or distraction, but not know what it is, why it's occurring, or whether it's OK to talk about. No one wants to seem like a wimp. This keeps many bowlers from figuring out why they're feeling the way they do, and from requesting appropriate assistance, support, or guidance.

Any competition-related feelings that come up are absolutely normal. Some of the most common are excitement, fear, nervousness, and anticipation. Just knowing what can commonly be expected can relieve some bowlers of the worry that their particular reactions might not be OK. The trick to staying in sync, though, is being able to control your energy and excitement levels to optimize your performance. Simply having a plan for how to handle competition excitement is, in itself, stress relieving. In the following sections I offer some user-friendly techniques for dialing in the right energy and activation levels.

FIND THE TIGER

**Survival is not about being fearless.
It's about making a decision, getting on and doing it.**

Bear Grylls, British explorer

Excitement, anxiety, and tension can show up in a variety of ways. At the most basic level, when a bowler begins to emotionally amp up in a competition situation, the mind and body are reacting as if risk or danger is present.

Fifty thousand years ago, humans played a different competitive game called survival. Imagine life as it was then. The competition arena was virtually everywhere. The game lasted as long as one could survive. Sometimes the threat was immediate—the growl of a tiger or a stranger with a club.

Back then, as now, when a critical moment appeared, the body went into a fight-or-flight response, causing blood to rush from the fingers, toes, and stomach to the big arm and leg muscles to prepare for action. Action-oriented hormones flushed through the bloodstream. Digestion stopped. Breathing became rapid and shallow. Fine-muscle coordination skills were sacrificed for large-muscle actions such as clubbing the tiger or climbing a tree. In your case, the pending action might be throwing a 15-pound ball for $100,000 or marking in a frame for a league championship.

The good news is that about three minutes after the event or threat passes, the body starts to return to normal functioning. Blood flow returns to the fingers and toes. Fine-muscle coordination returns. Digestion and other metabolic processes flow efficiently again. The game is over. In the wild, the score is humans one, tigers zero.

The problem is you often don't have three minutes to settle into yourself during a match. When anxiety, overexcitement, concern, or fear become part of your bowling experience, your body begins to do the same things it would do in a wilderness survival game. The mind and body activate the fight-or-flight response. You might want to win so badly that you can't sit still, for example, or your fear of losing might speed up your heart rate.

The reaction in your nervous system is similar to the one that would occur if a tiger growled in the bush. A problem occurs when you don't take the danger signals (for example, negative mental self-talk) out of the excitement response, and do not allow for adequate, full recovery and clearing from excitement.

THREE KEYS
TO MANAGING EXCITEMENT

There is more to life than increasing its speed.

Mahatma Gandhi

There are three keys to managing excitement in bowling competition situations. The first key is to recognize the thoughts, feelings, and physical reactions as they occur. Young or inexperienced bowlers don't always have a name for the excitement that comes with performance demands. Other bowlers might feel general anxiety but be unsure why it's happening. I have encountered this even with experienced players who are on television for the first time. They can become confused about the sensations in their bodies, and loss of feel for the ball. Worse yet is when athletes catastrophize or worry that nervousness will run out of control. This puts even more pressure on their bowling.

The second key is to accept competition reactions without negative judgment. Some bowlers get embarrassed or even ashamed that they have excitement and tension reactions. Some degree of body response should be expected when bowling in an important game or tournament. Top professional tour players talk about this phenomenon all the time. Common body reactions are diverse. They include queasiness, feeling hot or cold, difficulty taking full breaths, dizziness, and overly mechanical motions when trying to coordinate shots.

The third key is having a grab bag of strategies to reach into during competitive situations. Excitement management skills are like any other sport skill. They must be learned and then practiced regularly to make them useful. Instead of toning up muscles, you're developing your mental and emotional thermostats. This gives you the confidence to know you can handle any competitive situation.

MASTERING THE COMPETITION CYCLE

By failing to prepare, you are preparing to fail.

Benjamin Franklin

Of all the focus and regulation techniques, an ironclad plan for approaching shots under any circumstances is among the most valuable. Great bowlers know the secret by intuition. Bowlers who habitually fail tend to trip over the mystery. This is a tool that, once mastered, will deepen the well of confidence within you. This rare treasure, which I call the competition cycle, once mastered, can carry you through the toughest times.

Each shot, game, block, and tournament is part of a cycle of experience called the competition cycle. You can break the cycle down into five steps. Once you learn how the competition cycle works, you'll be able to recognize strengths and weaknesses in your mental game.

The cycle has five steps:

1. planning and intention,
2. execution and commitment,
3. observation without judgment,
4. reaction and emotion, and
5. clearing and recovery.

In this section we'll apply these phases specifically to shot making, but the formula, once learned, can be expanded to work in matches, or even a tournament block. These steps will also serve you in school, business, or any other time that committed action is called for.

Step 1: Planning and Intention

Step 1 for any shot is planning and intention. You can start this phase early. As you prepare for your next shot, you should have an idea of what you intend to do. Planning and intention should be part of your preshot routine.

Before your approach, make decisions about ball path, break point, rotation, ball speed, and direction. You can also decide how much you want to go for it, how free and athletic you want to be, and how much you're going to commit to your shot delivery.

Now is the time to ask and answer two of the questions from chapter 3: Am I present? What am I doing? You can't run on automatic in this sport. If you simply stand with your left big toe on the middle dot and throw over the second arrow, you better hope the lanes have been nicely blocked off for your convenience.

But even with house shots, conditions change. This means that, regularly and reliably, you have to check in. Ask yourself, What is the lane calling for? Where does it want me to play? What ball is going to hit best? What tilt, what speed, what shoe surface? These questions are all part of the dance between you and your bowling environment. Consider these factors or risk getting buried.

Also important in step 1 is the commitment to charge forth with your bowling. This is an either-or situation. You either bring a forward-moving, confident, intentional self, or you bring a tentative, cautious, fear-based self. This is your chance to commit to the best you can bring. Use your history, coaching, and experience—all your acquired wisdom—to make decisions. At this point you get to pick if you will be a lion or a mouse.

Two mistakes common in step 1 are too little and too much. Too little attention means inadequate preparation for your shots, which can result in sloppy shots, misplaying the lane, poor timing, or lack of concentration. Inadequate planning means you don't have a clear commitment to a dedicated shot. Too much attention occurs when you extend your planning into your execution phase. Bowlers often continue to think about how to bowl or the consequences of making or missing a shot as they move forward into their delivery sequence. This results in mechanical bowling and is a recipe for choking.

Step 2: Execution and Commitment

**A good plan violently executed now
is better than a perfect plan executed next week.**

General George S. Patton

Once you engage the motor gears, planning is over. The next stage is defined by total commitment to your plan. In this phase, let your training take over. Once you know what you're going to do, you have to trust that you can do it.

This step reflects complete and total surrender to what you intended in the planning phase. Don't spend a moment on thoughts of consequences, old shots, outcomes, or the audience. This step is about keeping a promise and demonstrating the total mental and physical commitment you have made to yourself. The lion is committed. The mouse thinks and questions.

More games are won and lost at this stage than perhaps any other. There are no statistics to measure this. But it might be better to throw the wrong equipment, or even the wrong line, with authority and conviction, than to play perfect balls and lines when unsure and hesitant. At least you can make moves and adjustments off of fully-committed shots.

Once you have settled in to your plan, you must believe in what you are doing—and act like it. Keep your word to yourself. It feels great to bowl, and to live, this way. If you end a tournament knowing that you stiffened up, lost trust in your plan, and held back on your own execution, it makes for a difficult recovery and can leave you with a competition hangover.

During step 2, the action phase, you may have one or two points of physical focus, such as balance, free arm swing, eyes on the mark, or any other element you need to focus on. These points of focus keep the whole mechanism coordinated. A focus point also gives your wandering mind something to do while you deliver a pure shot.

A heart check is called for here, too. You either bring it all, or you don't. As you move through your execution, the proof of your commitment should be obvious. You'll know immediately after the delivery if you gave your all. Ball roll and pin fall reveal your commitment level.

The biggest problem bowlers encounter in the execution phase is a failure to surrender completely to the shot. Whether they distrust their plan or have doubt in their ability to perform, bowlers are frequently infected with the carefulness virus. Overcontrol, and concern about results and score, get in the way of fully and freely rolling your shot.

In the execution phase, you must let go of conscious control. This will make you truly athletic. You have a plan—now go with it completely. If you don't compete with total commitment, success will feel like a trick. Failure will make you angry with yourself for holding back. Bowlers lose more sleep over not bringing their all than they do about whether or not they filled frames.

Step 3: Observation Without Judgment

One of the highest forms of bowling intelligence is the ability to observe without judging or reacting. Once you have mastered this step you'll have an essential self-improvement program, and an anti-choke mechanism built into your shot delivery cycle.

This third step is simple to understand but exceedingly difficult for most bowlers to execute. However, in my experience with some of the top bowlers in the world, this step has been among the most beneficial. This step—also called *awareness*—depends on your ability to maintain executive control over yourself.

One of the most important things you can do to consistently improve and repair your game is to keep an open mind and to nonjudgmentally pay attention after releasing the ball. As soon as the ball is off of your hand, stay awake and aware—no reaction.

Most bowlers simply cannot resist reacting to their shots as soon as the ball rolls off their hand. If you look at a bowler's face immediately after ball release, you'll generally see some form of either dismay or glee. Eyes jerk up and away from target lines; faces sometimes grimace as the ball rolls or skids.

In the briefest moment of time after you release the ball, you have maximum access to information about what just happened. There are three potential input sources:

1. The lane
2. Your body
3. Your freedom of motion (your heart)

Imagine waking up in the morning. For just a moment, if you're still, you have the best chance at remembering your last dream of the night. As soon as you do any other activity, such as brushing your teeth, there is interference. You lose your awareness of the dream.

The same thing happens after a shot. For the briefest instant, if you can keep the interference of emotion or judgment at bay, you have the most information possible about

- the way the lanes are playing,
- the way your ball is behaving,
- what your body did,
- your timing,
- whether you maintained focus and concentration, and
- whether you were free or overcontrolling.

The more open the screen of your mind, the better you can receive this information. The more cluttered your mind with reaction or judgment, the more difficult it is to receive the data, in which case you'll likely remain exactly as smart or as confused as you were before the shot.

The only thing you should be doing for about one or two seconds after you execute the shot is to keep your mind open. There's only one question to ask here—*What am I aware of?* The only real problem when making an errant shot is not knowing what you did.

A second enormous benefit to keeping an open mind is that it serves as an anti-choke mechanism during competition. It works like this. If the most important thing after a shot is what you're aware of, then concerns about results and how you appear to spectators fade into the background. You start to play for the love of the execution of the game, instead of sweating whether everything turns out every time, or whether you look good while you're doing it.

To be a great self-correcting, improving, learning machine you have to keep your reactions at bay for a moment. Stay present and aware after each and every shot. That way you can keep the best of your game flowing. This commitment to awareness also has yet another advantage of keeping your head in the game even through long competition blocks.

Step 4: Reaction and Emotion

Step 4 is the reaction and emotion phase. Something significant has happened. You rolled a strike, made your spare, or you missed. Unless you're made of stone, you'll have an emotional response to what has occurred. Your reaction might be subtle or intense, pleasant or noxious.

Reactions happen. Bowling arouses feelings. And feelings are how we know we're alive. That's all good news. No problem . . . within limits. First, withhold any reaction until you have completed step 3 (observation without judgment). Second, you have to act as if you've been there before, and will likely be there again. Until the match is over, there should be generally no emotional reaction that lasts longer than two to five seconds.

If you're living in your emotional reactions, your consciousness is likely still dwelling on the past—frames that have come and gone. Or you might be fretting about what's yet to come.

If you truly live in the moment, in the frame that you're currently playing, your reactions will rarely run you. Remember—you can own your reactions, or your reactions can own you. Ultimately, try to view your emotional responses as you view ball reaction. You can see your feelings from a distance. Your emotions will occur, but they're not really at the core of you.

There's no correct emotional response. However you respond, though, you have a choice to acknowledge your reaction or to stuff it down. If you manage your emotions well, they provide motivation in the form of positive feelings for successful completion of the execution and commitment phase of your shot (step 2). If you can be completely honest with yourself, the instant feedback of step 3 will inform you whether you brought your best game to the shot.

Step 4 has three primary risks: forbidding yourself to have any reaction, overreacting, and making rules about what you can and cannot allow yourself to feel. Some athletes and coaches believe you should behave like the Russian gymnasts from the 1960s: stoic, serious, and unfeeling. For most people, this is an unnatural way to react. Whether you throw a great shot, carry a backdoor strike, or chop a spare, you're going to have some emotional reaction.

Inhibiting reactions is like swallowing food that's inside a balloon. You have the food inside you, but you can't digest or metabolize it. Allow yourself the truth of your own reaction, exhale it, and move on. By the way, there are no good or bad feelings. Depending on how you rolled, and the pins fall, you're likely to experience a range of reactions. This doesn't mean you should act like a showman, or a robot, after the shot. Your game is not a demonstration for anyone else.

The alternative to having feelings is to be dead inside. Life without feelings is flat. Having a child, going to Disneyland, and throwing your first 300 game are all flat without some emotional life inside. Take charge, experience your experience, and then move on.

Sometimes emotions and reactions can rule you. There's a time for all things, including moving to the next phase of clearing and recovery. Letting strong emotions linger for too long is a luxury that can cripple the entire shot cycle. Getting lost in anger and irritation, or overreacting, diverts you from the learning and planning that are part of cleaning up your game.

Step 5: Clearing and Recovery

Everything in nature requires some form of recovery from mental and physical exertion to heal, reload, and prepare for what's to come. Training and competition are no exception. Step 5 is for clearing and recovery. Here you follow the laws of nature that demand rest and recovery before you can gear up for another maximum effort.

This is the time to cut off your emotions and reactions from step 4. You might decide to hang on to some aspect of the previous step to learn from the last shot, but then shake off any lingering emotional residue, and catch a moment of rest. No matter what has happened, say to yourself, *"That's what. So what? Now what?"*

This step is the equivalent of a weightlifter letting go of the bar completely before preparing for the next set, or a golfer taking a mental break while walking to the green. Although the golfer must be aware of what happened to the ball, she can exhale after the shot to finish the reaction phase, start walking, and then gear up into the planning phase again. All things in nature require some form of rest and recovery before gathering for the next maximum effort. Bowlers tend simply to run on automatic, rolling balls, making adjustments, thinking about past and future shots, and so on.

In weightlifting, you would never hang on to weights while attempting to rest between sets. Keeping your mind and body continuously running leads to energy erosion, mentally and physically. Clearing is essential to prepare you for excellence in the next shot or frame.

During a PBA telecast there's often a shot of bowlers sitting between turns, usually in some form of quiet repose. If you ask them, you'll discover they're not really paying much attention to their opponent, or to anything else going on around them; they are focusing on ball reaction. Many players employ sort of a working man's meditation practice, concentrating on simply breathing, relaxing, or even just enjoying being in such a wonderful bowling venue.

Divers, archers, gymnasts, and pitchers go through a similar sequence to let go of whatever just happened and refocus on what's coming next. Any successful athlete who must execute an offensive sequence without confronting a defensive player can experience this cycle.

The classic abuse of the entire cycle occurs most often in training. Bowlers practicing alone risk overlapping one shot into the next as they grab balls off the ball return and prepare to fire the next shot. By contrast, in league and tournament play, competitors get lost thinking about the last shot or immediately become concerned about the next shot.

An unfortunate example of not clearing and refocusing occurred during the championship match of the 2014 Queens in Reno, Nevada. Kelly Kulick, who has had a sparkling collegiate, amateur, professional, and national team career, had battled through the entire stepladder final to face the top seed, Maria Jose Rodriguez.

Kulick had been cruising along, averaging an astronomical 257 for her first three matches. But in the final, she did not strike after the fourth frame. Even so, the match remained very close in scoring. In the ninth frame Kulick left the 7-10 split. Uncharacteristically (Kelly is a superior spare shooter), she missed the corner 7-pin, failing to pick up a single pin on this nearly unmakeable split. But next, Maria missed her 2-4-5-8 combination spare in the 10th frame, ultimately forcing Kelly to have to double. Kelly left a corner pin on her first shot in the 10th frame, resulting in a win for Maria, 189 to 190.

That missed 7-pin might have made all the difference in the final tally. We can never know for sure, but Kelly might have succumbed to the disappointment of a pocket 7-10 at this critical juncture in the match, interrupting her normal recovery and shot preparation sequence.

To be successful, you must clear the shot to have a fresh experience the next time up, even in training. If you get accustomed to doing it in practice, you'll be more prepared to do it in competition.

A final trap in the clearing and recovery step is mentally going so far away that you get lazy about refocusing and bringing energy back to the planning and intention part of the cycle. Mental clearing need not take more than a few seconds. Grab some water, talk to a teammate or coach, breathe and rest—whatever works for you. Just make sure to gear up when it's time to turn the ignition key again.

PUTTING IT ALL TOGETHER

There's one more key step to completing the cycle. Remember the phase *awake and aware*? In the moment that you released the ball, you had a couple of seconds to become aware of everything you needed to know about your physical game, your mental approach, your timing, the lanes, and so on.

Information automatically entered your awareness when you were *awake* after your shot. This information then dictates what will become your primary adjustment or point of focus for your intention on the very next shot. In this way your game is a game of continual growth and improvement, whether you're practicing or competing.

Review of the Shot Cycle Steps

1. **Planning and intention.** You know what to do here because you've been paying attention, keeping your mind open to the kind of input that can occur only if you forestall your emotional reactions. Keep it simple and uncluttered. This is often a visualized, not a verbal, step.

The goal is to improve, and to achieve flow and freedom as you play. Make sure you intend to play freely and aggressively. Go after what you want.

2. **Execution and commitment.** Go means go. He who hesitates is lost. Keep your plans and intentions simple and focused. Then do it. Keep your word to yourself. Do what you said you would do, no matter how it turns out.

3. **Observation without judgment.** Stay clear, present, and aware after releasing the ball. You have a moment, just a brief moment, to have maximum awareness of your mind, your body, your execution, and the ball or lane behavior, after ball release. You don't have to plan what to think about. If you can stay nonreactive and aware, whatever you need to know will leap into the front of your mind. Your only limits are the limits of your understanding of your game.

4. **Reaction and emotion.** You are human. Feel what you want to feel. Recognize that you have a choice about what, and how long, you will have your emotional reactions. Keep it brief. Disappointment is over-rated. Beyond learning purposes, get rid of it. If there's good news, save (most of) your celebration for the end of the competition.

5. **Clearing and recovery.** Rest, recover, allow your body and mind to metabolize what has just occurred. Take what you learned in step 3 and cue up any adjustments for step 1 of the next shot.

Goals for everyone's game are to be confident, to be free, to learn and improve, and to course correct as we go. Enjoy the feeling of flow that comes from not overthinking your game. These steps, when practiced, will integrate quickly into a competition mental game habit. You won't have to think about employing the steps. This habit, once grooved in, will give you the confidence to peak your performance on demand.

KEEPING YOUR COOL

Nothing gives one person so much advantage over another as to remain always cool and unruffled under all circumstances.

Thomas Jefferson

A variety of techniques exist to regulate excitement and relaxation. The keys to good tension thermostat control can be initiated either through the body systems or through the thought system. The techniques that follow are valuable tips professional bowlers learn from sport psychologists. The way to decide which ones to use is simple: Pick the ones that work.

Bowlers feel more or less comfortable with different mental and physical synchronization techniques. Some bowlers are good visualizers but not so good at self-talk. Some techniques are easy to use anywhere. Some might be difficult to employ without help from a coach or partner, or a quiet place

■ Mastering the Shot Cycle
With Diandra Asbaty

**I've made the mistake of not being in the moment,
and thinking of who's watching, and not my own performance.
I know that if I'm being the best version of myself that I will be hard to beat.**

Diandra Asbaty, 2012 Queens title winner

Not many players, on either the men's or women's side of bowling, have been in more high-profile national, international, and professional bowling championships than Diandra Asbaty. Diandra has had to make "one shot for the money" countless times. When asked about a particular time that it mattered most, she can respond with 10.

Diandra holds the record for Team USA appointments at 16, and she has won gold medals individually and with the U.S. team at the World Championships and the World Ranking Masters. All told, she has won over 60 medals in international competition. She won the Queens title in 2012. She currently heads (along with Jason Belmonte) The International Art of Bowling, a unique bowling community training company.

The story has not always been pretty. "My first time on television was horrendous. It was the Queens in 2007. I fell flat on my face, almost literally. I was the number one qualifier at the Queens. I had bowled great all week and was undefeated. It was my first live show, and I was to bowl Kelly Kulick. They were running behind on the telecast, and the operations person told me that we would really have to get our match moving."

Diandra talked about what happened when she violated her own shot-cycle progression, "If I were who I am today, I would have done my job. But back then I thought that I had to be nice, and I rushed everything in order to help them. I rushed. I missed spares. I watched Kelly take the tiara. I was crushed."

The loss was really difficult for Diandra. "It's not the losing that's the worst part. It's knowing that you did not play your own game." She did not have a lot of time to reflect or gather herself. She had to fly to the World Ranking Masters the next day. Team USA coach Jeri Edwards took one look, and checked, "Are you going to be okay?" The answer was no, and then yes!

Three games into the World Ranking Masters, after rolling a 160 game, Diandra shifted. She realized she was going to be okay. She reset her intention and won.

The year 2012 was an entirely different story. Bowling against legendary Hall of Famer Carolyn Dorin-Ballard, Diandra was down 45 pins early. Never giving up, she had three shot clock violations. "I was not going to go on anyone's time but my own."

Going on her own time is an extremely critical part of the step 2 action phase of the process. Diandra has mastered the shot cycle. What she has learned has taken her to the top many times.

Photo courtesy of PBA LLC.

Step 1 is planning and intention. Most players think that planning means waiting until their next shot. This is not true for many champion players. Diandra doesn't even leave planning and intention until tournament day. In a way, that sets her up for success. She starts her visualization process early—very early. She sees what's going to happen, in her mind's eye, as she lays in bed.

Diandra is a huge believer in visualization. Here's an example. In 2004, the World Ranking Masters was going to be in Moscow, in the same arena that the Olympics were hosted. "Finals were going to be in this really great arena. I really wanted to be in the finals. I had known for months that I had qualified for the Masters."

"Every night, for three months, when I went to sleep, I imagined myself bowling in the finals. I saw the motion of the ball, and it was always a perfect shot. I saw my opponent but I couldn't see her face. I didn't know who it was going to be, and it didn't matter."

"When I walked into the finals, I felt like I had already been there—because I had, in my mind. I could have been petrified, but I felt calmness because I had already been there. And I ended up winning. And that is how it is now. I only focus on what I can control, so it doesn't really matter. It's amazing how powerful visualization can be and how powerful our minds are."

The planning and intention phase cannot be overstated. "Focus on your intention, and no one will beat you." Diandra sees the shot as it will play before she ever pushes the ball away. "You can see my eyes go up and down the lanes if you watch me on YouTube."

Diandra doesn't overly concern herself about excitement, or even nervousness. She knows that commitment to what she's doing trumps all things. "I'm not scared of being nervous. I know how to manage the nervousness. I breathe from my stomach. I drink a lot of water. I close my eyes and visualize. I enjoy the moment. I know that win or lose, it's pretty cool that I got there in the first place."

How would you like to feel like that with a ball in your hand?

Step 2 is the action step. You've decided what you intend to do, and you proceed with a committed action. You have essentially given your word in step 1. Now, when you feel prepared to go on your own command, you keep it.

After that, the trick is to do what only elite athletes tend to do: step 3—observe. To be able to see what just occurred accurately, without judging it right off the bat, might be the highest form of bowling intelligence.

Diandra speaks eloquently about this essential observational step. "You don't sometimes know what you've learned until later." She knows that you have to observe keenly to learn all that you need to in order to set up the planning and intention for the next shot. "I've learned not to judge it. You look at the shot objectively, based on the facts. Not anything emotional. You don't say, 'I'm an idiot' like most bowlers do after a bad shot."

When you operate in this manner, observing without judging, you're on the yellow brick road to success. "You make clearer decisions. You think more clearly. You make more informed choices. It's an obvious strength."

It's not just a shot that can be reflected on and learned from. It can be the whole tournament experience. "Because of that huge loss in my career, I gained what I needed. I would never have won without that. I wouldn't have been the athlete that I have become."

Step 4 is the reaction stage. Be careful here. Emotion is normal, but you don't want to let your feelings sweep you up, especially if they're negative, such as anger or frustration.

(continued)

Diandra Asbaty *(continued)*

Diandra is clear on this point. "As long as it's not going to affect you, and it's positive, you can react. The question is, how quickly can you bring yourself back? Try to forget about what happened very quickly, and get your intention back where it needs to be." In addition, Diandra cautions how your reactions can actually help the person you're bowling against. "If I see my opponent being negative, it empowers me."

And there's a time to just clear. Take some space to allow for resetting. Diandra relays one tip that has served her through the years in high-stakes competition. She never just crosses from one lane to the other if she has two frames to play in match competition. Diandra always steps off, resets, gets her intention and plan clear, and then plays.

At the end of our interview, Diandra had words of wisdom for everyone who wants to perform their best under pressure: "Sometimes the situation gets so big that we stop being ourselves." She has learned that in the moment that she's making a shot, that's the most important place to be in the world. Equally, before and afterward, it's not. "I got to the finals in the Queens in 2012. In the period between making the show and the show itself I had tears in my eyes. I knew what I had done to get there. No one else knew. I felt like I had already won. That's why it meant more to me than anything ever. I needed a strike to win. I saw my son's face (Madden). I knew that no matter what, my son would be proud of me, and my family would be proud of me."

"I looked at my target, and I hit it."

"There was a little girl who had a sign that said 'Diandra Rocks.' I knew that I had already won in a way. It's about how many people you affect along the way. I inspired that little girl. That was enough for me."

in which to use them. You might find some techniques natural, and others awkward or odd. Start with those that feel user-friendly, but try them all to discover which work best.

Breathing Skills

Within the shot cycle are opportunities to practice a wide variety of mental and emotional regulation skills. Probably the simplest of all body relaxation techniques is breathing awareness. You've got to breathe, anyway. You might as well practice it in a way that optimizes performance. Mindful breathing is especially useful if you're plagued with distracting or disturbing thoughts—such as preoccupation with aspects of your game, your shots, or your release—in the heat of competition.

These breathing techniques are easy to employ, and they really work! You already have a lifetime of practice getting the basics of breathing down, so adding these techniques doesn't take much time.

The first thing to do is to focus on the rhythm of your breathing, without changing anything. Merely notice the pace of your inhalations and exhalations. Simply turning your attention to breathing momentarily can help you ease tension. When you bring yourself to focus on your breath, you automatically bring yourself into the present moment.

But there's more to breath work than that. If you're anxious, frustrated, or excited, chances are your body is tight and your breathing is not calming and relaxing. Remember your wild tiger from early in the chapter? When your tiger growls at the outset of competition, you might find yourself taking quick, shallow breaths, or even holding your breath altogether. But during a high-stakes bowling tournament, you must do just the opposite.

Shallow breathing caused by a fight-or-flight response creates muscle tension and sends a message to the unconscious self. The brain picks up on rapid, shallow breathing and sends a warning message to your whole body. This is not a helpful message, especially when you're dealing with anticipation and excitement, not danger. Such a message to the brain can make it hard for you to relax and stroke your shots.

The good news is that by consciously adjusting your breathing patterns, you can bring relaxation and optimal focus to your entire physical system. You can also use your breath to energize your body between turns and games.

The shot cycle includes several phases in which you can use breathing strategically. During the planning and intention phase, breathing can help you get in touch with the internal part of your own spirit. For instance, in this phase, when things are moving too quickly, making yourself stop and breathe can help you organize your thoughts and get you ready to bowl. Breathing can also help during the execution phase.

Two particular techniques can serve to send oxygen all the way into your diaphragm, which will regulate your system to a degree. The first is a bit unusual. Consciously breathe deeply down the back of your throat. You'll find that you fill your lungs effortlessly, all the way into your abdomen. This kind of breath is *not* hyperventilating. Do it once during your preshot, or any other time that you're feeling overexcited. Sending oxygen deeply into your diaphragm signals your brain to get into the present moment, and eases worry. No one can breathe this way when in danger, and your brain knows this.

Another subtle and effective technique is to inhale normally; then, before exhaling, inhale a little bit more right on top of it. Once again you will find that this drives enriching oxygen deep into your system. This brings you into the present moment and eases your activation level; you'll also have extra fuel for muscular power.

When you hold your breath, you don't tend to feel your own experiences. By breathing consciously before or after you roll, you allow yourself to feel your natural athleticism. Finally, using deep breathing is a way to maximize the clearing-and-recovery process.

With practice, you'll feel a change in your tension levels. Breathing techniques are easy to take to any tournament, and are especially helpful to clear and recover. If you practice these techniques often, you'll feel a great sense of control over the relaxation response.

As mentioned, you should probably use some sort of breathing strategy as an important part of your preshot routine. Conscious breathing puts the body in flow and helps to shake off distraction. A key to making these techniques work is to go with total commitment to your shot following the exhalation. Linking a deep breath to your shot cycle serves as a cueing technique to relax, commit, and go.

Progressive Muscle Relaxation

Relaxing your body can have a profound effect on mental tension. For this reason, the experience of flow and grooving the swing can be influenced by simply learning to relax overly tense muscles. Progressive muscle relaxation (PMR) is a quick, effective way to take tension out of your swing response (Davis et al. 1995). This technique, in a radically shorthand version, is especially helpful if you have a difficult time relaxing your grip or allowing a free, loose arm swing.

In progressive muscle relaxation, you briefly overtighten your muscles, then release them into a relaxed state. PMR increases sensitivity to muscular tension and provides a sense of control over tension levels. Although PMR takes a little more time to learn than breathing techniques, once learned, you can use it quickly and selectively as needed. By the way, don't practice PMR right after eating because digestion can be adversely affected by the alternation of muscle tension and muscle relaxation. Also be especially cautious with neck, back, and other delicate areas to guard against overstraining. You should not feel pain.

Set aside just 10 to 20 minutes to learn this skill. Find a relaxing place where you are unlikely to be observed or disturbed. Sit in a comfortable place, or use a reclining chair with a head support. Once you have learned the technique, you can significantly abbreviate it, use it secretly, and implement it anywhere. There are longer versions of PMR (see Davis et al. 1995), but for competition purposes a shorthand version is presented here.

Tense the targeted muscle or muscle group for 5 to 7 seconds, then relax for 20 to 30 seconds. Don't stay too long in either the tension or relaxation phase. Too much time tensing can create problems, and too much time relaxing interrupts the flow of the exercise and makes it difficult to complete.

Many top bowling coaches emphasize the need to be free and easy with the arm swing and maintain a soft grip with the hands. Sometimes in the heat of competition the grip and arms can unconsciously tighten. The first area of focus addresses the arms and hands. Start by adopting an upper-body weightlifter's pose. Tighten both fists, tight, while curling arms inward to create big biceps. Imagine the biceps muscle is a big softball crawling up your arm. Hold briefly, and relax. You can hold for 5 to 7 seconds in practice session, but 1 to 2 seconds should be the maximum during competition. You want to feel and control the obvious contrast between tension and relaxation.

Many athletes do not recognize how much tension they carry in the jaws, forehead, and other facial areas. Relaxing and relieving these muscles can send a message through the rest of the body and ease the mind as well. Prune your forehead. Make it as wrinkly as you can. Your eyes are squinted slits. For a moment hunch your shoulders up to your ears. Tense briefly, relax, and repeat.

This exercise might seem odd, but you should practice it. During competition you can sneak in a quick spritz of facial tightening and relaxing that can help your face, body, and emotions calm down. Long competition blocks can be exhausting. If you're holding tension throughout the day, you'll be out of gas by the end. Taking mini relaxation breaks with the body can make all the difference.

You bowl with your legs. When your legs are wooden or mechanical, timing and leg bend can be jerky and stiff. To do PMR with the lower body, start by straightening your legs from a sitting position. Make duck feet by pressing down with your heels and, without using your hands, pull your toes back toward your face. Your shins will feel tight. Hold briefly, relax, and repeat (twice). This exercise is particularly useful during match play when you have two frames to wait for the next turn.

Body relaxation is especially useful when you don't have much time or when the pressure is on between shots and games. Remember to tense for a couple of seconds and then absolutely relax the targeted area. Do not overtighten or tighten too long during bowling. Your muscles should not get burned out from overtightening. Conversely, your mind and muscles should not become so relaxed during relaxation that you can't get the energy up for competing.

Imagery

You can use imagery in a couple of ways to gain a feeling of mastery during periods of excitement. Imagery, as used in competition, is using your mind to create a state of comfort in your body. The first use of imagery is best used for the period of time before you actually engage warm-ups and competition.

If anxiety, tension, or overexcitement are pressing on you before a tournament, or between blocks, imagery is a great way to let out some of the hot tension. Generally avoid relaxation imagery during the heat of competition; reserve it for in-between blocks and down times.

Use your imagination: visual, auditory, and kinesthetic (body feel). Imagine yourself in a safe, wonderful place—wherever works for you. We all have our own personal version of a safe place. For some, it's their beds. For others, it's a warm, secluded beach. It can be anywhere that feels safe, relaxing, and free.

Once you're mentally in your special place, bring all your senses to life— sight, taste, smell, touch, and hearing. What does the air smell like? What's the temperature? If the beach is your special place, imagine the feel of the grains of sand on your fingers and toes, the warmth of the sun, the sounds of birds and waves, and the taste of a cool beverage on ice. This one's especially useful if you're having difficulty resting or sleeping, which sometimes happens before competitions.

While visualizing, try using positive self-talk, such as, *I am healing, Warmth and calm are flooding my body and my self, I am reenergizing, Health is surging within me,* or *I am safe here.* See more on self-talk in the following section.

After a few minutes, come back to the present. Notice the feelings of warmth and relaxation. Carry these feelings with you. As with other relaxation and tension-easing techniques, the ability to shift into this mode at will increases dramatically with practice. Again, this technique is usually practiced away from the lanes. It has two benefits, it lets you de-stress, and gives you a sense of control of your overall relaxation response.

Effective competition imagery will relax and energize you even during tournament play. During competition, even as part of a preshot routine, you can imagine a warm glow within your belly. With this warmth, bring silent self-talk, and affirmations of confidence, athleticism, and well-being.

Target the technique to various parts of your body. Imagine relaxation in your arm for a smooth arm swing, feelings of power and strength in your legs, softness in your hands for your release, and positive emotions in your belly. It's a big confidence booster to know you can pull out this powerful tension-combating technique anywhere at any time.

Self-Talk

A final confidence and synchronization technique to learn is silent self-talk, or self-affirmations. When bowlers get into pressure situations in which they must strike or spare, they often use silent self-talk to direct the brain to cope positively with the situation.

You can use positive self-talk and affirmations to strengthen your mental game by rehearsing throughout the day. You might also include self-talk in step 1 of your shot cycle.

Self-talk can work for or against you. The worst thing you can do is say negative things such as *I have to have this shot, Don't tense up, Don't yank the ball,* or *Don't squeeze.* The subconscious mind often registers only the action word. Self-talk should always be phrased in positive terms. If you're accustomed to using "nots" and "do nots," simply turn the negative statement 180 degrees. Pick a phrase that declares the intention of the self-talk in positive terms.

Silent self-talk should lead to the desired focused state. Make yourself aware of your natural self-talk during bowling. This can be easy to notice while practicing or competing.

There are three easy steps to setting up your self-talk:

1. To get centered, try a basic mantra, such as
   - *I am relaxed and centered.*
   - *I am focused.*
   - *I am graceful.*
   - *I am present.*
   - *I am centered.*

   Pick one or two that you like and use them in practice. Really see if you can shift your focus and feelings with the use of positive affirmations. This is not a self sales job. You have to be able to authentically feel what you are saying at the deepest level. This technique is silent, effective, and always available in a pinch.

2. Once you can get your body into an effective athletic state, you can add a skill specific directive such as *Keep my hands soft and post my shot.*

3. Perhaps the most important step is to develop a mental picture, or feeling in your body, that's completely consistent with the self-talk you used in the first two steps. You should be able to call up this image or feeling readily and easily.

One vital note: Affirmative self-talk must not turn into a con or sales job. If you're silently speaking to convince yourself that you can play, this can be an indication of underlying self-doubt. Positive self-talk works only if you're willing to wholeheartedly go into the state of being suggested by your words. You must absolutely believe and know the truth of what you are telling yourself. Here's the sequence for your self-talk:

1. Know it.
2. Say it.
3. Be it.
4. Do it.

Once you're proficient at transformative self-talk, you have a something in your grab bag to assist you in any competitive situation.

You now have several go-to options for getting yourself in synch during both practice and competing. It's a fine craftsman who keeps his tools sharp at the office. When you gain mastery of these psychological tools, you'll never be lost when the tournament lights come on.

CHAPTER 5

Toughness to Overcome Adversity

When you're playing against a stacked deck, compete even harder. Show the world how much you'll fight for the winner's circle. If you do, some-day the cellophane will crackle off a fresh pack, one that belongs to you, and the cards will be stacked in your favor.

Pat Riley, NBA basketball coach

If you're going to play, compete, and survive to play on, you must be mentally tough. All sports are full of athletes with boat loads of skill who shrivel under a wide variety of challenges. Bowling is the same. Whether it's the ability to close out a tournament, deal with making errors, or handle the pressure of fans, coaches, and TV, the mentally tough player tends to come out on top in the long run.

The term *tough* is curious. You know toughness when you see it, but defin-ing it is tricky. In some sports toughness is easier to recognize than in others. Finding a tough football or hockey player is simple. You see the blood, the bandages, and how they repeatedly get back up after being knocked down.

Finding a tough golfer, gymnast, or diver is not as easy. These athletes don't bleed as much, and their aches and pains tend to be invisible. In bicycle racing we just *know* that racers' legs are burning up those hills, but often we can't tell whose legs are burning the worst.

What is toughness in bowling? Bowling has its share of disappointment, distraction, and despair, that much is certain. Injuries occur. And I never met a serious bowler who didn't want to quit at some point.

Mental toughness in bowling involves the ability to rebound after mistakes and failures, or to handle pressure. It involves concentration, and unshakeable confidence. Mentally tough bowlers have motors that never quit running. They are constantly driven by their motivation to get better after (Hinitz 2011).*

Here you'll have a chance to take a mental toughness inventory. You'll examine yourself in five areas of mental toughness. Be honest as you take this test. The results will give you and your coach the information you need to be a truly tough athlete.

INVENTORY

Every morning in Africa a gazelle wakes up. It knows it must run faster than the fastest lion, or it will be killed. . . . Every morning a lion wakes up. It knows it must outrun the slowest gazelle, or it will starve to death. It doesn't matter whether you're a lion or a gazelle—when the sun comes up . . . you'd better be running.

Christopher McDougall, *Born to Run: A Hidden Tribe, Superathletes, and the Greatest Race the World Has Never Seen*

For each of the following questions, simply answer true or false. Very few people's responses are black or white, all or nothing, for any of these questions. Decide which way you lean, even if it's only 60 percent to 40 percent.

I. Resiliency

1. I frequently worry about bad shots, missed spares, or other mistakes. **T** or **F**
2. I get down on myself during a practice or game when I make mistakes. **T** or **F**
3. I have no problem letting go of poorly-executed shots. **T** or **F**
4. If I start out playing badly, it's difficult for me to turn my game around before the end of the game or tournament. **T** or **F**
5. I get distracted by what my coach, teammates, or fellow competitors think when I make mistakes. **T** or **F**
6. I recover quickly from setbacks, mistakes, and bad breaks. **T** or **F**

II. Pressure Situations

1. When the stakes are higher, I do my best. **T** or **F**
2. My nervousness has kept me from competing to my potential. **T** or **F**
3. I play better in practice than I do when the competition begins. **T** or **F**
4. I might not like to admit it, but at times I get psyched out or intimidated by certain bowlers or other teams. **T** or **F**
5. I can keep my emotions and nervousness under wraps in pressure situations. **T** or **F**

*Adapted from D. Hinitz, 2011 (Jan.), "Tough enough," *Bowling This Month* 18(1): 35-37.

6. When the game's on the line for my team, I don't want the ball in my hand. **T** or **F**

III. Concentration

1. If the coach, or a teammate, yells at me, it really knocks me off of my game. **T** or **F**

2. When I'm bowling I get distracted by other players, exterior noise, and thoughts about the competition. **T** or **F**

3. Some players, such as league leaders, tour players, or champion bowlers, can overwhelm or intimidate me, or simply get into my head. **T** or **F**

4. Difficult or messy lanes or conditions (e.g., sport shots, burned-up lanes, reverse blocks) negatively affect my form, my execution, my confidence, or in other ways. **T** or **F**

5. When competition starts, I'm good at focusing on what's important and blocking out irrelevant stimuli. **T** or **F**

6. Just prior to and during competition, I think too much about things that could go wrong. **T** or **F**

IV. Confidence

1. One or two blown chances in a game or a missed spare does not shake my confidence. **T** or **F**

2. I compare myself too much to other players, including teammates and opponents. **T** or **F**

3. I'd rather compete against a good team and barely win than play a weaker opponent and dominate them. **T** or **F**

4. I'm a confident and self-assured bowler. **T** or **F**

5. I tend to be negative in my thinking when I play. **T** or **F**

6. I have trouble dealing with negative self-talk before or after rolling the ball. **T** or **F**

V. Motivation

1. If I fail to perform well in a game, I'm more motivated than ever. **T** or **F**

2. It's normal for me to practice and train at a high level of intensity. **T** or **F**

3. When I practice I think about how today's practice will pay off in terms of achieving my goals. **T** or **F**

4. Many times in practice I just go through the motions, rolling ball after ball without really stopping to focus, attending to what's happening, and learning. **T** or **F**

5. I periodically set clear goals for my improvement that are important to me. **T** or **F**

6. I feel that I'm a highly-motivated bowler. **T** or **F**

Score Yourself

We'll score the five sections of the test separately. Section I, resiliency, assesses your ability to bounce back after a setback. As you likely know, hanging onto negative thoughts about your bowling can only spell trouble for you. Bowlers who think constantly about what they did wrong, or what went wrong, tend to perform at a lower level. They also make more mistakes as competition continues. Score 1 point for each of your responses answered in the following way, and 0 points for the opposite answer:

1. F	3. T	5. F
2. F	4. F	6. T

Section II assesses your ability to deal with pressure situations. Bowlers who can manage the intensity of their feelings generally perform better in clutch situations. Players who can't tolerate intense situations will often fold. Of course, your motor will run higher in competition. You just want to make sure it doesn't run away with you. Score 1 point for each of your responses answered in the following way, and 0 points for the opposite answer:

1. T	3. F	5. T
2. F	4. F	6. F

Section III assesses your concentration abilities. In bowling, you must develop the capacity to tune out sights, sounds, and distractions, as well as deal with the down time between shots. Your concentration skills help you to perform at your highest level and to avoid choking or being psyched out. Score 1 point for each of your responses answered in the following way, and 0 points for the opposite answer:

1. F	3. F	5. T
2. F	4. F	6. F

Section IV assesses your confidence levels. Mentally tough bowlers keep bringing their best game, even when the breaks go badly for them and good for opponents. Mentally tough bowlers get even stronger under pressure. No matter how hard you work, if you're not mentally tough, your talent can be neutralized. Score 1 point for each of your responses answered in the following way, and 0 points for the opposite answer:

1. T	3. T	5. F
2. F	4. T	6. F

Section V assesses the fire in your belly—your level of motivation. Without adequate motivation, you can't sustain a drive to practice. You lose your energy for dusting yourself off when you stumble. High motivation carries you toward your goals no matter what obstacles are in the way. Score 1 point for each of your responses answered in the following way, and 0 points for the opposite answer:

1. T	3. T	5. T
2. T	4. F	6. T

This Inventory section adapted, by permission, from A. Goldberg, 2009, "Just how mentally tough are you?" [Online]. Available: https://www.competitivedge.com/athletes-%E2%80%9Chow-tough-are-you%E2%80%9D-0 [March 1, 2016].

Grade Yourself

If you scored a 6 in any section, that's an A+. Consider yourself extremely mentally tough in that area. If you scored a 5 or 6 in all five sections, you are a mentally tough force to be reckoned with. If you scored a 4 or below in any section, this indicates vulnerability, perhaps even weakness, in that aspect of your mental game. Be sure to share these scores with your coach.

Looking at the bigger picture, a total score of 26 or more shows overall mental toughness, and is a remarkably good score. If you're this mentally tough, just make sure to continuously improve your physical game, and no one will want to shoe up against you.

If you scored a 23 to 25, you rank as a B or maybe B+ in terms of mental game toughness. There are things you can do to reach A-level toughness. Your specific areas of weakness are highlighted to you in this inventory.

If you scored below 23, and if you're serious about your game, it's time to plot your own mental toughness boot camp. Your areas of focus are your lowest section scores.

If you want only to develop your physical game, and don't care about competing, then a low score on mental toughness might be OK for you. But if you want to play any kind of high stakes, improving your mental toughness quotient is crucial.

Whether you scored high or low on this scale, you would probably score similarly on your mental toughness in school, business, and other areas of life. Mental toughness is relevant in any area you seek to excel in. Do you have what it takes to excel? If you're ready to commit to solid 6s in all areas, you're well on the way to being tough enough.

BEING TOUGH*

When a man knows how to live dangerously, he is not afraid to die. When he is not afraid to die, he is, strangely, free to live.

William O. Douglas, Supreme Court Justice (1939–1975)

On Tuesday, November 5, 2002, at about 4 o'clock in the afternoon, Leanne Barrette (now Leanne Hulsenberg) was the most dangerous bowler on the

*Adapted from D. Hinitz, 2002 (Dec.), "Bowling dangerously," *Bowling This Month* 9(12).

planet. It happened during the final game of the qualifying round in the final PWBA event of the year at the Storm Las Vegas Challenge. Leanne entered the game 30 pins below the cut, while bowling on the same pair as the person who represented the make-or-miss cut number.

The only way she could prolong her life in the tournament was to throw a big number up there. The only way to do this, after a day in which the lanes were tough and consistent scoring even tougher, was to bowl with her back against the wall. Such a situation is like a street fight in which you're so outnumbered that the only way to succeed is through uninhibited, icy attack.

Hulsenberg had no choice but to throw caution to the wind, make her best guess about how and where to match up, and to bowl knowing that if she went down she would do it with absolutely nothing left in the bag. No regrets. Nothing remaining that could have been called up. No trying to play with perfection. No pointing. No overcontrolling. This was it.

The result was an incredibly exciting monster game. A string of strikes interrupted by the "big four" split, followed by a string of strikes, and this Hall of Famer showed what she was made of. She made the cut easily. If match play had started 15 minutes later, Leanne might have been nearly unbeatable (Hinitz 2002).

What makes great competitors like Leanne Hulsenberg so mentally tough? Players of their ilk achieve incredible results under the most challenging of situations. Whatever they have, can it be bottled? Yes, I believe it can.

Many of you reading this can relate to situations when you have been knocked down by the lane conditions, the approaches, poor pin carry, or intimidating opponents, or even simply by the lights coming on in a tournament situation. Mental toughness is knowing that no matter what gets thrown in your face, you'll persevere. Let's talk about ways to get there.

A paradox in bowling (and in other areas of life) is that the more you try to control outcomes, the more tense, frustrated, and anxious you're likely to become. In bowling, overcontrol looks like you're trying to manually influence everything, from your trained free arm-swing to oversteering your release.

There's a kind of control that's desirable that leans on consistency, accuracy, and intention. Then there's the evil kind of control that kills your game—when you attempt to force results.

AUTOGRAPHING YOUR SHOT

Live authentically. Why compromise something that's beautiful to create something that is fake?

Steve Maraboli, motivational speaker and author

Try this exercise on for size. Grab a pen and sign your name as you would if you were signing a check or credit card receipt, only do it larger. Now put your pen at the beginning of the first letter and very carefully trace over the original signature, taking extreme care not to slip off. Slipping off is considered a mistake, like throwing the ball into the ditch.

Now repeat the exercise. Write your name. Then write it again, on top of the first one, this time without thinking about it. Let it flow and trust it will be close.

How do the two compare? Most people feel tense or cramped when they feel pressure to trace the signature precisely. The tenseness leads to mistakes, or slips, that don't occur when the pressure's off. When you focus too hard on trying to prevent something from happening, you tense up and commit mistakes, whether it's tracing your signature or shooting a corner pin.

Just as you can sign an autograph with your signature, you can "autograph" a shot. That is the quality of executing freely, authoritatively, and athletically, without any "trace" of robotically trying to imitate perfect form. That back row of pins will grade you. Autographed shots seem to carry more energy, break up splits, and take out corner pins.

How can you improve control by giving up control, you might ask. Every accomplished bowler has had days when every ball is effortless. Racks of pins carry with uncanny frequency, and you hit your spares automatically. Have you given up control in these cases? No. Rather, you have transferred control from the thinking part of your mind, where lurks the ego, to the intuitive, subconscious part of the mind.

THE SAMURAI GAME*

I can handle anything.

**Motto screened onto the shirts
of 20-time collegiate champions Wichita State University**

True mental toughness is reflected in the following story. According to legend, Samurai warriors performed a ritual to prepare for battle. Knowing they would be facing another Samurai, one on one with a sword, the mental game clearly had to be inhumanly strong. Most battles involved one stroke with heavy swords. The Japanese had a saying: "While your sword is cutting me, my sword is killing you." Does match play get any more intense than that?

Before a battle, these warriors meditated, focusing on the absolute acceptance of death. This acceptance allowed them to fight with nothing to lose. If you're truly prepared to die, why not fight with total commitment? If they had not had complete acceptance of any possible outcome, including death, they would be at risk of flinching, trying to protect themselves, and thus withholding complete commitment. Any mental hiccup could quickly result in defeat. By knowing deep within they could accept any outcome, the Samurai could commit fearlessly to their performance (Hinitz 2002).

We tend to create what we fear. First, fears activate fight-or-flight systems that can lead to tensing muscles, squeezing and grabbing, and inhibiting

---

*Adapted from D. Hinitz, 2002 (Dec.), "Bowling dangerously," *Bowling This Month* 9(12).

follow-through. Second, consciousness and attention are drawn almost magnetically to the feared results and events. Fear of pulling and pointing the ball imprints "pulling and pointing" onto the mind. Fear of throwing a corner pin shot into the ditch creates the Panama Canal of ditches in the brain.

Fear of losing prevents you from reaching for greatness. Even if you manage to win under these circumstances—say, your opponent is even more fearful than you are, or he makes a mistake—you won't have the sense you can repeat the victory. Besides, bowling, like life, is a drag when played this way.

Once you train yourself to bowl without fear, you are bowling like a Samurai. If you're not afraid to "die," you avoid the bowling version of death—an overcontrolled, overthought game.

Let's be clear. I am *not* suggesting that you become OK with losing. The exact opposite is true. The point is that if you fear losing, fear being the runner-up, fear not making a shot, you invite all kinds of mental and emotional processes that put you at risk for failure. When you have made ultimate peace with yourself ahead of time—that is, you know you'll be OK, no matter what—you're free to execute to the best of your ability.

Once you can do this, will you always win? No, because you can't control how your opponent plays. In 2002, Norm Duke faced Dave Traber in the finals of the Cambridge Credit Classic on Long Island. The game ended in a dead tie. In the extra frames roll-off, Duke beat Traber, though both played like Samurai warriors. What else could Traber do? Probably nothing. Playing with the optimal mindset doesn't guarantee victory, but it does mean you're playing to the best of your ability (at least mentally), which often translates to winning. It makes for a far better pillow at night to know that you played a Samurai's game.

On that day, two Samurai braved it all, with nothing to lose and greatness to gain. Duke will be remembered for winning the title. But anyone watching will remember a no-holds barred championship—an unbelievably impressive show. Two dangerous bowlers gave it their absolute best. In score, one won and one lost, but neither was defeated. Traber left the competition knowing he had not lost because he was afraid to fail.

FEAR BUSTING

I have learned over the years that when one's mind is made up, this diminishes fear; knowing what must be done does away with fear.

Rosa Parks, civil rights activist

Everyone deals with fear. Some fears show up in a competitive environment; others live with you on a more pervasive level. But steps can be taken to address your fears and make yourself mentally tough.

1. **Acknowledge the truth.** You can't change what you're unwilling to face. This is a house rule of the universe. If you're tightening up,

acknowledge that fear—of not making shots, of not winning—is inhibiting your game. The first step is recognition and acknowledgment.

2. **Gain some perspective—*now!*** Once you have acknowledged fear, step back in your mind. This game, this match, this shot, this tournament is just an eye blink in your bowling life. In the big picture, none of this is huge, even if your ego is screaming otherwise. It's okay to compete as if the game is the most important thing in life, as long as you know in your heart of hearts that it's not.

   Armed with true perspective, you become dangerous. You accept the possibility of desired or nondesired results. Once you realize you can't lose in life if you give everything you have, you move beyond fear. They say angels can fly because they take themselves lightly. Take your bowling seriously, but leave your sense of personal value out of it.

3. **Compete with nothing to lose and everything to gain.** That's it. If you have something to lose, you become protective. If you have nothing to lose, you're free. It's that simple. Almost every bowler I've known has a story about how well he bowled once he knew he was out of the cut. Start that way. Think of what you can do with perspective like that.

4. **When hit by a fear grenade, reverse the effects.**
   - Use a clearing, deep-diaphragm breath as part of your preshot routine to tell your unconscious mind that all is OK now.
   - Shift your mind from negative images of nondesired results toward what you intend to have happen. Positive self-talk, especially positive imagery, can save the day.

5. **Decide what you're going to do, and then give it your trust.** Focus on what you intend to do. Make a decision to believe in yourself—what you're doing, the line you're using. Once you see clearly what you want to do in your mind's eye, fear takes a seat on the sidelines. At this point you become a very dangerous competitor.

6. **Make a distinction between caring about your bowling and worrying about it.** Of course you care about your bowling, making shots, and winning. Mental toughness says "care but don't worry." Observe the difference between worrying and caring. Read these two statements:
   - If I coach you, I *care* about how you are and how you bowl.
   - If I coach you, I *worry* about how you are and how you bowl.

   The attitude is vastly different.

If you need nothing, you are rich. If you have a sense of humor about life, every challenge becomes a dance with the universe. If you become desperate, you invite the demons of your mind to assault you. Now you're dangerous only to yourself.

A popular saying translates easily to bowling:

Compete as if you don't need the money or the glory. Love the game as if you've never known failure or defeat. Bowl as if no one is watching. Roll your shots as if each shot is a work of art. Play as if there's no tomorrow.

What a wonderful, edgy way to live your life. Think, *Six steps to Samurai.* You won't regret it.

LASER FOCUS
FOR MENTAL TOUGHNESS*

Concentrate all your thoughts on the work at hand.
The sun's rays do not burn until brought to a focus.

Alexander Graham Bell

Every bowler has had the frustrating experience of struggling to shake off the disturbances of competitive situations, be it noise, messed-up oil patterns, rude or aggressive players, or the pressures of high-stakes competition. All bowlers want to be able to deal effectively with anything thrown at them.

Many bowlers are bothered when they get to the bowling center on game day, and discover that conditions, internal and external, have shifted out of their comfort zones. If you're going to be a mentally tough bowler, you must be able to deliver shots no matter how much chaos is swirling around you.

Consider a scenario from a December, 2012, PBA tournament scene in Las Vegas. You can see instantly some of the focus problems that present themselves in big-time tournament situations. David Whitten, on BowlingDigital.com, cited on a blog by Jeff Richgels, commenting on the World Series of Bowling states (Hinitz 2013):

> Experiencing the bowling live was eye opening. Boy, these guys are certainly under pressure in this environment, and the distractions are enormous. The pinsetters were really noisy, people moving around on the sidelines, TV booms moving about, noise from the practice on the stub lane, interviews being conducted off to the side, and for some reason strange music would pipe in occasionally . . . I've concluded that this was essentially a signal to the bowler who's turn it was to chill until the music stopped. On top of that, the breaks after the 6th frame in the preliminary matches have to be a momentum factor (good or bad).
>
> If you ever wonder why TV rookies often struggle, this probably is a big part of it.

Reading this descriptive scenario, it's easy to picture the breadth of distractions that can pull a bowler away from pinpointing focus on pure shot

---

*Adapted from D. Hinitz, 2013 (Jan.), "Laser focus," *Bowling This Month* 20(1).

delivery. By the time you get to play for anything that matters, there will almost always be a kaleidoscope of input grabbing at your center.

Focus and concentration are skills that mentally tough athletes must master. Developing the capacity to focus effectively is one of the most important qualities of a resilient athlete. It's also among the least understood.

Most bowlers think that focus is simply concentrating on some part of their game for a long time—as if staring long and hard enough at their mark will improve their game. But bowling is more complex than that.

The ability to focus and deliver shots is one of the absolute staples of high-stakes competition. Yet having a go-to, iron-clad strategy for how to do this is not part of many competitors' mental game toolbox.

When a player gets to critical frames, games, and finals, her focus often scatters in ways that feel random and out of control. Like riding a horse without your hands on the reins, scattered focus can leave you feeling unsure, anxious, and unreliable—certainly not very tough.

At this point we will delve into the phenomenon of laser-like focus. You'll soon have the keys to one of the greatest secrets to bowling success. Once mastered, the confidence that comes with having your brain securely directing your steering system will allow you to deliver under virtually any competitive circumstances (Hinitz 2013).

Fields of Play

There are an infinite number of places that you can put your attention. But all of those possibilities can really be grouped into five areas: Your thoughts, yours feelings, your body, your spirit, the competition environment—including the lanes, the ball, and the approaches.

Your thoughts can range from your step cadence, to what's going on with the lanes changing, to awareness of the cut line, to whether or not you are getting lucky, and just about anything else.

Your feelings can go from flat, to elated, to scared, to nervous, to calm, to angry, to relieved, and so on.

Your body's physical cues can be anything from muscle tension, to leg fatigue, to hunger, and many more.

The environment always changes. Just imagine a tournament right now. You can easily picture and hear what is happening. Sweeps dropping onto the deck, balls rolling. Perhaps a player is stepping up out of turn. Examples are limitless.

Your head could go anywhere. If you master laser focus, what you are doing is deciding what you choose to key in on above and beyond all things. It might be as simple as just seeing your target or feeling balanced. Your choices are nearly infinite, so you must learn to attend only to those cues that will aid your shot delivery. And, you must learn to ignore the meteor shower of input that your brain, your body, and the bowling center can present to you.

Laser focus options are binary. You either focus on what assists you in rolling great shots, or you don't. Of all of the thoughts you could think, you must pick the best ones. Of all of the physical game variables, you must narrow the field. In short, you must focus on the most important thing (Hinitz 2013).

It Plays Like This

Let's say a bowler is about to start the last game of a six-game block. He needs to shoot around 220 to make the cut to the finals. Let's look at likely progressive shifts in laser focus of a successful effort:

1. He first makes a plan of attack for the lanes.
2. Having watched play on the pair of lanes ahead of time, he knows the area, angle, and speed with which to play each lane.
3. Knowing how important a coordinated push-away is, he pays particular attention to hand and foot timing just prior to beginning his first step.
4. He's also making sure that his arm and hand are relaxed.

He feels excited and nervous about the importance of the game, but instead of worrying about how nervous he is, he

- gets completely involved in having a good physical feel for the shot;
- has a nonjudgmental curiosity about the experience;
- has a sense of almost transcendent ecstasy, an experience outside of everyday bowling reality;
- feels an inner clarity, knowing exactly what he needs to do and how to do it; and
- looks eagerly forward to the feeling of flowing execution.

This is just one description of how flow can feel when your focus is on the few essential elements of great play. Not all of these experiences will occur every time. People can experience focus and flow differently. The one constant is that when you focus properly, you feel natural, at one with the universe. Flow is not a series of steps you can check off, but rather a feeling as natural, and as powerful, as the ebb and flow of the ocean.

On the Other Hand . . .

You are always attending to something. The question is whether what you're attending to helps or hurts your performance.

First, you might be generating negative attention that actively harms your flow, your rhythm, your faith in your game. Second, you might have mental laziness that accounts for general distractibility.

In the case of negative focus, you allow your thoughts to stray to destructive places that might include

- thoughts of the consequences of making or missing shots,
- thoughts of how well opponents are doing,
- doubts in your ability,
- fear of repeating past mistakes, and
- concern about what observers are thinking about you.

Negativity can be caused by mental laziness. You can't allow random thoughts to run amok. Whether you're thinking about work, school, relationships, or simply letting your mind slip, your performance will be significantly influenced. Your shots lose their integrity when you're not present for them. Remember, choice is power. Choose well.

Do You Need To Dial In or Dial Out?

One last thing about laser focus: A lot of players bowl best when dialed closely into the game for the duration of a practice session or competition. But not everyone is designed this way. Some bowlers require space to mentally wander between shots and games.

You have to know what works best for you. For some players they maintain their energy levels, and peak performance only by staying completely attentive to everything that is going on around their game, and on the lanes.

Other players need the break of conversation, meditation, looking around, or even daydreaming. Much like putting the weights down between sets in weightlifting, players who need to get away from their own gameplay for a moment put the game away periodically to be most effective. This decreases their anxiety and helps them achieve their best efforts when it's their turn to roll.

Sometimes coaches will get upset with players who do not seem to have their heads entirely in the game. But you have to be careful with this. Of course, if you are playing on a team you should be generous with your attention to your mates. But it really is okay, sometimes better, to put your own game aside for a bit. This allows for integration of information, rest, and a rejuvenated effort for the next shot.

Think of times you have practiced and competed really well. It should be apparent to you which mode of focus has served you best. Those who have a style of focusing, attending, and recovering that differ from teammates and coaches can be frustrating until you explain what you are doing, and how it helps you bowl. Just don't jump ship on those with whom you bowl. Communication about your operating style is key here.

THE MOST IMPORTANT THING*

Above all factors in competition, the most important thing is to keep your mind on the most important thing. Most players have never chosen a point of focus and held it for the entirety of a shot, until well after the ball is off of their hand. Here are some guidelines to help you attain laser-like focus when you bowl:

1. **Know what you choose to focus on.** If you're like most of us, you have about 60,000 thoughts a day. Each one either serves your purpose, or it doesn't. There's an internal universe, and an external universe, of possibilities. Train yourself to commit to a point of focus. Whether it be the lanes, empowering and coordinating thoughts, or some aspect of your body movement, live with your choice. You'll either fly or go down in flames, but you'll be playing with raw commitment.

2. **Focus only on what contributes to a great shot.** Remember that the only things you control are your thoughts, your visualization, and your physical execution—simply stated, this is what you plan, what you think, and what you do. If you can stand what happens after that, you can maintain laser focus. If you think you have to do more than that, your mind will skitter all over the place.

3. **Distractions happen.** Thoughts, noises, and events can have a gravitational pull on your focus. No big deal, right? Just deflect them and return to the most important thing—your laser focus. You can't get overly involved in distractions. You can observe them. You can be amused by them. You can be curious that they occur. But don't let them intrude into your point of focus.

4. **Learn to notice ever more quickly when you get off task, off purpose, off focus.** Then take effective action to re-focus your laser. Try cue words that reorient you, such as *relax, stay down, lion heart,* or *post.* Your actions will follow your cues with remarkable consistency.

5. **Develop a routine that sharpens your laser focus.** Perhaps try beginning your preshot routine earlier, with an intention to laser-in as the first step of it. Ask yourself, *What do I need to focus on in this moment to roll my best shot?*

Follow these guidelines to take you as far as your game can go. More than that, you'll be able to trust yourself to land your jet (that is, the ball) on the runway under any circumstances, no matter what distractions surround you. They could put a marching band behind you, and it wouldn't phase you. Lasering your focus prepares you to win (Hinitz 2013).

---

*Adapted from D. Hinitz, 2013 (Jan.), "Laser focus," *Bowling This Month* 20(1).

DON'T SHOULD ON YOURSELF

**When adversity strikes, that's when you have to be the most calm.
Take a step back, stay strong, stay grounded, and press on.**

LL Cool J, rapper, entrepreneur, actor

When things go awry on the lanes, bowlers might adopt the attitude that life is out to get them. Adversity seems personal. It might be a challenging sport shot, sticky or slick approaches, dirty back ends that slide the pins instead of trip them, an opponent who slaps his hands in your face after a strike, or any other bothersome circumstance. Adversity on the lanes feels that way because it's experienced as calamitous, afflicting, or antagonistic. Simply put, something is going on that you don't like.

By far, the most common thought process for bowlers who struggle with unpleasant conditions and hardships is that the difficulties somehow *should not* be there. The belief that life is supposed to be other than it actually is gets bowlers frazzled, frustrated, angry, and upset. Here are some of the classic beliefs of bowlers:

- There should be obvious breakpoints on freshly oiled lanes.
- The shot should be easier, or harder, or not so easy for lefties, or not so easy for righties.
- Other bowlers should wait their turns and not jump up on the approaches when you are up.
- The bowling center should be warmer, colder, quieter, better ventilated, better equipped, and have slower racks.

Notice the many occurrences of the word *should* in the preceding list. Instead of dealing with the *is-ness* of the situation, the bowler is dealing with one or more shoulds. The shoulds will kill concentration, feelings of well-being, and focus. Of course, the upside for many bowlers is that adverse conditions give them a good story about why they failed to win or didn't score well.

The first step in dealing with adverse conditions is to assess whether you can do anything to change the conditions. If you can, decide if it's worth doing so. Chances are this will depend on how bad the conditions or distractions are, and how much trouble it will be to change them. If something's bothering you, such as a bowler who doesn't know lane etiquette, and you think that you can intervene easily, then by all means make that happen.

On the more common occasion when you realize there's nothing you can do to change what's bothering you, you will be empowered by simply accepting the situation.

You need to ask yourself only one question: *What do I need to do to perform my best under these circumstances?* If you are busy constructing reasons for not excelling, you have already lost the game, regardless of the final score.

Accepting what can't be changed and then deciding how best to cope is generally the most effective course of action. In fact, even better, adopt the attitude that you invited tests to occur when you decided to be a competitive player, and that the universe is generously giving you what you requested. Once you learn to do this, you'll come to understand that many of the adverse conditions you encounter are really problems in your own thinking instead of problems in the world.

FIVE STEPS TO POWER

**However beautiful the strategy,
you should occasionally look at the results.**

Winston Churchill

We all have a choice of two positions in life: We can adopt the attitude of a victim, or we can take responsibility for ourselves. Victims feel helpless, persecuted, and targeted. Those who take charge of life feel empowered, capable, and free to create results. These five simple steps can assist you in developing and maintaining a responsible mindset:

1. Identify the source of frustration or irritation. Notice where the *should* or *shouldn't* is in your thinking.

2. Drop the *should*. Sometimes life is the way it is.

3. Once you have adjusted whatever you can, alter the conditions of the situation.

4. Once you have adjusted whatever you can, completely accept the circumstances, and go forth with your best effort. Again, by becoming a competitor you invited all of the things that could happen in competition situations to potentially come into your life. You asked to be tested. You can be victim to life, or remember that you are responsible for putting yourself where you are. Remember that you have the power to respond to anything effectively, instead of reacting reflexively. Choose the latter; everything works better that way. Whether you create your life or react to your life is a matter of how well you "C" (see)—create or react.

5. Assess whether your coping decisions have been effective and, if necessary, to try another adjustment. Check your thinking. Are you still living in *shoulds*?

Obviously, it's fine to have preferences on how life ought to be—but it is best to avoid demands. Virtually nothing that happens in the bowling center is personal. The rest of the world tends to be spectacularly oblivious to most of our requirements for order and caretaking. Alcoholics Anonymous has what they call a Serenity Prayer. With very minor adjustment, we can turn this into a Bowler's Prayer:

> Please give me the strength to change the things I can, the courage to handle the things I cannot change, and the wisdom to know the difference.

WORK OUTSIDE YOUR COMFORT ZONE

**Coming out of your comfort zone is tough in the beginning,
chaotic in the middle, and awesome in the end . . .
because in the end, it shows you a whole new world!**

Manoj Arora, author of *From the Rat Race to Financial Freedom*

The next important mental step is to get accustomed to playing outside your comfort zone of normal thoughts and feelings. To be mentally tough, you must embrace this one. People loosely throw around the term comfort zone as if there's a common understanding of what this entails. To visualize your comfort zone, imagine two parallel lines (see figure 5.1)

On the inside of your comfort zone are all the things that bring you security: familiarity, normalcy, predictability, the usual state of affairs, "the known." On the outside of the lines is unpredictability, fresh and new experiences, risk, feelings, life, and growth.

The problem with playing outside of the lines is that it can be unsettling if you're not used to playing there. The problem with playing inside the lines is that under anything other than normal conditions you might feel jerked out of your zone and feel helpless, overwhelmed, or ineffective. Of course, staying inside the lines also shuts you off from new experiences and possible growth.

To improve, grow, and prepare to master all competitive situations, you must embrace playing outside your comfort zone. The same rules apply in all of life. There's no coincidence there.

As an example of how much players like to play within their comfort zones, this quote was posted in one of the pro shops at the National Bowling Stadium in Reno: "I like to stand with my left foot on the center dot in the middle and throw over the second arrow." Even though the lanes were oiled for a different shot at the national tournament, the bowler was demanding to purchase a ball that would let him stay in his comfort zone.

As any moderately experienced bowler knows, lane oil patterns and bowling conditions can vary greatly from lane to lane, and even from frame to frame. If you get attached to playing a certain line with a certain ball every time, your scores will suffer because of erratic ball reactions and increasing self-doubt. The only way to succeed is to be willing to play with different equip-

Risk
_____

Comfort zone
_____

Greater possibilities

Figure 5.1   By imagining two parallel lines, you can help visualize your comfort zone with all the things that comfort you falling into between those two lines.

ment, on different parts of the lane, and using different hand positions and ball speeds.

We develop the flexibility to move out of our comfort zones in much the same way that we develop physical flexibility. When young gymnasts are learning to do the splits, they must stretch several times a day, pushing their legs just a little bit further each time. Bowlers should develop similar drills. For example, try playing strike shots over every single arrow in practice. Make yourself hit the pocket rolling over each arrow as a wind-up or wind-down exercise. In practice, re-create troublesome situations. Bowl next to recreational bowlers who don't know bowling etiquette. Play entire games with a plastic ball that has very little reaction.

Most bowlers can identify their weak links in terms of competition stresses. Have a plan ready for how to respond to each of them, as well as a plan to stay focused on your shot cycle, no matter what. This way you won't be caught emotionally off guard when things happen outside your comfort zone.

MINDFULNESS AND CONCENTRATION

**One reason so few of us achieve what we truly want
is that we never direct our focus.
We never concentrate our power.
Most people dabble their way through life,
never deciding to master anything in particular.**

Tony Robbins, motivational speaker

One of the most frequently voiced concerns for athletes in any sport is how to regulate racing minds and bodies. Whether it's leading off for your team, closing out the 10th frame for a victory, or rolling the 12th shot for a 300, the time that stressing about a shot always becomes paramount is when something that feels really big is on the line.

There are several holy grails in the mental game universe. Managing your physical and emotional activation level is one of them. And in the school of mental toughness, there's one universal quality that everyone recognizes: steel mind. Everyone applauds the bowler who gets it done when the heat is on.

Whether it's in our leagues, college tournaments, or the pro circuit, we all know players who consistently deliver the goods. Conversely, other players are known for not being able to roll reliably under pressure. The truth is that most competitors have, at times, been both characters.

When nerves start to thrum, you must have weapons in your arsenal that allow you to roll with confidence.

A STILL MIND IS A STEEL MIND*

**That's been one of my mantras—focus and simplicity.
Simple can be harder than complex:
You have to work hard to get your thinking clean
to make it simple. But it's worth it in the end,
because once you get there, you can move mountains.**

Steve Jobs, cofounder of Apple

Gaining control over one's mind has long been recognized as vital in any performance arena. In just about every religion and culture, from Christianity to the aboriginal outback, the importance of some form of meditation or mindfulness training has been highlighted. There are many benefits of mindfulness, and gaining control of your mental dragons is one of them.

Athletes, artists, and many others have tried to cultivate mental control in many ways. Most people have heard of, if not tried, yoga, tai chi, and meditation. Other practices for mental strength include art, music, dance, massage, sports psychology, and even the practice of sports like bowling itself.

When we discuss developing a steel mind, we're referring to a practice called "mindfulness" (Hinitz 2012). This strategy for improving the brain's ability to process emotional activation has an abundance of scientific support. But rather than get lost in scientific terminology, let's talk in user-friendly bowling language.

The steel mind we seek looks like this: Once again, you're at the cut line of a tournament. You have one frame to go and need only to mark and get a good count. You can feel yourself getting amped up. Your heart starts picking up a bit, you have some thoughts about how dialed in you are, how doable this is, how important the shot is, and so on. You're a little tight, not too tight, but you grab the ball a little.

The resulting shot leaves you with a 10-pin spare. You can play this game a little, so a single-pin spare is no problem. A few people gather around. Just make the spare and move on. The problem is that your hand is sweating a bit. Actually, the problem is that your brain is also sweating a bit. Heck, at this point it could practically be a 5-pin spare, and your system would be going off. (You know, who could miss one of these?!)

You might think that the goal at this point is to make the feelings go away, to buckle down to the task at hand, relax, and make a good shot. We see this approach fail now and then when we see single-pin spares being missed on the PBA telecast.

The truth is there's a more effective way to go about things, though it can be difficult to trust at first. Really, it's probably far less important to regulate your emotions than it is to regulate your attention, attitude, and physical tension levels.

---

*Partially adapted from D. Hinitz, 2012 (Nov.), "Steel mind," *Bowling This Month* 19(11).

COOL OBSERVATION

**The best way to capture moments is to pay attention.
This is how we cultivate mindfulness. Mindfulness means
being awake. It means knowing what you are doing.**

Jon Kabat-Zinn, spiritual teacher

Becoming cool requires two vital steps. First, you must corral the focus point of your attention. Many of the physical game tips for bowling simply give bowlers a place to put their minds. Regardless of the instructional value of these tips (and many are very helpful), having a place to put your mind elicits relief and confidence. Confident in the value of the tip, players avoid attending to distracting thoughts, and play with authority.

Second, you must suspend any fight to control your feelings. Instead, step back with an attitude of curiosity and acceptance of whatever thoughts and feelings are swirling inside of you. *You need not change anything at this point.* When you're observant and curious instead of fearful and judgmental, you'll naturally relax a bit. More important, you don't get involved in an internal battle.

In truth, the process you're going to practice has one purpose, and one purpose alone. We're striving to change your attitude, your self-confidence, and your patience. Whatever you want to do with the ball (up to the level of your ability), you'll be able to do, without all the mental interference that comes with believing you have to tell your body what to do under pressure.

STEPS TO MINDFUL FOCUS*

Mindfulness is another way of taking complete charge of your focus, attention, and tension levels. If you practice the following steps regularly, you'll almost surely get positive results in each of these three areas. But you must put in the time and effort. If you do, your performance in pressure situations will become remarkably normal and familiar. Your ability to marshal all your mental resources in a productive way will be readily available.

1. **Make time and space to clear interference.** This is the first step to quieting your mind. You must have a pattern and rhythm to this practice. No fooling yourself—you either do this every time, for real, or you do the fake-out routine, and try to pull this off only when you think it's important.

2. **Notice without struggling or panicking.** Remember, the reason you're doing this is so you can enjoy rolling great shots in any circumstances. At this stage you don't force anything in or out of your mind—but you notice everything. Take a look at the whole junkyard. In a moment you're going to have a mental yard sale, hanging onto the thoughts and feelings you choose to keep, and letting go of the others.

---

*Partially adapted from D. Hinitz, 2012 (Nov.), "Steel mind," *Bowling This Month* 19(11).

3. **Focus your concentration.** The next step is one that almost no one does naturally, yet it feels totally natural when you're in flow. You pick a point of attention and make that point the single most important point of attention in the world.

If you've been bowling for 10 years, you've probably rolled fewer than 10 shots in the following fashion. To employ this kind of mindful attention, you must believe and trust that you already know how to bowl. You're giving up control in order to gain control of performing with greatness.

If the most important thing is that you notice your breathing, then that's it—you focus on your breathing and trust your bowling. If the most important thing is relaxing your hand, then relax your hand at all costs and make that the only thing that matters. If the most important thing is zeroing in on your target, then that's it. That's all that matters. You could even pick a word or phrase that helps you, such as *thank you*, and make that the only thing that matters.

When practicing mindfulness, it's vital that the only thing you judge is your ability to value and concentrate on the one point of attention. Forget evaluating the quality of your shots. You can bowl. Trust this. Anything you need to adjust to bowl better will happen automatically, up to the point of your skill and knowledge base. Whatever you choose to attend to is what you concentrate on before, during, and after your shot. No judgment of anything else. Period.

4. **Achieve clear awareness.** This last step blends much of what we know about that which lets people perform beautifully, in flow, under any circumstances. Your task is to be aware of what's happening within, and around you, as you bowl. This part is extremely important. You are noticing the bare bones facts of what's happening. Notice the truth of the whole shot cycle, with no judgment, as you perceive things through your five senses, or as your mind sees them.

When you walk, you don't tell yourself to walk, yet you can notice everything about what it feels like to walk. The same is true for opening the refrigerator, and believe it or not, for your bowling. It's as if you're an outsider who gets to view what's happening. Whatever you see, you think or feel, "So what?" Once you become a skilled observer, virtually all negative thoughts or feelings begin to lose their power (Hinitz 2012).

Once you practice and internalize this process, you'll appear to have ice water in your veins. Your observation, curiosity, amusement, and confidence will make you a very dangerous bowler indeed. Need to step up in the 10th? "Hey coach, put me in. I'm good here!"

You now have a stash of training techniques for dealing with any adverse condition. But as with anything of value, you must earn the ability to use these techniques through patient and diligent practice. Once you gain just a bit of mastery, and begin to show improvement in your mental toughness, you'll be hooked and want to practice even more to become as tough as you can be.

■ Bouncing Back When it Counts With Rick Steelsmith

When you are pitted against the best in the world, you can't just partially commit. You have to be in it completely. If you are not fully committed, you will be done.

Rick Steelsmith, USBC Hall of Famer

Back in 1987, Rick Steelsmith was just out of college. As far back as anyone could remember, he was the first four-year collegiate All-American bowler. He had been part of winning the Junior College Nationals with Vincennes University and had won a national championship with Wichita State University.

Rick Steelsmith was bright, fresh, and had a backswing that went to the ceiling. His confidence went even higher. He had won everywhere he played and, at 22 years old, was not caught off-guard when he became the youngest bowler ever to win the ABC Masters. He played that scenario over and over repeatedly in his mind in the months leading up to the event. No one else was probably sur-

Courtesy of the United States Bowling Congress.

prised, either. Other men's and women's professional tour players, when asked about the greatest collegiate player ever, would overlap in exclaiming about Rick.

When asked about what his expectations were going into the Masters in 1987, Rick remembers: "I went there to win. I guess I was young, and naive and didn't really know any better, which, looking back, was probably a good thing. At Wichita State we won almost every time we bowled. You kind of get into a winning mindset from that, I guess. I had made Team USA prior to the Masters, and I was going to the Masters to bowl well, as well as enjoy the experience. I remember as the week unfolded thinking that things were kind of happening the way I had imagined it, and the way I'd imagined in all those practices as a kid, seeing myself throwing shots to win the Masters. I won a match, then another match, then another. Before I knew it, I had made the stepladder finals telecast, just as I had imagined. I ended up bowling well on TV and defeating Brad Snell for the Masters title."

"Then I went to Helsinki for FIQ worlds. Got two golds, a silver, and two bronzes. I won the individual all-events. I shot 300, which was the first 300 in FIQ history."

Rick was projected to be one of the giants of the sport. His record was sparkling, and his future looked brighter. He was a member of Team USA and already had gold medals in international competition.

Then one day, the music stopped. Rick headed out on the professional tour in 1988. Halfway through his rookie year, he competed at the U.S. Open. It was the

(continued)

next to last day, at the end of the day. The lanes were torn up and a little dry. Rick left a 3-6-10 spare. No big deal. However, he felt that he would have to get a little more speed on the ball to get down the lane.

As he reached through the shot, there was a pop in Rick's shoulder that could be heard by nearby competitors. Rick's life changed in that moment. His shoulder was torn. Rick finished the tournament somehow. He went to the next tournament, but he could not finish.

Eighteen months passed from when Rick hurt his shoulder to when he threw another ball in PBA competition. He first tried physical rehabilitation; then he had surgery. When he started up again, he used an eight-pound ball. He slowly built back to a normal weight. No one had had this specific injury in bowling before, so Rick patterned his recovery after baseball pitchers coming back from similar surgeries.

Speaking for himself and his doctor, Rick said, "We were both confident I would come back. But at the same time, I didn't know if I was going to be able to physically get the ball down the lane. That's the part people don't get if they haven't been through it. In addition, other people don't know that you're playing hurt. Every single day, I wondered if I could come back. At the same time, I knew it wasn't an option not to come back."

Back before the injury, Rick hadn't skipped any weeks. He bowled all the time. He had a high backswing and a closed swing. Doctors said the joint was tight. "Some things are good luck, and they come together. Some things are bad luck, and they come together."

"The tricky thing for me was I had just come down from the top of the mountain. Then I got my legs knocked out from under me. Anyone with coordination can come back physically. I had to change my timing, backswing, game. Technically, my game was better, but I wasn't the same bowler."

"I got a game back that physically could compete with anyone in the world. Anyone with coordination can come back physically. But the mental side of it was the difference. The mental side was the hard part. My quest, my determination, was to get that side back. It would be different if I didn't know what it was like to win. But I did know."

"There were days I didn't feel like battling back. There are times when you think, 'What the hell am I doing?' And then you wake up the next day and go, 'Oh yeah.' You have the days where you're depressed, where you wonder. But you wake up the next day and keep going. The depth of where some of that stuff goes. I don't think people realize. You don't know what tomorrow will bring."

Rick exercised the most powerful thing in his arsenal. *Choice.* He was faced with a clear fork in the road. He could quit, or he could persevere into the unknown, with no guarantee that he would ever win again. I was privileged to walk parts of this journey with Rick. At the end of the day, an indomitable spirit, and choosing to persevere, are what got him through this dark stretch of woods.

"You get to a point where you just don't make [quitting] an option. It beats you down, but you kind of don't let it be an option. You have that deeper thing that keeps you going. Deeper set. I told myself that unless I can't physically make that ball go down the lane, I'm going to keep bowling. I think that is the only way you can get through stuff like that. You have to have all your energy there in order to do athletics. When you are pitted against the best in the world, you can't just partially commit. You have to be in it completely. If you're not fully committed, you will be done."

Three years later, in 1991, Rick's ship turned. He won a PBA Doubles event with legend Teata Semiz. To be the best in the world for a week, and on finals day, was an indescribable reward. Even then, Rick felt that it was still week to week if he was going to be able to bowl. "It was like that [wondering if I would be able to complete a tournament] for seven years."

He iced his shoulder after every block for 10 years. In 1997, six years after his last title, Rick won his second major championship—the PBA national. Today that would be called the Tournament of Champions.

"The second one was on my own, and in a major. I was far enough into it that I had experienced all the junk and depression." The victory eased all of the struggles. "You know what? I just made it through all of that crap. The first one, I was week to week in terms of being able to compete. The second one, I was out there six years after that. I thought, 'I'm back as far as being able to bowl.'"

In 2013, Rick Steelsmith was inducted into the USBC Hall of Fame. He had walked the dark and difficult path and emerged into a lighter day. He had stared at adversity and truly bounced back.

"There again, you look at the progression of things. I was retired. My last title was in 1997. That was a culmination of all the things I did. It was kind of a humbling thing. One's perspective at the beginning, middle, and end of a career are vastly different. This honor is just more meaningful. Your whole career. Holy cow!"

"To me it just means that I did it. Looking back 20 years prior to that, I had those days. I didn't know if I would be bowling 20 years later. Hall of Fame wasn't even a thought. The thoughts I lived with are, 'Am I going to make it to tomorrow?' Looking back, I made it through that. I did it."

"Obviously, for anyone going through that (hard times), you have family, friends, support. You keep doing it because that's what you do, that's what you want to do; that was my life goal. What got me through was I was not going to let that not happen. You just kind of get the resolve."

And now? Rick still competes, and having turned 50 last year, he has the Senior Tour events to add to his schedule. In the meantime, he gives back. Rick is coaching aspiring bowlers in Wichita. Ironically, many of his students have no idea who's teaching them the fundamentals of the game.

Author's note: A half-hour after our interview, I received a text from Rick. Verbatim, it went like this: "I got a text from one of my students. He won the high school City League team and individual championships today. 753 series. Cool stuff!!"

Cool stuff, indeed.

CHAPTER 6

Mental Secrets to Making Spares

You didn't have to be a member of the Raccoon Lodge bowling team, bowled for dollars on TV or even seen *The Big Lebowski* on cable to know that Michael Haugen Jr.'s 215–214 victory against Chris Barnes in Sunday's H&R Block Tournament of Championships at Red Rock Lanes was something special.

Ron Kantowski, sports columnist

Here was the story on that historic day. After six frames in the final match of the Tournament of Champions in Las Vegas, Chris Barnes led Michael Haugen Jr. by 52 pins. I don't really know if anyone has ever come back from that kind of deficit to win in the championship round, but Michael Haugen did, and it was a big one for his career.

Somehow Barnes stopped striking, but that was not going to be an issue, mathematically.

Chris really only had to fill frames to win this one. Haugen Jr. changed balls, used a different ball on each lane, and started to light them up with strikes.

In the ninth frame, Barnes left a 10-pin. For a master player of his caliber, this is generally considered a tap-in. Barnes is a great spare shooter, and rarely misses a single pin attempt.

To all appearances, Chris stepped over to the ball return, picked up his plastic spare ball, and did not get fully set. His ball dropped into the channel to the right just before reaching the pin. Haugen Jr. rolled the first two strikes in the 10th frame and won the Tournament of Champions title.

Ironically, almost exactly three years previous to that event, at the 62nd PBA U.S. Open, fortunes were reversed. Chris Barnes needed a strike, then at least a nine-count, with a completed spare to win the Open title. He did exactly that, picking up the four-pin single-pin spare to edge Patrick Allen 213–212.

This is a dramatic introduction to the importance of spare shooting. Approaches to spare shooting, under various circumstances, deserve special emphasis. As you've just seen, spare shooting in competition is rife with tales of triumph and woe. Often a title is cemented by making spares. Conversely, many phenomenal bowlers can cite a championship slipping from their fingers because of a single missed spare.

MAKING SPARES IS THE KEY

All sports are games of inches.

Dick Ritger, USBC and PBA Hall of Fame

Striking at will is impressive in competition. But spares are often when you're seriously tested as an action player. Excelling at spares is the champion's game. As PBA star Patrick Healy once said, "I can't spot anyone 11 pins at this level."

Several years ago at the High Roller Megabucks Tournament in Las Vegas, PBA champion Mika Koivuniemi (then an amateur) chuckled while reviewing one of his matches as he advanced through the tournament. He told me that when his opponent missed a 7-pin spare early in the game Mika knew that he had him. Can you imagine giving a great player, or a weak player for that matter, an added booster shot by missing a spare? Painfully, most bowlers can.

TIPS FOR SPARE SHOOTING

Take time to deliberate,
but when the time for action comes,
stop thinking and go in.

Napoleon

Spare shooting is an area in which it's difficult to distinguish between mental and physical aspects of the game. At advanced levels it should be no more difficult to hit a single-pin spare with a plastic ball than to throw chewing gum in a basket a few feet away. It's like a 30-inch (76 cm) putt for a professional golfer. Yet even at the professional level easy spares are missed at crucial times, and in collegiate tournaments they are missed at a surprisingly high rate.

Spare-Shooting Tip 1: Commit to Seeing Your Ball Cross the Arrows at Your Mark

I know this sounds easy, but if you check yourself you might be surprised at how often your head and eyes jerk up. The mental part of this is the mistaken investment in the outcome, leaping ahead of the need to stroke through your line.

Believe it or not, it's fairly rare for the average bowler to be able to accurately tell you what board his spare shot crossed at the arrows. Most can tell you what they targeted. Most can tell you what they intended to hit. But few players can resist casting their eyes up to see their results simultaneously with the ball leaving their hands.

Keeping your head and eyes steady serves many purposes. It gives you a large point of focus, so you need not think about all your mechanics. It helps you plant and stay down at the line. And, whether you make or miss your shot, you get accurate feedback about where, and how, you're rolling the ball. Once your ball crosses the mark, it's natural to raise your eyes to witness what happened, but wait for that natural motion to occur.

Spare-Shooting Tip 2: Confidence Involves the Head and the Gut

Don't roll a spare shot until you know the strategy you're using will work. The profound importance of believing in your spare line can't be overstated, particularly on combination spares and double wood. It's amazing how many bowlers acknowledge that they knew they were going to miss a spare before they rolled the ball—and they rolled it anyway!

You either believe in your line or you don't. If you question what you're about to do, one of two things will happen. Either you'll execute mechanically (and poorly), because your subconscious mind knows you have doubt. Or else you'll unconsciously overcorrect. You know that you *should* roll it over a certain mark, but you don't trust your arm swing, or believe in the line, so you fudge it somehow by rolling it where and how your gut thinks it will work. This shows a lack of trust in your own judgment from shot to shot. Play the spare shot that you know in your heart of hearts will work.

Spare-Shooting Tip 3: Make Sure the Traffic Light Is Green Before You Progress With Your Shot

Self-starting athletes have a kind of starter gun in their minds. A diver can intuitively feel when to initiate her first bounce. A gymnast senses when to spring onto the apparatus. A *yes* or a *go* or a *now* occurs in the mind. If you can't feel this signal in your head, your response should be, *No, don't go!*

Bowlers who practice visualization refer to *seeing* the ball path before they go. For straight spares, you want to visualize a path back to you from the pin. For hooking spares, visually work back from your break point. You must be able to feel and see things in your mind's eye. Without this, it's difficult to have a self-fulfilling prophecy of success.

It's said that true commitment involves surrender to a choice. If you're still fighting belief in your lane-play decision, you have not surrendered, which makes the *go* signal in your head a no-go, or a con job.

Spare-Shooting Tip 4: Value Your Best Effort More Than a Perfect Result

Imagine this scenario. You somehow leave the 2-4-5-8 bucket (unfair, I know—the universe must bear a grudge). As you prepare to roll your spare shot, you hear the click of a pistol hammer being drawn back. "Spare or die" says a familiar voice. Whose voice is it? Yours, of course.

Many athletes who are self-demanding perfectionists have a judge and executioner living in their unconscious mind. If you have extensive self-punishing thoughts or feelings following a miss, you know they are there.

"Extensive" means anything that lasts more than a few seconds. If there's self-punishing talk like, "You @#%!" after a bad shot or missed spare, a desire to avoid looking bad in front of others, or even a feeling of increased pressure because of the importance of the spare for total score," you might be flirting with "gun to the head" bowling.

If you're afraid to fall in this game you'll fall far more frequently. If you're willing to risk falling in order to fly, you have a shot at flying. The bottom line is that if you can't stand to miss, then the pressure you feel will make you shovel and steer instead of sweetly rolling the ball.

If you're going to be killed in your own mind for missing a spare, you're not free to bowl. Yes, you might roll your shot, but it probably won't have your signature on it. Your internal self-talk must be as supportive as you would say to an eight-year-old doubles partner. "Come on give it your best. I'm with you no matter what." This kind of encouragement must occur consistently.

This is especially important after an errant shot. If you kick your own butt after a miss, you end up reinforcing your fears of the internal hangman on the next one. You must know you're going to be OK upfront, and then you're truly free to cut loose.

Spare-Shooting Tip 5: Feel It, Do It

It would be easier to execute spare shots if the pins would take a jab at you first. Then you could react, respond, and wipe them out. The problem is the pins are just sitting there. There's nothing to react to, so you must move into action on your own. A great way to do this is to start with brief visualization, and then add *feel*.

Oddly enough, despite the term, *visualization* is not just visual. You can picture your ball path and roll as a form of visualization. Feel is a way of imaging with the body. Some people do this by doing a practice swing with the ball before actually setting up and going. This is similar to golfers taking a practice swing, or gymnasts moving their bodies through imaginary routines before jumping onto the equipment. When you do this, your natural and trained skills can come into play.

Having a sense of how your body will feel when you execute a shot gives you an internal point of focus and a way to generate action in a sport that does not give you the luxury of reaction.

Spare-Shooting Tip 6: Let the General Run the Show

There's something about shooting spares that invites bowlers to get lost in the mechanics of rolling the ball. If you're thinking about all kinds of body parts, timing, and movement, you risk overriding your automatic setting with your manual transmission.

Imagine the general of an army issuing orders. There are two approaches to take. He can talk to every private, corporal, sergeant, and lieutenant in order to execute a plan. Or he can trust that his troops have been through boot camp. This means issuing one or two general orders and trusting they'll be carried out.

Issue one or two general orders and call it a plan. Typically, what works best is to have one physical key and one *heart* key. Your physical key coordinates your entire body—head, balance, soft hands, whatever. Your heart key surrenders full commitment to the shot.

Experiment with these spare-shooting tips to see which serve you best. Sometimes committing to one or two of them works better than trying to keep all five in mind.

It's a Wrap

Don't brood and moan over your spare shooting because you miss one here and there. This only causes all kinds of mental loading that's best avoided. We all make more than we miss. We all miss a big one now and then. Take the stress and drama out of your spare shooting. If you follow the tips, you'll hit most of your spares and can quit worrying about the few that you miss. This is way better than feeling you must strike every time to survive.

SPARE-SHOOTING FORMULA

**Everything must be made as simple as possible.
But not simpler.**

Albert Einstein

The success or failure of any tournament or league night experience often boils down to spare shooting. Strikes come and go, but perfect games are still statistically unusual. Everyone who picks up a ball at the beginning of competition can expect to need to make some critical spares during the match.

Champions in any sport have simple formulas for executing key skills at critical times. In fact, you can probably think of several formulas for success that you use in your everyday life. When you have a formula for success—in any activity—you have no need to rely on special gifts or talents. Whether it's making chocolate chip cookies or toning abdominal muscles, if you follow a good formula, the end product is just about ensured.

The good news is that there's a formula for spare shooting that produces great results. But be warned: A shift in normal thinking might be required. You will need a true openness to adopting a new perspective on how to succeed. Although this formula might look elementary, it is critical for mastering the mental game. Learn this elegant secret inside and out, and it will never desert you in a time of need.

Notice that I use the term *formula* and not *system* at this point. For the bowler looking for a reliable spare-shooting plan, I will present an earthquake-proof spare system later in this chapter.

Many strategies exist for moving right or left off the strike line or lining up with a plastic ball on preestablished marks. Most physical spare-shooting directions are simple and effective. The problem that competitors encounter is not that they can't decide what ball to throw or where to throw it. The problem is they often overthink and tense up when shooting single pins and combination spares that are well within their ability level.

Bowlers use many strategies for handling spare-shooting anxiety. Deep breathing, muscle relaxation, visualization, and self-talk all have proven success. Later in the chapter we'll add some of these techniques to the mix for effective spare shooting. But underlying all techniques is this basic formula:

Staying in the present + intention + mechanism = ultimate spare shooting

At first glance, this formula is hardly earth shattering. It might even seem obvious. Once translated into bowling terms, however, it's the only spare-shooting magic you'll need. To unlock this formula, you must fully understand and internalize the terms.

Stay in the Present

When your strike shot does not net 10 in the pit, you'll likely experience a flash of disappointment. The thoughts and self-statements aroused will significantly affect the next ball you roll, either positively or negatively. Here are some examples of negative thoughts:

- Upset thoughts and feelings related to throwing the bad shot
- Concern that a strike was very important in that particular frame for personal or team scores
- Pressured thoughts about having missed the same or different spares
- Anxiety about the importance of making the spare
- Lack of confidence in executing the spare shot

Instead of wallowing in negative thoughts, choose instead to use positive thoughts and self-statements, which leads to confidence in your spare strategy, trust in your execution, mental preparation for throwing a good shot, and mental adjustments to physical setup and lane play based on the strike shot. We'll discuss positive self-statements in more detail later in the chapter.

A fundamental distinction exists between great spare shooters and the rest of the field. The great ones stay in the present when they go to execute. You have three options: living in the past, present, or future frames. The mental frame you put yourself into will determine your emotions, your tension levels, and, often, your confidence. Basically, tell me what you're thinking about, and I'll tell you what you're feeling. Anytime you're not living in the present frame, your spare shooting is at great risk.

**The most honest form of filmmaking
is to make a film for yourself.**

Peter Jackson, film director

Think of the frames of the game as frames in a movie. Each frame is broken further into split frames for the first and, if needed, second shots. You can identify orientation in past frames by some key symptoms. Watch out for thoughts of unfair pin fall, anger, irritability, hopelessness, or helplessness to carry the pins. Frustration is a mental and emotional clue that you're not shaking off disappointing bowling results.

You have to deal with what is happening in the frame that it is occurring. Do not get involved with what you think was supposed to happen on your first shot. Don't get caught up in the outrage of having left an unfair pin or combination spare. Also be careful of retaining self-punishment or anger at throwing an errant shot or reading lane conditions incorrectly. Such thinking patterns trap you in past frames.

Any attention to the consequences of leaving a spare is living in past or future frames. Such problems manifest as anxiety, fear, distrust, or lack of confidence in your ability to deliver a good shot. Even excitement about an upcoming shot is a way of living in the future, unless managed well.

Flow, peak performance, and maximum effectiveness come with living in the present frame. In the present frame you can briefly acknowledge any thoughts or feelings about leaving a spare and having to pick it up. Beyond that, the shot cycle, including the preshot routine and awareness of the ball, body, and lanes, must be in the present.

Imagine the captain of a ship leaving shore, dwelling on what might have been forgotten and left behind. The ship might be on course to crash and the captain won't even notice. Dwelling over missed spares in the middle of a game is like sailing out to sea while still staring ashore. This is not a responsible way to steer a ship. Staying completely aware of what's happening now promotes the best chance of successful navigation, at sea and on the lanes.

The only place to be is *right here, right now.* Don't bother chasing away past and future thoughts. Those thoughts are like little cartoon bubbles floating past the inner mind. Simply decide to orient to what's happening now. An effective way of doing this is to focus on two aspects of the spare shot: the shot cycle, including the preshot routine, and the finish.

As discussed in chapter 3, the first step to staying in the present is establishing your preshot routine. You need a regular and reliable sequence of thoughts and behaviors that precedes every practice and game shot. Staying with your preshot sequence can be incredibly calming and reassuring.

The second key to staying present and aware in spare shooting is to give extra attention to finishing the shot well. Decide to deliver each shot with perfect follow-through, balance, and intention (discussed next). If you're fully committed, aware, and feeling good about what you brought to finish the shot, you're probably shooting your spares in the present frame.

Have Intention

Most people use the word *intention* all the time without being clear about its true meaning. Many athletes make the mistake of confusing ideas such as hoping, wanting, and wishing with the power of intention. Competitive athletes who count on ideas like hoping, wanting, and wishing will likely go broke. For our purposes, intention is the absolute commitment to getting something done, under any circumstances.

Most people's commitments evaporate when obstacles appear. Consider how New Year's resolutions seldom make it into March. To make the spare-shooting formula work, you must understand total intention and commitment. Real intention is the deepest of deep-seated desires. It's the one thing that keeps you going no matter what feelings or obstacles appear. You either have committed intention, or you don't.

You can see the distinction between true and false commitment by examining an athlete's self-talk. The mind hears whatever comes after *I.* For instance, if you say to yourself, "I hope I make this 4-pin," your mind focuses on *hoping* instead of on *making*. The same applies to "I want," "I fear," and "I wish." The mind responds to the verb. In effect, you become a hoping, wishing, wanting person; that is not the mettle with which champions are constructed.

Say, "I *will* execute this shot" or "I *intend* to roll a great shot." Your mind now focuses on "I will" or "I intend." Such self-declaration of intention has the best chance of getting the subconscious mind to respond.

If you lack true intention, your mental game can get rocked by overthinking, fear, anxiety, and external factors such as noise and other distractions. Without true intention, the everyday earthquakes of training and competition will shake the spare shooting right out of you.

You can identify whether you have true intention to get better at spares. Simply look at your results. See what you're doing to excel at this skill. Intention and results go together like the head and tail of a coin.

It might be said that wanting and wishing are "intention lite." They work until significant resistance appears. In this formula, intention is far deeper even than willpower. For those who don't reach their goals, perhaps a more compelling intention took precedence: for instance, being comfortable, satisfying cravings, or responding to a habit. Real intention always makes itself known. The way true intention is developed or known is that no feeling of discomfort dissuades you from your stated commitment.

At the level of shot execution, intention is both subtle and clear. State your intention to focus, visualize the shot picture, and freely allow your arm to swing with total follow-through. Then it's simple to observe from both the inside and the outside whether you brought your intention to life. This is a black-or-white issue, everything or nothing. You either surrender to your intention to be free with the shot, or you go with an intention to protect yourself and play it safe.

Use the Right Mechanism

People often think mechanism means a machine or a machine part. In a way, a mechanism is a tool, the means to the end of any effort. It's the way you get where you're going. In bowling, mechanisms include balls and ball surfaces, drillings, and weights; hand positions; ball speed and rotation; spare lines; shoes; wrist braces; tacky and slippery substances for hands and shoes; towels; and mental game tools such as visualization, preshot routines, shot cycles, and relaxation.

Think of mechanism as any of the hundreds of methods or tools that take you to magnificent spare shooting. There's never just one single mechanism for any spare—or for any bowling goal, for that matter.

Bowlers frequently confuse mechanism with what it takes to score and make spares. They think if they just have the right ball, the right spare strategy, and the right preshot routine, they'll succeed. Advertising works the same way. Advertising tells us that if we drive the right car, drink the right beer, or use the right credit card, life will turn out grand. Ads say nothing about making things happen on your own. In bowling terms, the right ball won't shoot your spares—you have to shoot them.

Champions are people who can overcome feelings, fear, and external conditions to get results. Pick a mechanism—equipment or physical technique—and bring full intention to making it work for you. If it doesn't work, reevaluate your tools and strategies, adjust it as needed, and go at it with full intention again. The correct application of intention plus mechanism will overcome doubt, lane conditions, and even pesky bowling gods.

MAKE SPARE SHOOTING WORK

Do what you want that works.

Toba Beta, author

Intention plus mechanism plugs in perfectly to spare shooting. To accomplish great spare shooting, you must first get some basic mechanisms in place. Decide whether or not to get a spare ball. Establish a basic spare system, such as the one developed by coach Susie Minshew, shown later in this chapter. Determine at which spares to throw straight, and at which to hook the ball.

Let's look at how total and complete intention opens up spare shooting. Many bowlers mistakenly think that the more they need to make a shot, the better they'll do. It is true that for some competitors, focus increases with importance. If we look closely, however, we'll see that what's really enhanced is commitment to focus, not shot-throwing ability.

Success in spare shooting, as in every other part of the game, depends on making the right commitments. Often competitors commit to calming down and trying to make nervous or anxious feelings go away. Another common effort is to banish distracting or negative thoughts. This directs mental and emotional energy to trying to make a thought or feeling vanish. This is not only extremely difficult to do, but it's also a detour from positive and useful intentional thoughts. The best plan is to pick the intentions that will most powerfully match your spare-shooting plan. Adopt one or more of the following tactics. They'll serve you well.

- **Commit to swinging freely at all costs.** When the stakes are high, or when a spare is particularly challenging, the tendency is to try to point or fit the shot. But being careful only serves to change your natural stroke and to threaten results instead of ensuring them. A free arm swing gets the ball on line with the maximum amount of energy and the greatest chance of going where you want to send it. When they must make a spare or hit a strike to win, bowlers become increasingly vulnerable to trying to control the entire ball path. But muscling and pulling the ball down only increase the risk for errant shots.

- **Decide on the spare line and trust it.** Once you've decided where to throw the ball, all debate is over. Unconscious questions about whether it's the best line will cause subtle deviations and corrections as you approach the foul line. Every time you leave a spare in practice, you can be thankful for the opportunity to practice this one as if you were in the most intense competition. The principle of deciding absolutely on a spare, or breakpoint line, remains the same in any situation.

• **Commit to maintaining your poise and executing athletically.** Spare shooting can be analyzed from top to bottom. Not coincidentally, that is frequently the problem—thinking instead of accessing the feel that the trained mind and body can deliver. The issue of heart and spirit can be determined by a single question: *Did I like who I was when I threw that shot?* After you roll the shot, you should feel that you could spin around, face the settee area, and say, "That's the person I am," and feel good about it. If you're an overthinking, tight, careful person while you bowl, you won't want to sign your name to the shot, whether you make it or miss it.

FINISH WELL

A bad completion cannot be changed later.
Zhuangzi, *The Complete Works of Chuang Tzu*

If there's just one aspect of the physical game that intersects perfectly with the mental game of spare shooting, it's finishing the shot. The commitment to completing the shot with a free arm swing, easy release, and perfect finish can clear out the tendency for overthinking and plow through anxiety, allowing for proper mechanics without even having to think about it.

This is an aspect of spare shooting easily observed and reinforced during practice. It takes discipline to keep the finish of the swing in the forefront of your intention. The commitment to finish well keeps you from shoveling, pulling, or otherwise muscling the shot. In addition, if you have difficulty balancing and finishing well, you have information that something is amiss earlier in the shot sequence.

You must decide upfront to demonstrate the guts, athleticism, and commitment needed to post your shot. Make this promise no matter what thoughts or feelings are swirling in your head. There's always a fundamental choice: Do you try to make thoughts and feelings go away, or do you throw more of your mental energy into how to feel about the act of shooting the spare? You can do a sort of spare-shooting inoculation by making this decision before ever stepping up on the approach. Choose guts, grace, and athleticism over carefulness, and watch your spare shooting percentage shoot up.

SPARE SYSTEMS BY SUSIE MINSHEW, USBC GOLD COACH

Susie Minshew is a USBC Gold coach and two-time United States Olympic Committee coach of the year, known for her experience, wisdom, and world-class expertise in bowling instruction. Here she presents a spare-shooting system (a mechanism) that's immediately practical and easy to apply to your game.

The importance of a solid spare game can't be exaggerated. No one can strike enough to overcome missed spares. There are 1,023 possible spare combinations, 249 of which occur commonly, and there's much more room to make spares than to carry strikes.

The pin, at its belly, is 4.75 inches (12 cm) wide. The ball is about 8.5 inches (21.5 cm) in diameter. So, with the exception of the 7- and 10-pins, there are 21.75 inches (55 cm) of room to make a single-pin spare. Of course, the only part of your ball that touches the lane is the middle of the bottom, so technically you have 13.25 inches (33.6 cm) of lane in that 21.75 inches (55 cm) of space. Any way you look at it, it's more than a foot (30 cm) to make a spare! How do we ever miss one?

Crossing the lane right to left is a mystery in today's game. Though you might get away with shooting left-side spares with your strike ball in league, on tournament competition shots it works far more rarely. If it does, it's a cruel cosmic joke that will desert you at Nationals or the city tournament. It's nearly impossible to predict when your strike ball will hook. One time it hits the spare, the next it misses left. You think it's you, so you adjust to stop doing something you weren't really doing anyway. Blame the lanes and keep on throwing a ball that reacts to them.

Some elite players change hand positions and use their strike ball for spares. The purpose of changing hand positions is to make the strike ball act like a plastic ball, changing rotation and roll, "killing the shot." This type of rotation will not respond as much to lane conditions as one with more axis rotation. This takes lots of intense practice to use effectively.

Wouldn't it be much simpler to use a ball that ignores lane conditions? Polyester balls have a slow response to friction and behave in a predictable manner. A polyester ball is going to go where you throw it. Period. That's the ball motion you want.

A spreadsheet is available from www.strikeability.com that computes your conversion percentages to help you identify and focus on the spare groups you're leaving. A link to this spreadsheet is available at www.HumanKinetics.com/Hinitz/SpareConversionsCount.

THE SYSTEM THAT WORKS ALMOST ANYWHERE YOU GO

There are two essential requirements for a great spare-shooting system. First, you need a system that's easily employed, requiring no deep analytics. Second, you need a spare system that will travel across oil patterns, as well as continents. Coach Minshew provides a choice of user-friendly systems here.

First Shot

The first of the four spare shots is the 4-pin, the 7-pin, or the 4-7. You'll be shooting both pins whether both pins are there or not. The inside of your left foot covers the 10th board. Your target is the 2nd arrow. You'll be crossing the 2nd arrow at an angle going right to left toward the left corner of the deck. Since you're playing right to left, you'll walk right to left, finishing farther left than the board on which you started, probably around 15.

Second Shot

The second spare shot is the 2-pin or any of its combinations—the 2-4, the 2-5, the 8, the 2-8, the 2-4-5, the 2-4-5-8, or the 4-5. Move five boards left of your 4-7 alignment so that the inside of your left foot is on 15. Your target is still the 10th board at the arrows. You'll be crossing it going right to left, as with the 4-7, but with less angle. You'll also walk right to left, sliding farther left from the board on which you started, but not as much as the first shot, landing on about 17. Since you have a place to stand for the 7-pin (the 10th board) and a place to stand for the 2-pin (the 15th board), what will you do when you leave both of them? Just split the difference and stand on 12½!

Third Shot

The third spare shot is the 3-pin, the 9-pin, or the 3-9. This is the first time we're going to move the target. Since this is a right-side spare, we'll move to the left side of the approach. Stand on the 30th board, and target the 17th board between the 3rd and 4th arrows. You might walk a bit left to right but not much—maybe a board or so.

Fourth Shot

The fourth spare shot is for the 6-pin, the 10-pin, or the 6-10. Again, you want to put the ball on both pins whether both pins are there or not. Your feet are on 35, and your target is the same as for the third shot. You should land on 32 or 33. Any farther right, and you'll likely miss. In fact, I beli-eve the second most common reason people miss this spare is because they walk to the middle of the lane (the number one reason is a lack of concentration).

Since you have a place to stand for the 3-pin (the 30th board) and a place to stand for the 10-pin (the 35th board), where would you stand if you left them both? Why, 32½, of course. Interestingly enough, between 2005 and 2010, this spare, called the-baby split, was converted on only 17 of 35 attempts on the professional tour on TV! Tables 6.1 and 6.2 are a summary chart of the basic spare alignments.

The Fourth-Arrow System

This is a very simple system—you shoot everything from the fourth arrow! Oh, it might be around 17 for one player and 22 for another. The point is that

Table 6.1 Basic Spare Alignments for Right-Handers

Number	Spare	Alignment
1	4, 7, 4-7	10th board, 2nd arrow
2	2-pin or combinations: 2-4, 2-5, 2-8, 2-4-5, 2-4-5-8, 4-5	15th board, 2nd arrow
Special	2-7, 2-4-7	Split difference between 2-pin and 4-7 alignment
3	3, 9, 3-9	30th board–17th board
4	6, 10, 6-10	35th board–17th board
Special	3-6-10, 3-10, 3-6-9, 3-6-9-10	Split difference between 3-pin and 4-7 alignment

Table 6.2 Basic Spare Alignments for Left-Handers

Number	Spare	Alignment
1	4, 7, 4-7	35th board–18-20th board
2	2, 8, 2-8	30th board, between 3rd and 4th arrow
Special	2-7, 2-4-7, 2-4-8, 2-4-7-8	Split difference between 2-pin and 4-7 alignment
3	3-pin or combinations: 3-5, 3-6, 3-9, 3-5-6, 3-5-6-9	15th board, 2nd arrow
4	6, 10, 6-10	10th board, 2nd arrow
Special	3-10, 3-6-10, 3-6-9-10, 6-9-10	Split difference between 3-pin and 6-10 alignment

the target is generally in the middle of the lane and is the same regardless of what spare you get to shoot. You just move your feet.

Let's take the 6-10, for example. Place the inside of your slide foot on 35. You might need to adjust right or left a bit depending on your body size. There are three critical things here. One is that, of course, you're always going to clearly "see" your ball path across the target toward the 6-10. Another is that your feet, hips, and shoulders are perpendicular to your intended ball path, not to the lane, a slightly open alignment. The third is that you must end up on 33 or so, making sure not to walk toward the middle of the lane.

For the 3-pin or any of its combinations, scoot right a couple of boards to 32 or 33. Once you get this alignment figured out, you'll easily be able to tell how much to adjust to make the 3-10 or the 3-9. You'll be sliding no more than a board or so right of where you started. If it doesn't feel right, try it anyway. Notice where you slide to determine if that starting alignment feel of it not being "right" is misleading. Remember, the truth is at the line. How it looks from your starting stance is just perception.

For the 2-pin or any of its combinations, start at about 25, and for the 4-7, at about 20. Get that right heel closed to force your body perpendicular to your intended path. For both of these spares, you'll slide 2 to 4 left of where you started.

If you're accustomed to shooting left-side spares from the right, you'll perceive that you have less room with this method. It's true that you have less lane. However, keep in mind that if it didn't work, people who make their living bowling wouldn't use it. You can get used to it. Maybe you need to face two or three lanes left or feel like you're taking your first step dead left. It doesn't matter what you do to help yourself get the feel as long as you get it.

So, for this system, your target stays the same, and you just move your feet about 5 left for each shot. Table 6.3 is a chart of the fourth-arrow spare-targeting system.

Table 6.3   Using the Fourth Arrow as a Target for All Spares

Shot 1: 4-7	Feet 20, eyes 20
Shot 2: 2-pin, etc.	Feet 25, eyes 20
Shot 3: 3-pin, etc.	Feet 30, eyes 20
Shot 4: 6-10	Feet 35, eyes 20

LEFT-SIDE SPARES FROM THE LEFT AND RIGHT-SIDE SPARES FROM THE RIGHT

Whatever system you choose must become comfortable, and your confidence with that system will escalate. When the system fails (doesn't matter why), or your belief in it fails, you need alternatives.

Let's say you always throw crosslane at left-side spares. Today, for whatever reason, it's not working. Your normal alignment misses left.

Get radical. Move left, and instead of visualizing the shot going crosslane, adjust so your body alignment is parallel to the channel and square to the lane. Roll your shot *down* the boards instead of up the boards. This means you're going to play the hook instead of fighting it.

Although not generally recommended, since you'd be playing in an uncharted area of the lane, it could be possible that because this side is smoother, your spare ball will behave more predictably. Playing the left side of the lane for left-side spares is sometimes necessary, and often desirable.

Occasionally you might need to shoot right-side spares from the right side of the lane. When you miss a right-side spare to the left, your inclination will be to move more inside in an effort to find oil. On long oil or a sport shot, that might not be the right move. Sometimes you need to move to the outside to find hold. Move outside and line up to shoot the 6-10, for example, across the 10th to 12th board. Yes, there's not much available lane. Yes, you might miss. You're missing now. Might as well give it a try. This is also an excellent alternative for shooting right-side spares if you're having difficulty keeping your footing on the approach.

Try them all. Experiment with each system. Mix and match. You might use one system for right-side spares and another for left-side spares. Spare shooting might be the most critical part of your game. You'll never strike enough to make up for having no strategy for spares.

VISUALIZING SUCCESS

To keep us focused on our Olympic goal, we began ending our workouts by visualizing our dream. We visualized ourselves actually competing in the Olympics and achieving our dream by practicing what we thought would be the ultimate gymnastics scenario.

Peter Vidmar, 1984 Olympic gold medalist

Visualization is a key mechanism for spare shooting. Think of visualization as a spare-shooting time machine. You stand in the present, engaged in imagining a future that has not yet occurred (Vealey 1986). You complete the spare in mind and body as if you have already succeeded. This gives you an opportunity to prove that seeing into the future is possible.

A point of clarification is called for here. We have just discussed the importance of staying in the present to achieve great spare shooting. Why is it OK now to discuss living in the future? Here's the distinction. The negative aspect of living in the past and future has to do with consequences—that is, thinking about the results of made or missed shots. Usually, frustration, worry, or anger is present if a shot was missed. There might also be anxiety, excitement, or fear about a shot yet to be taken. In each of these cases the wonderful or difficult feelings have to do with what did, or will, happen.

Visualization works. Not just a little. I mean visualization *really* works. Of course, we could say the same thing about vitamins, exercise, and bringing flowers to your spouse. Nonetheless, for all these good things, there are two kinds of people: those who do what works and those who don't.

Visualization works so well that it's astounding how few bowlers have found the discipline to fortify their visualization skills (Hinitz, 2005). This easy-to-pack, easy-to-teach, easy-to-learn skill, is commonly neglected— except by the richest, most proficient, competitors in all sports.

How Visualization Works*

Visualization is not merely visual. The act of *seeing* what your body or the ball will do before it actually happens can involve any or all of the five senses. Research shows that when you visualize bowling your brain uses the same

*Adapted from D. Hinitz, 2005 (June), "Visualizing your success," *Bowling This Month* 12(6).

activating processes that it uses in actual physical practice, even if you're only seeing, and feeling, in your mind's eye (Weinberg and Gould 2015). This is key. Your brain doesn't know the difference between thinking and feeling what you will do when you bowl, and actually going through the physical motions. (Incidentally, this principle also works for learning new bowling skills.)

Simply put, visualization makes the brain achieve more, leading to physically self-achieving more. Three things happen when you visualize:

1. Your brain is programmed to let anything into your awareness that will help you accomplish your goals, be it body position, shot execution, or tournament results.

2. Your subconscious mind is awakened to problem-solve the results you seek. In fact, if you let yourself engage in the practice of visualization throughout the day, your subconscious works around the clock. Any part of your game can improve. You'll start feeling what to do, and practicing your match play at odd times—when you're walking, when you're showering, or even (oops!) when you're working.

3. Visualization creates new levels of motivation. Once you picture and feel the greatness of successful outcomes, you'll unexpectedly draw an amazing phenomenon from inside of yourself. You will have heightened awareness about any movement or action that you take that is, or is not, in the direction of your goals.

Your brain is amazing. At any given time, as many as eight million bits of information are running through it. Obviously, you can never attend to everything that your brain is capable of registering.

When you visualize, your brain looks for ways to provide matches for the pictures your mind is generating. As powerful as this is, it only works if you provide your brain with specific, realistic, and compelling images.

If you give your brain the image and feeling you intend to experience as you release the ball, your brain will go to work to ensure that your body does everything it has trained to do in order to make that feeling actually happen. If you give your brain a picture of the ball path, or of ball rotation, then it will seek out and mobilize everything in the mental and physical storehouse to make it happen. If you don't have the physical ability to execute what you're seeing, then you'll be driven to find the coaching or training to learn it.

The Process*

Visualization is so simple, effective, accessible, and cheap that bowlers keep looking past it for something more expensive and hard to learn. Can anything that will make you champion be this easy? The answer is yes. The play that is your visualization takes place on three stages:

---

*Adapted from D. Hinitz, 2005 (June), "Visualizing your success," *Bowling This Month* 12(6).

1. Your body
2. The ball
3. The competitive setting

Your Body

You can decide ahead of time how you intend to feel during any part of your approach and delivery. Try this exercise right now. In your mind's eye, picture standing in the ready position with the ball in your hand. Where is the weight of the ball? What is your hand and wrist position? Imagine the flex in your knees and the balance in your body. Feel the ideal push-away. The ball has its own motion now. Feel the pace of your steps. You go into your slide step. Feel the balance. The ball drops through the slot. Most important, notice everything about what the ideal release feels like. See what your eyes see. Feel what your hand feels. Feel the perfect body position. Feel the tug on your fingers.

If you move in a dedicated way through this exercise, you'll almost feel as if you're actually bowling. Meanwhile, your brain barely knows the difference. Your best experience of bowling is being grooved in for future use. You can also practice visualizing the most important aspects of your approach and release.

The Ball

Imagine standing on the approach facing any oil condition you want to play or practice on. There are two things to visualize here. The first is always ball path. You don't have to see a skinny little line here. Bill Hoffman, the great amateur champion (and former Team USA member), laughed in a conversation with me about picking specific boards to hit. He said that he picked his ball path to the break-point area and let it fly. But it's no coincidence that he's one of the most accurate bowlers you'll ever see in repeating his shots.

Pick a path. Some people imagine a painted 4- to 8-inch (10–20 cm) swath. Others "see" in other ways in the mind's eye. Importantly, you must visualize in a straight line. If you see a curved line in your mind, you risk bending your arm, or in some other way distorting your pure shot in order to make the ball curve on the path.

Second, visualize the ball speed, roll, and tilt. Depending on your ability and experience, you can see the ball doing whatever you want it to. But there's a caveat here. As famed coach Bill Hall notes, no amount of visualization will take the place of practice and skill development. If you see yourself doing something to the ball that your body has not yet learned to create, who knows how you'll contort yourself to make it happen?

On the other hand, you can in fact stretch yourself into new skills and abilities through visualization. You need to have a mental picture of a player

■ Making Spares With Bill O'Neill

**From the pro level to the extreme amateur, keep it simple.
It's still the same game that you knew it was when you got up there.**

**Bill O'Neill, seven-time PBA champion, U.S. Open champion, international gold medalist,
three-time collegiate player of the year**

Bill O'Neill has seen a lot in bowling. He's one of just a handful of players who has known the experience of being a collegiate national champion, a professional tour champion, and a gold medal winner in international competition as a member of Team USA.

Now a seasoned veteran, Bill was for a period considered by many to be the best bowler on tour who hadn't won a professional title. He had been in the finals a lot, "10 or 12 times," but had never closed it out. That all changed in 2009 in Detroit, when he faced Ronnie Russell on the television final.

Bill had already defeated Walter Ray Williams Jr. in the round of eight to make the telecast. His first opponent was Hall of Famer Amleto Monacelli. The lanes were tough, and neither player scored well, with Bill shooting "170 something" to win. To prevail in the end, Bill knew that his whole game, especially his spare game, was going to have to be solid. "I just wanted to avoid splits. When the lanes are hard, you just have to believe in yourself. You're not going to shoot 240 or 250. You just have to trust yourself." It seemed like a good plan, and it was. As in so many other venues, Bill O'Neill emerged a champion.

Bill O'Neill is so rock solid in his spare game that he's a clear and obvious choice for exploring mental tricks for making spares. Ironically, what Bill does and recommends is so simple that it doesn't qualify as being a trick. He starts with a preshot routine that does not vary. It's a way he creates familiarity and a sense that he has done this thousands of times before. "That's the idea of the preshot routine. Keep everything the same, strike shot or spare shot. That's why I take a deep breath—it gets me back to the place of mental calmness. I know that I've done this 100 times."

"First I put my hand down and dry it off, get some air. I then wipe off my right shoe and my left shoe so there's nothing on my shoes. I wipe my ball off. It's part of my routine. I don't want to change it." Added to that routine, Bill creates a sense of certainty for himself: "I get myself set. I kind of adjust myself, wiggle myself into a spot that feels right, look at my target, and go."

"I try to make sure I take a big deep breath. I try to make sure that right before I step up on the approach I let out a big exhale and get it all out." Most important, he believes in himself. "I trust that everything that I work on, and that my ability hasn't gone anywhere. No matter what the situation, everything is still equal. From the pro level to the extreme amateur, keep it simple. It's still the same game that you knew it was when you got up there."

Bill recognizes that for many players, as they advance, the excitement and the nervousness can be part of the experience. You don't have to have ice in your veins to be a great spare shooter. And you must hold on to your preshot routine as part of your spare-shooting ritual. "When I step up there, I might think about just one thing. If you think about more, it's not good. Depending on how I'm bowling that moment, that one thing could change. Of course it's anxious, but you learn over time how to handle the anxiety. You have to train your body and your mind that everything is the same. You go through the same routine every time."

As far as technique and strategy go, Bill O'Neill favors rolling straight at almost every spare, except for perhaps some combinations, such as a 2-8 spare. "I'm a guy who likes to shoot spares straight no matter what. Ninety-nine percent of the time I'm shooting straight at everything. You take all the variables out of play when you do that."

Although a plastic ball might be the obvious choice for most straight spares, Bill no longer travels with one. To conserve his arsenal, he's worked on, and mastered, coming up the back of the ball to shoot his spares. "Because with overseas travel I could only take six balls, so I wanted to learn. I haven't noticed any negative effects of that."

Bill emphasizes minimizing the mental interference that can be part of the spare-shooting process. He's leery about taking too much time to overthink things, or to consider being too perfect. "When I start hanging out up there too long, the hand sweats, and different things go through my mind. The over-analyzing of everything is bad. When you're competing, there's just no need to go out there and over-analyze."

Bill's clear intention paves the way for him. "I'll get this eerie calmness that comes over me. I just know that I'm going to do what I came to do. You have to be that way in order to be successful."

Conversely, when you allow your mind to linger in other places, that doesn't play well. "When the doubt creeps in, you get out of rhythm and time. It doesn't always go 100 percent according to plan. The weakest part of my game is when I'm over-analyzing too much."

Of those rare times when Bill or another professional misses an easy spare, he suggests some common human factors are part of it. He emphasizes the need to be completely present, but not perfect, when shooting spares. "There could be a lapse in concentration. Some people leave a ring 10-pin and are angry that they have to shoot it. Then they just go up, and they aren't even there. When it goes bad, you get down on yourself. It's good to remember the right things to do."

**I just know that I'm going to do what I came to do.
You have to be that way in order to be successful.**

Bill O'Neill

That seems like a good plan!

executing what you want to, and imagine your own body doing the same thing. You can also be your own model. It is perfectly fine to be the only player you have in mind. As long as you stay aware of what your body is doing as you execute your shots, and take liberal doses of great coaching feedback, this is precisely how great athletes become even greater in their physical games.

Most important, don't spend a lot of mental energy telling your body how to make ball speed, roll, and tilt happen. True enough, when learning new skills, you'll have to focus on how to make your body parts work together to achieve the necessary movements. But once you have it going, the program in your mind will run itself. With enough practice, it will be just *see it and do it.*

The Competitive Setting

This one is fun—the visualization field on which daydreams are made. Pick anything here. If you're a touring pro, see yourself on TV. See yourself executing a premier shot in the 10th frame in match play to win. See yourself playing the first frames of a tournament, or the last game to make a cut. See yourself being interviewed, or accepting the winner's check.

Imagining competitive situations and settings will train and prepare your mental and emotional reactions for actual situations. If you do this enough, and I strongly recommend that you do, by the time you show up for real, you'll have been there so many times in your mind that the familiarity will both relax you and make you feel supremely prepared for everything and anything that's going to take place.

Seeing yourself winning, accepting awards, being interviewed, and so on does two other things as well. First, it creates an internal attitude of expectation that you will arrive in those very circumstances. Once the mind accepts these scenarios, it allows you to perform in a way that will create the visualized outcomes. Do you have these outcomes every time? Of course not. The key is that you will not choke yourself off short of something that the mind has already trained itself to endorse as a reality.

Second, when you visualize success, your subconscious tends to push you toward people, activities, and training that will make those results occur. You'll also get subconscious nudges away from activities and people that might try to steer you away from your visualized goals. Of course you can always override these subconscious messages. But if your intention is strong and clear enough, you'll listen to these messages, not ignore them.

THROW IN THE KITCHEN SINK!

I'm to the point that I can see it, feel it, and then do it.

Kendra Gaines, PWBA champion and former Team USA coach

When using any of the three recommended visualization areas (the body, the ball, and the competitive setting), add sounds, physical feelings, and sensory sensations that would be present in the real situation—even smells and tastes. Remember, it's not always visual. Any way that you imagine these stimuli in your mind will work.

Add the jet fuel of passion, intensity, or excitement, if you choose. This way, when your physical system gets activated with the intensity of the actual bowling situation, you'll have the expectation of positive visualized results. This should help convert anxiety and fear into productive anticipation and excitement.

Many bowling champions live their lives backward with the magic of visualization. They create the future in their mind, and then they go make it happen. Few bowlers fully appreciate how *little* the past must determine what happens on the very next shot or game. It takes courage to live this way until you realize that the only thing you end up having to trust is you.

CHAPTER 7

Raising Peaks and Filling Valleys

**When you're in a Slump, you're not in for much fun.
Un-slumping yourself is not easily done.**

Dr. Seuss

Virtually every player who has taken on the rigors of competition bowling has had dark periods when her game goes stale. Perhaps you feel stuck in terms of personal improvement. Maybe you come close but just can't seem to win. The energy and excitement associated with competing are let out of the balloon, and you might not feel like going out to get beat up again.

Sound familiar? If you have been at this game for a while you've probably had some version of a slump. Something must change, but for the life of you, you can't come up with any other plan than to plow through until the sun starts shining on your game again.

Waiting for a shift in the bowing weather might work, but that's an extraor-dinarily passive approach to changing one's life. In this chapter we'll address the phenomena of slumping, burnout, injury, and dealing with adversity in general. There's no reason to wait for your fortune to change when you can be an agent of change yourself.

HOW DID THIS HAPPEN?

**Losing streaks are funny. If you lose at the beginning
you got off to a bad start. If you lose in the middle of the season,
you're in a slump. If you lose at the end, you're choking.**

Gene Mauch, professional baseball player and manager

All paths to mastery include steps that are dark, disheartening, even scary. If the path is long and meaningful, you'll suffer at least short periods of fatigue, loss of direction, and stumbling. In this chapter we'll explore those stutter steps and what to do about them.

Bowlers in slumps often worry, become concerned, overanalyze, and expect continued problems in the game. Self-punishing thoughts about being a bad bowler or being stupid might surface. Feelings of frustration, anxiety, low-level depression, and anger are common during slumps. Typically, bowlers in slumps worry about how long the slump will last and whether they'll be able to shake it.

A slump is a trend of events infused with negative meaning. Whether the slump is triggered by mental, emotional, or physical causes, bowlers tend to see patterns and develop belief systems about them. Slumps are a natural part of the competition and improvement process. They are a test of character and commitment.

Slumps can be beneficial (though they never feel that way) because they might be an opportunity to cure something that isn't working in your overall game. Slumps also cause athletes to examine training habits, stress levels inside and outside of bowling, and overall burnout. Slumps can reflect a period when training, learning, and competing are all being digested and metabolized. This can be a hidden part of your growth as a bowler.

The results of slumps might not be pretty. Some players quit or give up the game for a time. They lose confidence. Their enjoyment of the game plummets, and the feelings from the slump leak over to other parts of their lives. But it doesn't have to be this way. If slumps can be recognized for what they are—part of the overall process—they can be brief, nondistressing, even productive.

Here are three typical examples of slumping:

- You miss the cut in two or three tournaments in a row.
- You don't feel connected to your swing for a week or more.
- You have lost your zest for the game for one or more weeks.

Other markers of slumping are strings of missed spares, inability to carry strikes, and a stretch of low-scoring outings.

The belief systems that often accompany these occurrences can be disempowering.

- I can't play anymore.
- I'm bad at spares now.
- I'm sick of bowling and can't get motivated to practice anymore.

Here's a hypothetical question, one that might have been real for you. If you missed two easy spares in a game, and then were presented in the next game with a similar spare opportunity, what do you think? Would your chance of making that spare be better or worse, considering what happened previously?

The truth might surprise you. So, before you answer, consider the following. If we switch sports for a moment and look at basketball, 91 percent of athletes and fans believe a shooter has a better chance of making a basket after he has made two or three baskets rather than missing two or three. But the facts run contrary to intuition. A shot taken after a series of successful shots has no more probability of success than one taken after a series of missed shots. A recent history of makes and misses does not affect the success of the next shots. This is why confident players keep shooting, while those who lose their confidence do not.

Back to bowling. It seems like many bowlers are only two consecutive bad shots, or sometimes two bad tournaments, from some sort of meltdown. If your belief system allows you to crumble after a couple of misses, you're on the slippery slope to slumping. You must be willing to play through your misses. You must know the reality that the very next shot, strike, or spare can be the most effective one.

YOU HAVEN'T LOST IT

**I was in a very deep, dark slump,
and I needed to find a way to get myself out of it.
I had to force myself back out into life,
back out into experiencing things.**

Shania Twain, musician

So what are you saying? You lost it? You no longer know how to bowl? The game you once loved has no juice anymore? When thoughts like these occur, they are based on belief systems. None of them is true—unless you make them so.

In reality, being a bowler is like being a tuned instrument, a piano or a guitar. A musician doesn't tune up his instrument and expect it to hold in tune over a lot of play. Strings stretch and change, and get out of key. As a musician you listen, and adjust accordingly.

The same is true for all aspects of your bowling. You must "listen" to your physical game to keep track of what's in tune. You should track exactly why you have missed spares, and confidently employ working spare lines. You must find the heart of the game, and the heart of the player that you are when at your best. Ultimately, you must continually retune.

LET THE HEALING BEGIN

Nothing in this world can take the place of persistence. Talent will not; nothing is more common than unsuccessful people with talent. Genius will not; unrewarded genius is almost a proverb. . . . Persistence and determination alone are omnipotent.

Calvin Coolidge, U.S. president

The saying goes that time heals all wounds. But time alone has never healed anything; time only makes space for healing agents to work. Although a break might sometimes clear the fog, a slump is like an athletic flu. Something's going on. It helps to identify the source of the slump and make decisions on the best actions to take.

By this time you probably know your game pretty well. You know your game tendencies, your habits, your typical emotional responses, and your physical game. But maybe you haven't taken the time to really take an inventory of these aspects of your game. There are some steps we can take here to begin to find your way out of slumping (Worthington, 2015).

Step 1: Your Emotional Barometer

If you're not stewing, fuming, weeping, or boring yourself to death with your malaise, you're probably not in a slump of any kind. Prolonged feelings of hopelessness or helplessness are an indication that your bowling, and your excitement level, are four tires in the mud. And you, who haven't been able to find your tire chains, are to shift to all wheel drive. They say that rock bottom is good solid ground. Sometimes we have to fall long enough and hard enough to have the drive to make the changes we need to make.

Bowlers change their games and their attitudes for two reasons:

1. It is so unpleasant to be flailing ineffectively at the game.
2. Some part of their brain knows that flying is possible, and that it feels way better than flailing, even if you have to blow out your comfort zone to do it.

Realistically though, at the end of the day, for most bowlers, the yuck of staying stuck is the basis for making positive moves. It finally just feels too bad to suffer for any kind of prolonged weak, flawed, or ineffective bowling. That is if there is any part of you that wants to feel and perform like a champion, you have to put a name to what is choking you into submission. This is vital, for what you can put a name to, you can put a frame around. What you can frame, you can deal with!

Some physical and emotional sources of stuck-ness are release, timing, emotional reactions, your nervousness, and your fear of making adjustments. If you are not aware of whatever it is, and if you cannot name it, you are generally condemned to continue your patterns. I almost hate to say this, but oftentimes you really have to hate what you've been experiencing to tap the deep well of commitment you need to get through the heavy weather of a slump.

Step 2: Find the Thinking, Training, and Competition Patterns That Have Locked You Down

Here is the thing. You have two possible stances for what landed you where you are:

1. You are a victim of stuff going wrong for you all the time.
2. You have something to do with what is happening in your life.

If you are a perpetual victim (option one), your primary move is probably going to be to wait for the world to wake up, get things straightened out, and possibly for it to come begging for your forgiveness. You might want to pack a lunch, you're going to be waiting for a really long time.

Option two is called taking responsibility for your life, all of it. If you are going to err, err on the side of being overly responsible. At least you have power and choice from that position. From this empowered stance you can take your brain and your game apart. You can look at how you train, how you think, and what your reflexive reactions to positive and negative results are.

The answer is always going to mental, physical, or emotional. But this can be a tough mirror. No one wants to stare at the blemishes in their own reflection. Yes, you might have a little embarrassment when you look at what you have done to land you in the pothole you found, but give yourself a pat on the back. It takes extraordinary courage and character to look at the flaws in any part of our selves. I have tremendous respect for anyone who goes at this process authentically.

Step 3: Take the Pain and Discomfort

Lean into it. We have talked about truly examining what you have been doing. It's you, the good, the bad, and the ugly. Maybe you get to bypass the discomfort of this part of it, but probably not. As discussed earlier, when you admit to something you don't care for in yourself, it's a bit of a butt kick. There are some pretty painful things that can show up in your looking glass. Mental game breakdowns can feel like character flaws. Physical game tendencies can make it seem like you just can't play, or that there's a low ceiling on your game. Imperfection can be a bitter pill to swallow, even if your philosophy is that it's OK to have to strive to get better.

Here's the good news. Just as noticing skin blemishes might make you wash your face more often, noticing a blemish in your game can be the platform you use to harness your horses to pull yourself out of the mire.

Step 4: Be Smart. Know What You Know... and What You Don't

You figured out what you have to change or adjust. Or you didn't. If you have it, and you have the internal fuel to get moving you have two ways to move with this:

1. Put your necessary training and competition changes into immediate action.
2. Ask for observations, feedback, and coaching from someone who has the chops to direct you.

Look, if you already knew what you had to do, and had the self-discipline to move on it, you would have been at least part of the way through this slump already. Whether we know it or not, most of how we think, act, bowl, and react, is discernable to our best friends, our bowling buddies, and to a good coach. Maybe you just need someone else to tell you the truth. And what's more, you are not going to hear much that at some level of consciousness you didn't already know.

Step 5: Go After It With a Vengeance

Warriors attack. Make a decision to blow past your feelings, your laziness, your anger, or whatever your personal gremlin is. No one can do your sit-ups for you, so to speak. To bust your slump you have to get moving no matter what you feel like. Just do the right things. You don't want to get all hopped up to start painting, and then paint the wrong wall.

Get moving. Even if you are not perfect (you're not), once you put plans into action you are either going to get better, or at least you will see more clearly what you need to do to move to the next level. Secondly, when you put your heart into this, you will know that you paid your dues. When you shoe up, your inner self will say, "I paid my dues. If it's my day I deserve to be paid off!" You are nobody's victim. Welcome to the show.

The slope into a slump has a key ingredient—it's called blaming. PBA Champion Mike states that as soon as players look outside of themselves, they're on the way to being stuck. "A lot of guys scapegoat. They blame other things. They don't take responsibility." Then slumping players complain. "A lot of times guys will get down on themselves. Then when they do have the chance, they don't perform." Mike's prescription is simple, but sometimes difficult to do, "You have to analyze each game, work with it. Eventually you have to let the mistakes go. Move on."

■ Digging Out of My Slump
With Mike Fagan

**I'm the type that wants to know why.
I want to do better next time.
I want to know what I have to do if I get in that situation again.**

Mike Fagan, 2012 USBC Masters champion, 2015 PBA World champion

Photo courtesy of PBA LLC.

Mike Fagan knows what it means to work through hard times. He knows what it's like to have to run on faith until results can catch up. And he knows what it's like to take a shot to the mouth, get up again, and complete all 15 rounds, still standing. He is a champion's champion, but it hasn't been all sunshine and roses along the way.

The 2015 PBA World Championship titlist first joined the PBA tour in 2002. Things looked good right off the bat. His third week on tour, at 21 years old, he led qualifying in a tournament. He didn't win, but the very next week he was second in qualifying before losing to Tommy Jones. Given that racing start, no one would have thought that it would be 2008, six years later, before he would win a title—a PBA doubles event with Danny Wiseman as his partner, in his 108th PBA tour event.

It was two more years later that Mike captured his first singles title, when he beat Walter Ray Williams Jr. at the Dick Weber Open. It was two more years again before Mike won his first major title, the 2012 USBC Masters, and became the Bowling Writers' Bowler of the Year. Notably, in order to win the Masters, Mike had to overcome a fifth-frame 30-pin deficit to Chris Barnes (Chris had beaten Mike in his first television finals back in 2003). It would be three more years (2015) before Mike would capture his next major tour championship, the PBA World Championship.

There were several hard knocks along the way. Mike made the television finals in 2003 at the Empire State Open, but lost to Chris Barnes. Liz Johnson became the first female to win a PBA event when she beat Mike in 2005 at a regional tournament. In 2009, Jack Jurek won his first title in 14 years when he beat Mike in a roll-off at the Shark Championship. And Mike just missed winning consecutive major titles when Pete Weber struck to beat him by a pin at the U.S. Open in 2012.

Back in 2007, when Mike still hadn't won on tour, things were tough. He even thought about leaving the professional tour. "In the beginning of 2006, I made two shows in a month. I thought that I was doing well. Then I didn't do anything. Although I never actually choked on the show, I had some bad TV experiences. I contemplated quitting and getting a job. I was just treading water. I wasn't close to where I wanted to be. I hadn't won anything, although I'd had several close calls. I was contemplating going back to school, or getting another job. It was a decision I had to make."

Sometimes it's those moments when things look bleak that we find another gear, and a new purpose. "I think I had to focus on the good things in my life. I was young and healthy. Instead of just getting out there and bowling, I started setting goals for myself." For example, "I want to win Bowler of the Year—how do I do that?"

Interestingly, when you talk to Mike Fagan, he never references any of the times when he faced adversity as being in a slump. His attitude, intention, and plan are like a recipe for anyone. "I don't like to make excuses; maybe I should have won sooner, but I was getting so much better."

Mike advises, "When you're in a slump, go back to basics. When you're on the pro level, every single shot can be a breaking point. You can only rely on yourself to a certain extent. Up until I was about 25, I didn't rely on many people. I was kind of self-taught. That only got me so far. Yes, my eye for the game and natural ability got me to the pros. In order to succeed, I wanted to change how I approached the game."

"I was more proactive. I found coaching. I did video work with Mike Jasnau in Reno. Seeking coaching at the highest level can do wonders. You can't just do what you like to do. You have to execute properly, making sure every single step is right on the money. Coaches, video, they help you make sure that you are right there every step of the way. I was told forever that I had a great game. I had to go to the best people in the game, guys like Del Ballard and Del Warren."

Mike knows that the game comes and goes for all kinds of reasons. "Bowling can be such a different game depending on the pattern. Houses you play in can be comfortable or not, depending on your game. The approaches vary. How you are throwing the ball varies as well." So many factors come into play. "The fact that we're on a season kind of schedule can be an adversary. We're on a staggered schedule. We're not bowling every week. Sometimes you're at the mercy of the qualifying format. Sometimes you take a week off and you're not as sharp as you once were."

> **I've been reflecting about my career;**
> **it's good to review the ups and downs and what brings you back.**
> **Change is something we all have to do.**
>
> **Mike Fagan**

There's nothing wrong with taking a break from the game. Players can get stale, lose their feel from overtraining and overcorrecting, and simply need to see things from a different perspective. "Getting away from it for a bit of time is not a bad thing, either. Take a week or two or however much time you need. Come back to it when you're ready. You'll be fresher, and more apt to learn and get back to your game."

Popping out of the down times can happen just as tumbling into them does. Taking charge of how to find your way out is essential. "I'm the type that wants to know why. I want to do better next time. I want to know what I have to do if I get in that situation again. A hot streak is all about getting comfortable. When a player finds it, it is usually for a while. Players doing well are good for weeks, not just one time."

Mike is a Master's champion because he has mastered three essential components for working through tough times: patience, perseverance, and developing proficiency. "There were tough stretches of my career. I changed ball companies. I changed philosophies about lanes. It took a little longer than I thought to come around. Things just hadn't come together. I knew I was close. I had to remain patient. I know how hard it is to win. I felt good about my game, and I waited for that wave of breakout to come by."

Trust yourself. You can break through, too!

CREATING YOUR FUTURE

There are two primary choices in life: to accept conditions as they exist, or accept the responsibility for changing them.

Denis Waitley, author, motivational speaker, consultant

I have never met someone who was slumping who did not contribute to the darkness with negative self-talk and destructive thinking patterns. This makes self-talk and thinking habits critical for early intervention. Bowlers who sink into the mire of slump negativity are often victims of "stinkin' thinkin'."

The excellence process is like a path with subtle, sometimes hidden, obstacles. If you're really alert and know what to watch for, you can recognize the danger signs and avoid tripping into a slump trap. Recognition also affords the opportunity to see when a slump trap has snagged you and to take action in freeing yourself. Watch out for the following common mental traps often encountered on the path to excellence.

Mental Trap 1: Negativity About Your Self

Bowlers who are mentally sinking tend to see themselves in a negative light. This might not seem like an earth-shaking revelation, but slow down and consider this point. It's nothing to make a face, swear, or experience frustration about a bad shot, game, or competition block. However, bowlers who are in emotional slumps or struggling with the physical game are likely to attack themselves repeatedly. When their performances are not up to standard, they think something is fundamentally wrong with them. For example, a bowler who misses a lot of spares in a given week or month might get down on herself as a bowler, maybe even as a person, and create a negative self-image.

A negative self-image destroys confidence, and might lead to the emergence of hateful self-fulfilling prophecies. Bowlers start to question their ability to carry shots and complete spares. Their feelings of embarrassment about their performance contribute to bad feelings about themselves. They then experience pressure as they attempt to avoid these negative thoughts and feelings.

In this developing scenario, bowlers start to press and tighten to force better bowling. This further compromises their natural stroke. Instead of bowling for the great feeling of executing like a champion, competitors shift focus to avoiding aversive feelings and messing up further.

This negative feedback loop results in a downward spiral. Negative self-evaluation leads to difficult feelings such as frustration, depression, and anger. Thoughts such as "I stink" or "I shouldn't be out there" or "I can't bowl" are common. Pressure increases because of these unpleasant thoughts and feelings. Muscles tighten. Shots are forced. Scores go down. The pattern continues. Some bowlers even start to experience fear before rolling shots.

Mental Trap 2: Pessimism About Change

Bowlers who are slumping physically and emotionally tend to be pessimistic about possible help or change. When a bowler is in a slump, everything goes through the negative filter in the mind. The result is that no matter what's happening, the data is processed negatively. The bowler might have decreased faith in coaching, little confidence in the ability to perform the next time out, or a sense of helplessness that anything will make a positive difference.

In addition to focusing on their shortcomings, bowlers stuck in slumps see outside influences in negative terms as well. Lane conditions are bad or unfair. Life itself is picking on them. Nothing can help. They are like cartoon figures with rain clouds over their heads while everyone else gets sunshine. Even bowlers who think they're open to assistance might really be shut down to accepting help.

Mental Trap 3: Negativity About the Future

Bowlers who are struggling often think negatively about their bowling futures. This trap makes slumps even more oppressive. In addition to difficult thoughts about bowling and about the effectiveness of intervention, these bowlers are pessimistic about things turning around in the near future. This sense of hopelessness drains energy, drive, and enthusiasm.

When falling into a slump, bowlers can become frustrated, angry, depressed, and self-punishing. They feel bad about themselves, don't know what to do, and don't see any relief on the horizon.

A true slump is defined as a pattern that becomes seen as a lasting reality to the individual. In fact, it's not the bowling itself that puts the bowler in a slump. It's the way the bowler thinks about bowling skills, the game, and the possibility of bowling greatly in the future that defines a slump. At this point, the bowler needs to identify the slump and cure it before it becomes overwhelming.

LOOKING INTO A CRACKED MIRROR

When I discover who I am, I'll be free.

Ralph Ellison, author of *Invisible Man*

As we are seeing, slumpers are often hamstrung by thinking distortions. The thought patterns discussed in this section are highly correlated with feeling stuck and decreased performance levels. Consider the expression, "perception is reality." The following bad mental habits are the danger zone. Check to see if you're prone to any of them.

All-or-Nothing Thinking

If you're an all-or-nothing thinker, you view bowling in black-or-white terms. You either bowl great or feel bad. Anything short of perfect performance is unacceptable. If you don't win or make the cut, the outing is a failure. You have strong reactions to errant shots or not carrying the corner pins. The panorama of normal life that includes great, good, and weak performances is lost on you. Good and bad are the blanket descriptions for shots, games, and competition blocks.

The reality is that you're never the same bowler from day to day. Sometimes you have a feel for timing. Sometimes you can see where the shot needs to be played. Sometimes you clear the thumb more efficiently. And sometimes while one aspect of the game is strong, positive, and in the forefront of your consciousness, another part of your game has regressed.

You might feel great on some days, but even on the days that you think you're completely horrible, you're not. You're simply awake and aware of certain mental and physical aspects of good bowling, and unconscious of other aspects. Ease up and notice the nuances of your game.

Overgeneralization

If you tend to overgeneralize, you might exaggerate anything that you view as unsatisfactory. For example, you see one missed spare, a bad practice day, or a weak tournament as a bigger problem than it really is. You overgeneralize the nature and extent of your bowling difficulties and see your mistakes as part of a never-ending pattern. You might see two missed 10-pin spares in one outing as a general problem in spare shooting and turn it into a much bigger problem than it really is.

When you overgeneralize, you forget the positive elements of growth, progress, and execution. You don't recognize that stumbles and falls occur on the path to mastery. Poor outings cause you to lose sight of the improvement process.

Dismissing the Positive

Rather than seeking out negativity, as some slumping bowlers are prone to do, you might simply dismiss good shots, positive elements of overall execution, and even lucky breaks. If you suffer from this mental pattern, you forget, dismiss, or explain away the upside of the game and competition experience. In this way you find supporting evidence for your self-doubt.

Dismissing the positive kills hope, and sabotages the understanding that growth in bowling is a process of ups and downs like any other excellence process. You basically keep yourself down, perhaps because you think you don't deserve better.

Are you the kind of bowler who scowls when others compliment you or rejects positive input? This is a possible sign that you suffer from this mental pattern. You are left with only the negative aspects of your game.

Catastrophizing

Catastrophizing is like personal fortune telling. If you think this way, you blow up problems and mistakes bigger than they actually are, and you predict that things will get worse, and last a long time. You fret over aspects of your bowling, thinking that problems and mistakes mean that bad events and outcomes will continue to occur. You enter league night and tournaments with feelings of fear and pessimism. Every poor shot, game, and tournament becomes evidence of the truth of your catastrophic thoughts.

Shoulding

As we discussed in chapter five, when self-talk includes the words *should, shouldn't, must, mustn*'t, and *have to*, trouble is a storm cloud on the horizon. This is the language of perfectionism that leads to guilt, frustration, and self-directed anger. When you believe you're supposed to strike every time, pick up every spare, and never throw errant shots, you're setting yourself up for a guaranteed letdown.

Perfectionist thinking is exhausting. It leaves you feeling perpetually inadequate. If you're not already in a slump, *shoulding* will help to create one.

Labeling

Labeling occurs when you use one or two words to describe yourself, your ability, or your bowling. It's a way of overgeneralizing that leaves out details that would provide a balanced perspective. Calling yourself a failure, saying "I'm terrible," stating that your bowling stinks, or declaring that your bowling sank the team are all ways of wrapping up a whole self-judgment in a word or statement. This is another way of viewing only the negative parts of experience. If you believe yourself, it takes only a few repetitions of labeling to land you in a slump.

If you recognize yourself in one or more of these thinking styles, you're at risk for the kind of mental pressure that leads to a slump. Remember— perception is reality. Athletes are anchored in their thinking and experience by the self-talk they employ. The good news is that knowing that self-talk creates reality is one of the keys to breaking free of your chains.

RECOVERY FROM THINKING ERRORS

**There is nothing either good or bad
but thinking makes it so.**

William Shakespeare

Some bowlers are able to pull out of slumps after only a few weeks. Other bowlers are more entrenched. Luckily, there are quick and clear steps to correcting the kinds of thinking errors that can condemn you to a lengthy slump. Here's a five-step approach for curing slump-bound thinking patterns:

1. Identify the ways you talk to yourself (self-talk).
2. Observe the impact on your confidence and how you feel.
3. Choose effective things to say internally (change your self-talk).
4. Observe changes in thoughts and confidence caused by the new self-talk.
5. Practice the new and effective self-talk and self-concept.

If you write down your thoughts at each step, you'll have a record of what you're thinking and how you're acting to bust the slump. You'll likely see desirable changes in execution after implementing these steps.

Step 1: Identify the Ways You Talk to Yourself (Self-Talk)

If you know that you're contending with prolonged frustration, loss of confidence, or declining energy and enthusiasm, you have likely fallen prey to one of the thinking patterns listed previously. Read through them again and make a self-diagnosis. If you can't see it in yourself, ask a coach or someone close to you. They might have observed one or more of these patterns when you talk about yourself or your bowling experience.

Step 2: Observe the Impact on Your Confidence and How You Feel

You must notice and truly acknowledge the impact your talk and thinking patterns have on you. The words you use to describe yourself and your experience tend to determine your feelings. Feelings tacked on to negative thoughts are what make slumps so difficult. Frustration, irritation, depression, anger, and hopelessness are some of the most common experiences that accompany slumps. It's time to change all that.

Step 3: Choose Effective Things to Say Internally (Change Your Self-Talk)

At the very least, this will allow for a truer, less distorted experience of the process of competing and improving. Look again at the thinking patterns that apply to you. Start by sifting out all-or-nothing statements. Instead of statements such as, "I always stink," "I'll never get better," "Nothing I do makes a difference," or "I was terrible," modify your language. Adaptive self-talk can take many forms depending on what has happened. Here are some sample positive self-talk statements:

- "Shake it off. Every shot is a new moment in time."
- "Everyone has an errant shot (or game) periodically."
- "Focus. Make a good shot."
- "Just because I don't have the good feeling today does not mean I can't bowl."
- "Getting better is a process. I won't always have my A-game."
- "Let me attend to the aspects of the game that I'm doing well."

Any phrase or idea that avoids all-or-nothing thinking, or that makes room for positive aspects of experience, is a good way to direct your thinking. However, your adjusted self-talk must be both true and able to be embraced at the deepest levels. This has to be real, not a sales job. Otherwise you'll feel that you're merely cheerleading for yourself.

Look at reality. Bowling and skill development is a process. Nothing about you or your bowling can be accurately described in black-and-white, all-or-nothing terms. You can acknowledge that you didn't care for the results, but avoid extreme statements. Anything described in absolute terms is not going to help you, and probably isn't true. If nothing else, compliment yourself on effort, commitment, and being on the field of battle instead of just spectating.

Step 4: Observe Changes in Thoughts and Confidence Caused by the New Self-Talk

If you've done a rigorous job of examining and changing self-talk, then thoughts and feelings about yourself, and being in a process instead of a slump, will also change. The result is often a dramatic positive shift in physical execution.

Changing self-talk must not be a con job. You must walk in truth here. Don't just parrot phrases. You're not selling yourself something. You're transforming yourself as an athlete. You must see an actual positive shift in how you think about yourself and your bowling. If your thoughts and feelings have not changed, it's probably because you're not applying yourself wholeheart-edly or don't believe in the new point of view. You might have to go back and repeat the steps. Just like developing other skills, walking through this process takes practice before it becomes effortless.

Step 5: Practice the New and Effective Self-Talk and Self-Concept

If you're still stuck in negative thoughts and feelings, take another run through the steps. Consider asking to someone help you. Make sure you write down the thoughts and feelings at each step. This will ensure that you're following the process properly, and that you're tracking your thoughts. Write down self-talk thoughts, feelings, beliefs, and challenges, as well as your new feelings and beliefs. Review and practice your notes. The proof is in the pudding. If this technique works for you, you'll soon see mental game shifts in how you experience slumping, and this will free up your bowling.

FEEDBACK IS A GIFT

Feedback is the breakfast of champions.

Ken Blanchard, author and management expert

People often simply advise a bowler to wait for a slump to subside, as though it were a weather pattern that came with the wind and will leave on its own. Slumps happen for a variety of reasons, but they are not random events that occur because of bad luck. Unless you discover the contributing factors, you might not be able to exit your slump, or fend off the next one. We reviewed self-talk in the last section. Now it's time to introduce a potent intervention called feedback.

Many people don't distinguish between feedback and criticism. Others define criticism as negative reflections, and feedback as positive reflections. Feedback in its purest form, however, is completely nonjudgmental.

The most familiar feedback generators are cameras and video recorders. Despite your reactions to hearing or seeing a recording of yourself, neither machine makes judgment. The camera and video recorders don't suggest that you should sound like Frank Sinatra or Celine Dion, or that you should lose weight and tone up. The video camera doesn't say that your bowling is good or bad. Machines are pure reporters. They simply generate feedback.

Similarly pin fall is a feedback generator. It is impersonal. Single pin spares that fall down tell you that your spare line, or execution, was effective. Racks that don't carry, and spares that are missed or chopped, are simply raw infor-mation. Overall, the pins tell you how well you are rolling the ball, whether you have made the right ball and surface choice, and whether you're bowling on the right line. The pins don't mock or comment on any aspect of you as a person. They are pure feedback about your bowling effectiveness.

Criticism, on the other hand, always carries a "should" or a "shouldn't" with it. Criticism thrives on perfectionist thinking. It paints you as good or bad. Either way, it's judgmental.

If you're camped in a slump, feedback from outside sources might be essential to help you make decisions about what to change. Your only other option is to draw from your own thinking processes, which, as we have seen previously, can be far from helpful at this point. You've already tried everything available from the inside out. Getting a view from the outside in is the next option.

There are several ways to obtain an outside-in point of view. One is to pretend you're viewing yourself from the spectators' position. Imagine every part of your approach and delivery. Is your arm swing free? Are you staying down and balanced at the line? Are you grabbing the ball? Did you hold onto nonjudgmental awareness until the ball was well off of your hand? These are the sorts of questions to ask and answer.

It's helpful to have a checklist of physical and mental game elements that you can scan for performance cues (figure 7.1). Better yet, ask someone to shoot video of you bowling, and zero in on your approach and delivery. Indisputable visual evidence is a powerful tool for diagnosing and treating the physical parts of a slumping game. The best tool of all is a trustworthy, knowledgeable coach who knows how to communicate with you effectively.

You're responsible for developing your own checklist. Write down all the important elements, and ask your coach, training partner, or teammate for feedback on what you might be missing. If appropriate, add the observers' notes to your list. Bring the list to practice and make sure you cover all the elements. Awareness is king. You can only consciously change those parts of your execution that you can feel. Add elements as your awareness grows.

Physical Game

____ Balanced at the line

____ Free arm swing

____ Good hand position

____ Leveraged release

____ Proper follow-through

____ Decided on a point of focus and stayed with it before, during, and after the shot

Mental Game

____ Visualize ball path and rotation

____ Commit to wide-open execution

____ Use positive direct self-talk

____ Stay in the present moment

____ Go through complete preshot routine

Figure 7.1   Performance cue checklist.

From D. Hinitz, 2016, *Bowling psychology*. (Champaign, IL: Human Kinetics).

Bringing the list to tournaments might provide a backup cueing system if your game seems to be off and you can't pinpoint what's happening.

One of the most difficult things to do as a bowler is to listen to feedback nonjudgmentally and use it to change things that are either outside your awareness or outside your comfort zone. Bowlers seem to be naturally drawn to doing what's familiar to them. It can be challenging to think or move in an unusual way or to consciously execute a skill differently.

Some bowlers can hear, integrate, and make use of feedback. Others are too closed-minded or proud to open themselves to outside input. Being coached is an art. Are you open to feedback? This is the most important question to answer in breaking free from a slump, as well as in moving forward in your overall improvement.

Strive to be open to doing something different. Imagine you're trapped in a raging river, about to be pulled under. Would you keep your hands on a log in the river, or would you reach for the hand of someone on firm ground? The risk of letting go of comfortable or familiar ways of thinking, and of executing shots, might be necessary to break free of habits and techniques miring you in a slump.

PERFECTION VERSUS EXCELLENCE

Strive for continuous improvement, instead of perfection.

Kim Collins, world champion sprinter

Let's go back to a concept introduced earlier in the chapter. Those who suffer slumps often fall prey to perfectionist thinking. Perfectionism breeds self-criticism, hyperawareness of flaws and errors, and personal demands of winning and striking every time. It leaves no room for human factors.

The thinking traps identified earlier are all about perfectionism. Perfectionism causes frustration and self-condemnation. Many bowlers experience slumps because they think they're not supposed to go through the normal learning curves. These slumps are total mental creations born of unrealistic personal demands for performance. In a nutshell, perfectionism helps to create the psychological hell that is the slump.

Every competitive bowler has a choice: perfection or excellence. Excellence is marked by intention and commitment, not by perfect results. Excellence recognizes that any journey includes exploration, pitfalls, and successes, and that growth is a process. Athletes with an excellence orientation see learning plateaus as part of the growth curve; they don't deteriorate into slumps.

Excellence is human. Perfectionism is robotic. Excellence involves learning. Perfectionism demands first-place, strike-every-time, inhuman bowling.

Here's an illustration of how your motivation differs depending on whether you've adopted an excellence or perfectionist perspective. Imagine a gold ring hovering over the middle of a big pit. Your desire is to leap and grab the ring, which can bring you honor and wealth. Perfectionists have two thoughts. The first is an awareness of the stakes involved in making the grab. The second is to avoid missing and the punishing thoughts associated with falling. In effect, the perfectionist grabs to avoid the pain of failing or losing the prize.

A player committed to excellence leaps for the ring with total commitment, heart, and intention. It is fun and exciting. The test of the leap is rewarding in and of itself. Fear of falling is not a consideration because he knows it's an illusion. The value of the experience is in bringing everything possible to the effort. Continual effort and intention are the essential ingredients in a process that's ongoing until the end of the player's involvement in the sport. In excellence, a slice of heaven on earth is the feeling of flight during the leap for the ring.

Bowlers who have an excellence orientation are like artists always seeking to improve the stroke. The search is for the experience of greatness, not because the ego demands it, but because it naturally feels great to master anything. Feelings of joy, pleasure, warmth, and excitement accompany excellence. Execution with heart is the turn-on from this perspective.

Table 7.1 compares slump-bound perfectionism with an excellence-oriented process.

Every thought and reaction while bowling is a choice; every choice has consequences. From this point of view, all difficult periods can still be part of the path to excellence.

CHANGE YOUR STARS

Life isn't about finding yourself.
Life is about creating yourself.

George Bernard Shaw, author

Have you made a decision to move through this thing? It must be worth it because you're going to endure the discomfort of busting out of your comfort zone. If you have the same elements of heart that champions have, you can slump bust—and the payoff is a slice of athletic heaven. A slump is just a stage stop along the way to becoming great . . . unless, of course, you quit. But that's not you. You keep going.

Take responsibility for everything that occurs in your bowling. Slumps happen to people who see themselves as victims of circumstances. The path of mastery demands that you take ownership of all your consequences and results.

With intention and positive practice techniques, growth is inevitable. In fact, the only thing that seems certain in the universe is that everything changes. By busting your slump, you're just speeding things up a bit.

Table 7.1 Comparison of Perfectionistic Bowling and Excellence Bowling

Perfectionistic	Excellence
Must bowl great in order to feel ok	Always brings the best to every game and shot and feels good about committed effort; pin fall is a bonus
Feels increasing pressure as the stakes get higher	Feels increased energy and excitement when the stakes get higher
Is self-critical and punishing after an errant shot or a weak game	Reviews play in order to learn and make corrections; irritation is fleeting
Is triumphant when striking; angry or enraged when missing	Ties joy to bringing best effort
Has fun only when winning	Frequently has fun while bowling
Worries when not winning or scoring	Understands that everything is part of the growth and improvement process; does not worry about stutter steps along the way
Ties ecstasies and agonies to good and bad shots and games, wins and losses	Keeps correcting and improving through the ups and downs of bowling; has both passion and perspective
Has to win; believes that winning and losing define who he is	Thoroughly enjoys the competition experience and brings out the joy of winning; naturally wins and improves by focusing on the process
Chokes based on pressure	Makes mistakes based on being human
Lives and dies by wins and losses	Sees winning and losing as part of a much bigger picture
Expertise	Mastery
Demands that choices and guesses be right every time	Is willing to explore new methods, techniques, and strategies
Trial and error are associated with fear of failure	Takes risks in order to facilitate learning, growth, and ultimate success
Has feelings of frustration and anger	Has feelings of mastery, power, and well-being
Need for control limits discovery	Is creative and spontaneous
Judges based on individual shots, games, and tournaments	Accepts all aspects of the growth, learning, and improvement process
Is drained of energy	Is energetic and excited
Has constant doubts	Plays in an uninhibited way; shots just flow
Looks only at whether or not perfection has happened	Sees all of bowling and life as a learning, improvement process

HANDLING ADVERSITY

Strength does not come from winning. Your struggles develop your strengths. When you go through hardships and decide not to surrender, that is strength.

Arnold Schwarzenegger, actor, politician, body builder

Much that happens in the world of bowling is really, really hard. Most of this does not get discussed. Maybe you think that what happens to you doesn't matter that much. Maybe you're old school and don't want to complain. Maybe you just don't know what to do.

Really challenging stuff happens sometimes. I've never met anyone older than 18 who hasn't figured that out. The thing is, the hard stuff can take so many forms. The obvious ones are injuries that take you out of the game for a little while, or maybe for a long while. There are other ones, such as choking on an opportunity and having to live with the results, losing cherished friends and teammates in any number of ways, and of course, there's always aging.

We'll look now at what happens when you get hit with one of life's ice balls. There's a remarkably predictable set of responses that athletes have when adversity hits. So if you have ever been "beaned" by life, read on. There's always a way out of the woods. The only problem is that sometimes the way out is *through* the woods.

Getting Hurt

Bowling is unique in the sporting world. Players have an asymmetrical approach to delivering the heaviest object in conventional sports. Even if you're a fitness buff, with great core strength and a balanced body, enough repetitions can break anyone down. The types of injuries that show up range from toes, to fingers, to hips, to lower backs. When it's a minor injury, such as stress on the thumb or toe, it's hard to know how to react. It's amazing how such a little thing can cause major alterations in your bowling. You wouldn't think a pinky finger could matter so much. When the injury is more serious, like a lower back or a knee, things get more involved. First of all, you can't bowl—perhaps you can, but it's not easy. If you're sidelined, you must endure the misery of not being able to play. Worse, there's often the fear you'll never return to your normal self.

Bowlers react to injury with various emotional reactions: denial that anything's wrong, anger about being hurt, depression about being out of the game, and many others. Here are some guidelines for helping you accept, recover from, and learn from an injury (Goldberg 2015):

1. Your brain needs to know what is wrong, and where to go to work. When you have pain it's like an immediate text message to the brain, "Hey, there's a problem here. Check it out. Could you get some

neurotransmitters and hormones moving to provide some assistance please? Umm right now would be good." That's what pain does for you. The brain texts back, "Got it. Thanks for the pain. I know exactly what is needed. I'm on it."

2. But, if you numb out or disconnect from physical or emotional injury with pain killers, pretending nothing is wrong, or thinking being tough is better than healing, your body might not have the time, tools, or techniques to self-repair. If you numb your feelings with denial, minimization, or alcohol, you cheat your brain and body of a fighting chance to get the problem handled. And of course, check with your doctor. He went to school a long time to know about how bodies break down and how they heal.

3. You have to acknowledge the realities of the situation, nothing more and nothing less. You may have to talk to a physician or a coach, but gather full and complete information on what's wrong. You will also need to detail the steps needed for recovery. Any time spent on what could have, or should have, happened is time wasted.

4. Your new goals will be the steps needed for your recovery. You have to know what you are doing next, and then what you are doing after that, in order to get better. Then do it. A plan with no accompanying action is called a fantasy. It's got no weight and no power.

   Your mind and your body are one system. There is a reason that placebo drugs often work as well as "real" medicine. What you believe in wholeheartedly influences how your body responds to everything, whether it is a spare shot, or your own body's healing response. Stay positive. Injury and disease processes tend to heal and mend better and more quickly when your attitude is solidly in the right direction. Even if you falter in your positivity, get back on it with your best attitude; it matters.

5. Hang in there. As the Buddhists say, "You can't push the river." Find patience as best you can. It's not always noble to play through pain; often it's the exact wrong thing to do. Sometimes you must go slowly to heal faster.

Losing

Losing can be really tough. Legendary college basketball coach Dean Smith once said, "If you make every game a life and death proposition, you're going to have problems. For one thing, you'll be dead a lot."

Losing is hard for a number of reasons:

1. You train hard, and sometimes it feels as if there's no payoff.
2. You might not be getting what you want out of your results, and this can lead to some real questions about how good you really are.

3. You might be bowling well in practice, but messing up in competition. This leads to potential thoughts about your mental game, or your worthiness as a champion.

4. You really wanted to win a significant event. You know that making some form of the show is special and rare. It matters to you, and you didn't get what you came for.

Bowling is exactly like life. You can do everything "right," and still stone an 8-pin or wrap a ten. Just like getting bumped by a tailgater even though you followed all of the driving rules. On the other hand, every now and then you whiff at a shot, and still roll the 2-pin forward, or something else fortuitous happens, even though you rolled an errant one. Just like life, you can make a wrong turn, and end up meeting the love of your life (it could happen!).

When you catch a break, enjoy it. There is no shame in getting dealt a good card. But when it goes the other way, keep your head straight. Your emotions are like a train, or a bull. They are relatively easy to control, turn, or stop when you intervene early. But if they get up to speed they run out of control. Your negative thoughts can be the same. If you catch them early, you can turn them. If they pick up speed, they can own you (Walton 2009).

You have two choices here when things don't roll your way. You can live at the mercy of reactions that feel like they run you, or you can take charge. Understand that there is a "you" that is still observing and experiencing your thoughts and feelings. Don't let the negative ones gather momentum. If that happens you are basically shaving mental and emotional IQ points. There is virtually no fun in this experience.

If you just allow the negativity to play on you, your image of who and what you are is at risk for hopping on a water slide that goes down. What happens next is that you start to expect bad stuff to happen, and you see yourself in a light that is anything but that of a champion.

If you say "I stink," you will stink. If you say, "I get to make the show, but I never win," you'll likely never win. If you say, "I'm a choker," you will choke more often. The power in your self-diagnosis is profound. If you catch this early, you can turn the train. If not, it's a rocky ride.

Succeeding

Bowlers who succeed have a very different progression of adaptive thoughts. By far the most important thing, during times when you're not accomplishing your purpose, is to objectively find the truth of why you didn't get what you wanted.

The bottom line is that if you really learn what you need to, every shot, every game, every tournament, then you are a self-improvement machine. Your confidence builds because you know that you're getting better every time you compete. This is a critical point. Players who live in regret over what happened, who self-punish and self-doubt, create pressure for themselves. Instead of competition being fun and exciting, it becomes an arena to keep trying to prove they are not the player they fear they are. Most of those fears center on four themes:

1. I'm not a good enough bowler at a physical game level.
2. I'm not the stuff true champions are made of.
3. I am not destined to be a winner. I'm a runner-up kind of person.
4. I'm unlucky.

The cure here is to boldly tell the truth in each of the four categories. Almost mathematically, to the degree that you have the courage to tell the truth, you can have the possibility of change and success. Let's look at the items in order.

First, regarding theme 1, there's plenty of objective data available about your skill level. All you have to do is get feedback from any reputable coach, or watch video of what you're doing. Maybe your game is limited. Perhaps you struggle with certain oil patterns or transitions. You might not have the speed control, ball command, or understanding of where and how to play that would put you in the champion's seat. All that's really needed here is accurate analysis, and a commitment to get better at what's weak in your game. This doesn't guarantee you'll win, but you'll have a much better shot at it.

With respect to theme 2—I'm not the stuff champions are made of—for better or worse, players tend to get results consistent with what they think they are. Most people don't remember that famed champion Carolyn Dorin-Ballard had three years between her first title in 1991, a doubles title won with Lisa Wagner, and her next title in 1994.

What happened after that was transformational. During her best year on tour (2001) Carolyn won seven times. One could argue that her physical ability suddenly took a quantum leap. But that doesn't make entire sense, given the stellar physical skills of some of the other players on tour with her at that time.

More likely, what happened instead is that Carolyn's idea of *what* she was (not *who*, but *what*) shifted to champion. She won because she expected to win and knew she deserved to win. With each win, she reaffirmed what she already knew about herself.

The same is true of Walter Ray Williams Jr. the all-time professional titles leader. Walter Ray once lamented to me that he was disappointed in his Horse Shoe world championship results. He won the world championship six times, but said that he felt that, having gone to the championships fifteen times, that he should have won more. *That*, is knowing you are a champion.

If, however, you think you're not a champion until you actually win, it's going to take a lot longer. You can be *proving*, or you can be *being*. Being a champion upfront will reduce your chance of choking and increase your excitement when you play.

As for theme 3—I'm not destined to be a winner; I'm a runner-up kind of person—remember that whatever you believe you are, you'll find ways of affirming that for yourself. If you believe you're always a runner-up, you'll never win. You'll start choking or missing spares. You can change your stars in an instant, but most players don't understand that.

Finally, regarding theme 4, if you believe that you're unlucky, you'll find plenty of evidence to prove it's so. On the other side of this, bowlers who insist they are lucky tend to create lucky breaks for themselves. They tend to have the following traits or behavior patterns.

1. They're good at creating, picking up on, and acting on life's opportunities, both planned and unplanned. They see opportunities all around them.

2. They make "lucky" decisions by checking their gut and taking action.

3. They expect good things to happen, and the world seems to line up for them. Even when bad things happen, they turn them into good things.

4. They are resilient, shaking off bumps and bruises and learning lessons from short-term misfortunes.

When you live like this, positive things happen. You bowl better, and when it's your day, you allow winning to come to you.

YOUR FORMULA FOR SUCCESS

And once the storm is over, you won't remember how you made it through, how you managed to survive. You won't even be sure, whether the storm is really over. But one thing is certain. When you come out of the storm, you won't be the same person who walked in. That's what this storm's all about.

Haruki Murakami, author

Your formula for success is grounded in the way you deal with adversity. Virtually no one gets through their bowling life (or their outside life) unscathed. The point isn't to shoot 900 every time, or to win every time you shoe up. Nor is it to go through your athletic career imagining that you'll never hurt, grow older, or lose flexibility.

No. The target is to have a way of showing up and facing up, and sometimes growing up, that allows you to stare down adversity until it says, "I get it and I give. I brought my game, but yours has me beat." Only then will life step aside, take a bow, and admit you into the champion's circle.

Do you have what it takes? You wouldn't have made it to this spot if you didn't. Trust that you're on your way.

BURNOUT

**Burnout is nature's way of telling you you've been going through
the motions, your soul has departed; you're a zombie,
a member of the walking dead, a sleepwalker. False optimism
is like administrating stimulants to an exhausted nervous system.**

Sam Keen, *Fire in the Belly: On Being a Man*

On the path to mastery of any sport or discipline, most athletes encounter the mental and emotional grinch called burnout. Burnout jumps you when you're in the middle of pushing forward toward personal and team goals. It lurks where there's repetition, stagnation, and exhaustion. Burnout can numb even the most excited bowlers. To deal with this mental trap, you must be able to spot the signs, recognize the symptoms, and take early action to avoid it.

Burnout is the hidden undertow of the serious athlete. It sneaks up on the bowler, sucking energy, excitement, and enthusiasm, and insidiously drowns competitive spirit. Ironically, burnout tends to strike those who strive the hardest for high achievement. Many athletes affected by burnout drop out of their sports or simply limp along with ever-declining performance.

Burnout vulnerability can be highest at the end of league season, during a swing on the professional tour, or after weeks and months of training. The problem is that bowlers confuse what might be a temporary condition with a fundamental change in their feelings about the game. The other problem is that burnout sometimes occurs when competition demands are still present. This can rob the bowler of feeling able to, or interested in, competing well.

The prime targets of burnout are bowlers who have worked hard on their games by training frequently, practicing diligently, and taking few training and competition breaks. These bowlers put great emphasis on achievement and winning. As a consequence, they often spend a lot of time at the bowling center, enter most tournaments, and bowl in multiple leagues. For those on the professional tour, time for breaks and recovery can be limited.

Certain personality characteristics put some bowlers at higher risk of burnout than others. The first we've already discussed extensively in this chapter: perfectionism. Perfectionism is the personal demand that every shot and game yield the desired result. You leave yourself no room for errant shots, learning along the way, or recognizing that growth and improvement is a process.

The second personality trait that can put bowlers at risk of burnout is overconcern about what others think. To the degree that you need other people's approval and acceptance while you play, you're in bowling jail. It's difficult enough to focus and deliver in a competitive environment without directing attention outward.

Bowlers who feel they must deliver for teammates, or fear making mistakes in front of others, often find their pilot light of competition fire blown out. It's natural to want to do well for the team and to want to excel on the bowling stage. The problem occurs when playing the game for the attention, approval, or acceptance of others dominates. It's no fun playing while trying to avoid making mistakes instead of reaching for the stars.

Still other bowlers at risk of burnout are those who set goals so out of reach that they're continually frustrated and let down. Setting lofty goals is helpful and motivating. Setting goals that you're unlikely to achieve is an invitation to burnout. Raising the bar can motivate training and improvement. Raising the bar so high that you never clear it cheats you out of the periodic reinforcement of successful goal achievement.

Another significant personal risk factor for burnout is constant worry about bowling performance. This makes it difficult to live in the present moment. Anxious worry and concern always involve having your mind in the past or future. This orientation takes its toll in useless expenditure of adrenaline and energy. It's no fun playing when you're not even there for the game.

Finally, all athletes must attend to their personal health. No engine can run well with sugar water in the tank. Bowlers can bowl without being muscularly toned or aerobically fit. Because of this, too many bowlers act as if they don't have to follow the same rules for peak performance that other athletes follow. This illusion of invulnerability can put the bowlers at risk for not getting adequate sleep, not following the rules of proper nutrition, and not controlling the consumption of sugar and alcohol. The human mind and body are a system. If the system gets overrun physically, the mental part of the bowling machine suffers a greatly increased risk of burnout.

Signs and Symptoms

Some of the signs of burnout are straightforward; others are insidious and sneak up with little warning. An individual or team might perform with excellence through the early part of the season, and everyone might be in competitive shape, but something is off just a touch. It can be hard to put a finger on. Energy and excitement are down. Motivation to excel is a memory. Painful losses to less able bowlers can become more frequent. One of the ways you know you're burned out is an overall loss of interest and enthusiasm for bowling, particularly if you were once committed to the sport.

Burnout is characterized by mental, emotional, or physical exhaustion. It can leave you feeling that someone pulled the plug on your energy source. Shots are lackluster. The physical and mental games, once crisp, become dull. Bowlers are particularly susceptible when they have dreams and goals of winning and continually fall short.

You could ask whether not making cuts, not scoring, and not winning leads to burnout, or whether burnout leads to worse results. The answer appears to be a circular dance. As mentioned, repeatedly failing to reach lofty goals can be tiring, frustrating, and draining, all cardinal features of burnout. On the other hand, burnout itself tends to lead to negative thinking, which leads to disappointing bowling. However it starts, once you detect an emerging pattern, it's vital to interrupt it.

Bowling burnout can be hard to detect because it happens over a long time span. Burnout is different from the flash of disappointment after a poor outing or the bitter taste in your mouth after really wanting to win a tournament and falling short. Those are sharp, difficult, unpleasant reactions.

What distinguishes those feelings from burnout is that disappointment, hurt, anger, and frustration occurs, then peaks, and then clears up. You know you don't have burnout if the feelings pass, leaving you with renewed enthusiasm to bowl. If your interest in bowling doesn't rejuvenate, burnout might be the culprit.

You might also be suffering from bowling burnout if you're not feeling like practicing anymore, you have a loss of interest in being coached or receiving feedback, or you're feeling overwhelmed by responsibilities outside of bowling. Figure 7.2 is a short checklist of common burnout symptoms.

Watch out for a lowered interest in hanging out with teammates and bowling buddies whom you normally enjoy. Burnout can leave you feeling uninteresting as well as uninterested, particularly with respect to sharing bowling experiences.

Preventing Burnout

Recognizing the signs of burnout and working to prevent it from happening can go a long way toward improving your game. Setting a realistic vision, resting, and following a good diet and exercise are just a few ways to help prevent burnout.

Set a Realistic Vision

Challenge yourself, but refrain from burying yourself with suffocating goals. Take a good, old-fashioned look in the mirror and honestly appraise your bowling. List your personal goals, and then ask yourself if they're properly calibrated. If your expectations are too rigid, then you're placing yourself in a personal pressure cooker. If your mission is not properly aligned with your commitment and ability level, a loss of energy and enthusiasm are bound to follow.

Rest

Take breaks from training and competition periodically. Every organism in nature has three fundamental needs for survival:

1. Growth
2. Maintenance
3. Repair

The mental psyche follows the same rules. If you're always driving hard at bowling, your mind and body will be striving to simply repair and maintain equilibrium. No healing and recovery will have space to occur. There's no growth occurring, much less fun.

None of these symptoms necessarily indicates burnout; symptoms can have different sources. The important thing is to watch out for patterns that endure over long periods of time. Be honest about whether you've been pushing too hard with unrealistic goals and no recovery periods. Some of these symptoms can also indicate medical problems, so checking in with a physician is advised.

Check the symptoms that apply to you, with a score on each item of 0 to 4 (0 = not at all; 1 = rarely; 2 = sometimes; 3 = often; 4 = very often).

Loss of enthusiasm for the game _____

Lack of interest in practicing skills _____

Reduced experience of fun while practicing or competing _____

Continued disappointment at not achieving goals _____

General fatigue _____

Ongoing mental and physical fatigue while bowling _____

Declining confidence in various aspects of the game _____

Pervasive irritability with self and others _____

Physical breakdown, colds, nagging injuries _____

If your score is 0-9, there's little indication of bowling burnout. If your score is 10-18, there's need for concern only if your score is concentrated in two or three areas. If your score is 20-27, be on the alert. Burnout is a real threat for you, especially if two or more areas are scored high. You might want to consider taking corrective action. If your score is 28-36, burnout is likely affecting other areas of your life as well as your bowling. Take corrective action right away.

Note: This inventory is an overview of burnout symptoms. It's meant to be intuitively useful. It has not been validated through controlled scientific tests and must not be used as a formal diagnostic instrument. Use common sense in deriving meaning from the results. Also make room to consider any challenges, changes, or losses that might have a disproportionate influence on you at the time you take this inventory.

Figure 7.2 Possible symptoms of burnout.

From D. Hinitz, 2016, *Bowling psychology*. (Champaign, IL: Human Kinetics).

No matter what activity you dive into—bowling, school, or relationships—periods of stepping away are essential for easing stress and providing perspective. Even in business environments, holidays, weekends, and sick time off are built into the system. The same rhythms apply to athletes. Needing time off is not a sign of weakness. In fact, trusting yourself enough to step back momentarily from training and competition patterns can be a sign of strength and wisdom.

Some bowlers subscribe to the training philosophy that the more frames, games, and hours they practice, the better they'll be. Some coaches believe this as well. If practicing 10 to 15 games is good, then 25 to 30 is better. Such ideas are refuted by motor learning. Physical and mental breakdown can result (Weinberg and Gould 2015).

Concentration is less sharp when practice involves unlimited time and games. Training can become monotonous. Practice time might transform from an opportunity to an obligation. Look at a parallel example from academics. If a student is told to study for three hours, she might sit in one place with a book in front of her, but her attention has plenty of time to wander. Studying goes on so long that it becomes a drag. But tell that same student she has one hour, and one hour only, to study, and her focus will sharpen. Study time becomes a privileged activity, and boredom and burnout are avoided.

Follow a Good Diet and Exercise

Naturally, as mentioned, food, diet, and exercise come into play as well. When the rest of the machine is well taken care of, the mental, physical, and emotional components have the best chance to rest, recover, and improve. Attitudes toward physical care and well-being often reflect general attitudes about other aspects of life.

Balance in these three areas can't be emphasized enough. Athletes in other precision, individual sports, such as gymnasts and divers, understand this. These athletes have a hard time performing when their bodies or mental games are not razor sharp. Many bowlers seem to be slow in catching up to other athletes regarding a belief in the competitive advantages of taking care of themselves.

Bowling has a mischievous trap built into it. Bowlers can be overweight and have bad wind from smoking, but still roll a powerful ball. Some of the legends of the game, past and present, were periodically heavy drinkers.

Poor health habits influence bowlers in two primary ways. The first is the subtle energy drain that results from being out of shape. An athlete must be in denial to think that his game is not affected by physical conditioning, particularly over long competition blocks, or over a long season. It simply takes extra effort to move when you're out of shape.

The second effect of improper diet, drugs and alcohol, and inadequate rest is on the emotional energy state. Susceptibility to fatigue, irritability, frustration, and overall lack of resilience is all part of being physically taxed. Long periods of time living and competing with inadequate fuel and recovery is another source of burnout.

Making changes in training styles and schedules can rejuvenate tired routines. Practice with friends. Participate in dollar pot games. Play for sodas. Get some fresh coaching perspectives. Allow for rest days between intense practice sessions. Anything that shakes off the staleness of overtraining and too much unconscious repetition can send fresh blood into a dragging season.

Curing Burnout

If you're fatigued at the bowling center and sick of bowling, or if you're already bowling worse because your mental game has declined, or if you're thinking of quitting, then burnout might well be the problem. If the diagnosis fits, there are three basic intervention options.

1. **Simply to do nothing.** This seems to be a surprisingly common choice. The reality is that most people keep operating within their comfort zones. This means that they deal with life by doing what's normal and usual.

Without waking up and doing something different, you might be condemning yourself to a continued slide into the burnout doldrums. Some people define insanity as doing the same thing repeatedly and expecting different results. Taking option 1, doing nothing, is leaving it up to time and hope to cure burnout. Dining on hope alone might well leave you starving.

Some athletes quit at this point. This is a drastic measure that requires no shift in how they handle whatever triggered the burnout. Since no shift has been made, chances are they'll burn out on their next endeavor as well. Meanwhile, teammates and bowling buddies lose. The quitter loses something he once loved.

Quitting doesn't allow growth as an athlete. Remember that the way you participate in sports tends to reflect your overall approach to life. Sometimes quitting is a long-term drastic solution to a short-term problem that could be effectively addressed otherwise. We'll deal further with the issue of quitting later in the chapter.

2. **Take a break, not a retirement.** Note that taking a break, structuring some recovery time, and allowing for mental and physical healing is far different from quitting. All healing occurs during down time. Plan for time off to make room for refueling. If this is your plan, however, you should make a good effort to figure out what led to the burnout in the first place. As discussed earlier, possibilities include overtraining, a heavy competition regimen, critical self-judgment, and continually falling short of high performance goals. Don't just rest up and go back to doing all the things that landed you in the soup in the first place. Make conscious and committed choices on how to keep your razor sharp.

3. **Get a hand from someone who can act as a guide in this situation.** Isolation is the accomplice to burnout. Find a coach, friend, family member, or sport psychologist who can help you pull back from the game, and get perspective on how you have approached it.

Sometimes merely airing out the experience of burnout with someone who's safe and supportive can jumpstart the recovery process. Acknowledging symptoms and talking about them is like an inoculation against the burnout virus. Some change in thinking, training, or competing patterns is going to be called for. An army of at least two on the recovery side is infinitely better than going it alone.

Bowling burnout is far easier to prevent than it is to cure. If you're an ambitious competitor, excited about bowling, and bent on taking the game as far as you can, make sure to protect yourself from overrunning your mental, emotional, and physical engines.

IS IT TIME TO CALL IT QUITS?

"Most people give up just when they're about to achieve success. They quit on the one yard line. They give up at the last minute of the game, one foot from a winning touchdown."

Ross Perot, politician

Every now and then you'll see a bowler slam his bag down and declare, "I'm through with this!" Particularly toward the middle or end of bowling season you see players threaten to quit and never come back. Fortunately, most of these declarations pass with the speed of a player's frustrations and disappointments. But sometimes the feelings of wanting to quit persist.

Have you ever wondered if you should still be in the game? Do you ever think the unpopular thought that maybe your time has come and gone? Perhaps quitting has occurred to you. This experience can be an awful part of your sporting life. And it's not uncommon.

It seems to me that most people who have played or coached the game of bowling for any length of time have thought about leaving the game. The reasons are varied. Some, even at the professional level, wonder if they're good enough to play. Others feel, or fear, that they're not getting any better. Nagging injuries can finally nag too much. Burnout can sneak up on anyone, even those who take precautions.

In this last section of Raising Peaks and Filling Valleys we'll look at an underbelly of the game of bowling—the desire to run, to quit. More important, we'll examine strategies for moving through these unpleasant weather patterns. Sunnier skies almost always await, though it seldom feels that way when you're in a bad rut. But for positive-minded people like us, there's always a way through.

Why Quit?

There are typically only a handful of reasons that players want to quit the game. Topping the list are

1. pain—physical, emotional, or both;
2. life change, such as marriage or having a child, and
3. boredom.

Pain

We've looked at pain already in this chapter. When your body hurts, it speaks to you. However, what you think it's saying might be off the mark. Pain signals that something is wrong, but what exactly is wrong can vary widely. Perhaps something's incorrect or inefficient in your approach or delivery style. There might be an imbalance in your muscular system. Some old or chronic injury in your body might have been aggravated and reappeared with little notice.

Before you quit or have surgery, you have several other intermediate options. Of course you should consult a physician to help you determine the cause of your pain. Yet, beyond this, bowlers often treat their injured bodies improperly. They fight through the pain, making an injury worse. They fail to adjust their form, further exacerbating the problem. Or they don't lay off long enough to fully heal. (*Why not rest instead of quit?!*)

Pain at the emotional level is a more complicated issue. The first thing that one needs to know is that when anything in us hurts, the mind searches rapidly and repeatedly for answers and solutions to the problem. The subconscious mind doesn't care about rationality, practicality, or sometimes even consequences. It just wants you to stop hurting.

If you're disappointed with your progress or achievement level, the mind says "leave" as one of its varied options for feeling better. If you feel pressure or stress around any aspect of your bowling or competing, the mind sees quitting as a relieving possibility. Remember, though, that you are not your mind. Your mind might run around on you, but you don't have to obey it. There's no emotion you have that can't be worked around.

Life Change

Any change is stressful. Whether it's a wonderful new job or relationship, or a difficult loss, the human organism responds as if it's facing a stressor. When we're faced with change, some part of us seeks stability in order to find peace within.

Here's where your game comes in. Bowling can be a wonderful constant in any life that is being whipped by changes. The winds of change, loss, and pressure blow these elements into your life, whether you invite them or not. But bowling offers consistency, constancy, and the peace of familiarity. You have your buddies, your ball, and the game. When everything happening around you picks up speed, you always have bowling.

Boredom

Boredom is a lack of investment or interest in what you're doing or experiencing. When that happens, the fun, challenge, and reward of playing the game has flattened out, at least for a time. The cure is to breathe life into the game again. Whether it's a marriage, a job, or the game of bowling, you have to keep it new and fresh, or else it will wither.

You have to find energy and life in improving, playing for something, or rediscovering the invigorating feeling of stretching yourself to be great. Boredom is a challenge; it says to you, "Wake up, for gosh sakes!" We're either busy getting better, being powerful or graceful, and having a heck of a great time, or . . . well, the alternative is to fall asleep at the wheel, go through the motions, and die on the vine. These rules apply to every part of life.

You Have Company

When you look around the bowling center, nearly everyone is confident, chipper, and into their games. It might be hard to believe that virtually everyone who has been serious about taking anything to the top has had despairing moments. But it's true. There's probably no one who hasn't wanted to shut their game down after a bad league, a bad tournament, or a difficult run of subpar results.

Times can be tough. Expense to income can be out of balance. Just about every athlete has some form of a 2 a.m. awakening when everything feels like it's too much. It's not uncommon for there to be times when negativity, self-doubt, and limiting beliefs about your possibilities come to the surface.

The good news is, you have company. There's virtually no experience in bowling, or bowling discouragement, that has not been shared and worked through by thousands of bowlers before you. Take heart. This sport is supposed to be hard sometimes; if it weren't hard, everyone would just breeze through, never testing their physical, emotional, and mental muscles. How rewarding would that be?

Quit the Limiting Beliefs

If you're struggling, hurting, and fed up, you almost certainly have unconsciously subscribed to a set of beliefs that's limiting you. As we saw earlier in the chapter, everyone, whether they know it or not, holds on to ideas and blueprints about how life, and therefore, bowling, are supposed to go.

The way you react and respond to anything is based on your underlying belief system. Some of your beliefs will uplift you. Some will bring you down. But, most important, when you don't know what these beliefs are, instead of you running them, they will run you—sometimes into the ground. Here are some common ones (Douglas 2016):

- (A) Bowling is not supposed to test you, or (B) bowling is supposed to challenge you.
- (A) I am supposed to play with classic form, or (B) I can put my own style into my form.

- (A) You must win, lead, score high, or (B) every now and then a person can stumble, and then fight his way back up.
- (A) I should always be unfailingly competent (e.g., know which ball to roll, which line to play), or (B) bowling is a sport of research and development. You figure it out as you go, both short term and long term.
- (A) I'm never good enough, or (B) I am okay with learning, growing, gaining skill, results, and wisdom as I go.

Looking at this list, note that the (A)s will make you miserable. They're full of judgments, absolutes, and criticisms. The (B)s leave room for excellence, improvement, and being human.

Discovering the potentially limiting beliefs that you live by is really important, particularly if you've been discouraged or ever had thoughts of quitting. Here's a way to see what yours might be. We are going to do a bit of free association. Grab a sheet of paper and write down the following initial phrases (Douglas 2016):

- I am
- I must
- Bowling is
- Bowlers are
- Life is

Now record virtually whatever initial thoughts or ideas show up right after the statement. Whatever comes to you immediately, positive or negative, is perfect. Don't think about it; just repeat this process three times. You are generating useful information. Your answers, if they were reflexive, can reveal a lot to you. Notice if what you write is empowering, or if it is a limiting belief.

FREEDOM

The way out of the oppression of limiting beliefs is to learn how to challenge the destructive ones, like so:

- Challenge the negative or judgmental beliefs. They likely come from old messages that you were taught somehow.
- It should be easy to see how the negative thoughts keep you down.
- Turn any negative belief 180 degrees, to something that is both true and positive (you must truly endorse the positive belief in order for this technique to be effective).
- In addition, find examples of the positive stance.

This exercise really works if you can really get behind the empowering thoughts, you practice disputing negativity with truth and positive statements, and you bring this to your bowling.

The turning point in the process of growing up is when you discover the core of strength within you that survives all hurt.

Max Lerner, journalist and educator

Is life challenging and hard sometimes? Of course. Is bowling hard sometimes? Do you lose your feel for the game sometimes? Do you flat out play badly sometimes? Do you go stretches without getting better? Again, and again—of course! The game is rigged. The advantage is to the ones who can figure out that the only way through the fog is with a light, a heart, and a will. (I believe that's you!)

CHAPTER 8

Team Building

All right, they're on our left, they're on our right, they're in front of us, they're behind us . . . they can't get away this time.

Chesty Puller, WWII Veteran, when surrounded by eight enemy divisions during battle

They say that there's no *I* in team. And it's common knowledge in sport that talent alone doesn't win championships, at least not repeatedly. Most athletes can name teams from any sport that were loaded with ability yet failed to take home the big prize. In bowling this happens at all levels of play.

It really does pan out that the team that plays together best *as a team* performs consistently better, especially when it counts. This has been demonstrated at the highest levels in recent years in the U.S. team's international success at both the junior and senior levels.

The good news is that team building can have a significantly positive impact on players' performances. The bad news is that most team-building efforts do not work or last long. The reason that team building often falls short is that it is technique-driven experiential exercises (e.g., challenge courses) and team-building activities tend to be one-shot deals.

Like the development of any other skill, team building is a process. You must decide to engage the disciplines that will pay off dividends in the long run. Whether you're bowling USBC nationals, tournament doubles, league, or collegiate bowling, playing as a team can take you to the top. Conversely, when bowlers don't play well together, choking, slumping, bickering, and other negative aspects of bowling can easily present themselves.

But this is no child's play chapter. The elements of team and doubles play are essential and often hidden. In this chapter we'll look at what makes great teams great, what goes into developing team chemistry, and how to make yourself into a top team player.

WHAT MAKES A TEAM A TEAM

**Everyone is trying to accomplish something big,
not realizing that life is made up of little things.**

Frank A. Clark, American politician

Take a moment and list the best teams in any sport. Now, to that list add the best teams you have played on. Looking over your list, do all the teams have the following attributes?

- Team members had a common goal, usually winning a title.
- The team had confidence in one another to play to the best of their ability.
- The team instilled a sense of safety in performing in front of one another.
- The team had good communication skills.
- The team looked within for support, not to outside influences.
- The team understood how to work with differences in personality.
- The team had faith in its coaching.
- Team members developed the skill to compete well.

Now let's look at something that's not immediately obvious. Most people look at athletic teams in simple terms. They see them as either good, average, or bad. But if we look more closely and we examine the attributes mentioned previously, how many of them involve skills, and how many involve ways of being together?

The first seven attributes involve ways of being. Only the last one is about actual ability and skill. So we might say that around 85 to 90 percent of what makes great teams great is the way they embrace being on the team, not merely their skill. Sports are filled with stories of talented teams that did not fulfill expectations. Now you have a clue why that can happen.

Common Goals

The first and most important aspect of team building is the establishment of common goals. If every player is not on the same page, your team is weakened. It's not enough to say "we want to win." Everybody wants to win. The team that wants to win most doesn't win. The team that commits to do what is necessary to win does.

The coach and the team establish both goals and methods. Training schedules, fitness expectations, meeting attendance, and performance expectations must all be in line. It feels great to be on a team when you know you're up to something great. When you look around, it's awesome to see that all of your teammates are willing to make sacrifices to reach for the golden ring.

Confidence in Each Other to Bring It

Few situations in sport are as frustrating as being on a team when you know a teammate is dogging it. As athletes, we can forgive misses, we can forgive lane-play errors, we can forgive nervousness, but we can't easily forgive a teammate who brings less than maximum effort. An essential team agreement that requires 100 percent buy-in is that every teammate shows up for every shot, every time.

Interestingly, this agreement actually relieves pressure in competitive situations. When team players know that simply doing their best is what's expected of them, they don't sweat made and missed shots so much. Players understand that as long as they're not careless, or mentally taking frames off, they are welcome in the team lifeboat. They understand they can be less than perfect, which is amazingly stress relieving.

Safety

Safety in a team setting is comprised of three factors. First, you must know that whether you play great on a given day or have a rough outing, you won't be judged or rejected. Every athlete knows you have both kinds of days. You should never turn around after a shot and see annoyance or disappointment on a teammate's face.

Second, safety is in knowing that your teammates have your back. Although it's common in all groups for people to talk about one another, teammates must not engage in negative conversations about each other. Trust is violated when you don't feel that everyone on the team has your back.

Last, we feel safe when we need not prove anything to our teammates and coaches. Once we trust that our teammates have faith in us, that they know what we're capable of, and that they see the greatness in us, we're free to play safely in front of them. In fact, we can play better with them than we might otherwise play.

Communication Skills

Whenever two or more players are playing together, bowling knowledge, intelligence about lane conditions, and coaching benefits are more likely to be improved. Conversely, when teams play as individuals rather than as a unit, they tend not to share, or benefit from, collective knowledge.

The first point of sharing involves extra sets of eyes, and various levels of experience, chipping in to the pool of knowledge. For example, it's hard to see what your own ball is doing up to the midlane. We can get fooled about which lines of play are most effective. And it can be really difficult sometimes to feel what's out of whack with your own physical game. A teammate can often see a little hitch in your delivery that's outside your own awareness.

Looking Within: Concentric Circles of Attention

At young levels of play, such as youth leagues, it's common for kids to look at their parents after shots and to go to mom and dad for coaching tips. This behavior thins out as players advance to high school age. Yet even at the college and professional levels it's not uncommon for family, ex-coaches, and bowling buddies to draw attention away from your bowling and your team.

There are four concentric circles of attention when you play doubles or team bowling (see figure 8.1). The first, of course, is your awareness of your own shots, the way the lanes play, and how your body is moving. The second is purely with your team. You watch them. They watch you. You share, support, and problem-solve together.

The third circle of attention involves your coach. Although the coach is part of the team, she's also one step removed. The coach watches you, supports you, and problem-solves with you.

The last circle is the fans and family who have come to cheer you on. You might actually need to practice not looking at them immediately after shots. As tempting as it might be sometimes, it undermines the team if you leave the competition area to receive coaching or support from an external source. On some teams, members formally agree to forego external coaching and family contact during competition.

There's technically one other circle of influence beyond the four we've identified: your opponents and their fans. Ideally, you'll train yourself not to be affected by this circle. Even if the circle is huge—the rest of the world

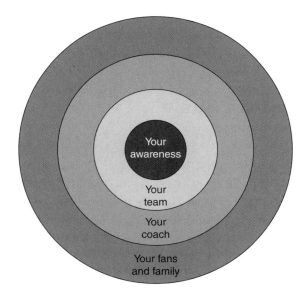

Figure 8.1   The four concentric circles of attention.

rooting against you—anyone who's not supporting your team should receive no attention from you or your teammates. Your team is its own universe.

Personalities

Great teams are not comprised of identical personality styles. It's highly beneficial to have diversity on a team. The problem is that under stress we almost always expect others to act and react in the same ways we do.

For example, after missing a shot, some players like to talk about it, some like to be left alone for a moment, some seek coaching immediately, and some can refocus their attention on their teammates right away.

Some teammates like to socialize together, and others like to keep their private lives separate. Some will come to you directly if they have a problem. Some tend to internalize irritations. Some are jokesters. Some can't take a joke.

The best teams are made up of teammates who recognize and appreciate each other's personality differences. There's no demand that anyone else be like us. Nothing about other players' behavior styles is taken personally. No one gets bent out of shape about other players' eccentricities.

Coach Leadership

Great teams defer to leadership. On any team, natural leaders emerge. On teams with coaches, players accept that being coached means surrendering to the wisdom and direction of your leader. Great teams have natural or formal leaders, and they follow them.

Skill

Some people think that great skill is based primarily on genetics. But most athletes know that skill is a combination of genetics, environment, commitment, training, practice, coaching, and experience. Exceptional teams certainly must be skilled. Yet even the aspects of being skilled involve qualities of personality and character.

The Point of It All

Team and doubles play is often significantly more exciting than solo play. The group energy is infectious. The shared joys and hurts add spice to our bowling experiences. Titles that have been jointly earned are prized because we become one another's living journals for success.

Must be present to win.

Motto of 20-time national champion Wichita State University

They say that sport is training for life. In the elements of team play presented here, you'll find principles for success in virtually anything you do with a partner. But our purpose here is to start with bowling. Give your team a quick scan to assess how the team stacks up on the seven attributes just discussed. When your team has them all, it can have it all.

TRAINING PRINCIPLES OF WORLD-CLASS TEAMS*

Doctors and scientists said that breaking the four-minute mile was impossible, that one would die in the attempt. Thus, when I got up from the track after collapsing at the finish line, I figured I was dead.

Roger Bannister, the first man to break the four-minute mile

In any team competition, several teams might have the talent to win the title. But, beyond talent, only a few teams realistically have a chance to take the crown. You might ask, Doesn't everyone have an equal chance? Well, not really. It's rare for a team to possess the essential characteristics to take the team all the way to the finish line. How can we say this? Many tournaments involve dozens of collegiate teams, international teams, league teams, or doubles teams. Why don't more of them have a chance?

From a sports psychologist's perspective, only a few teams have prepared their bodies, minds, and games to take the prize. Almost all of the players on a team might have come out of their home centers as the best individual players. But team bowling is an entirely different rodeo.

What does it take to be world class? More important, can your team develop what it takes? In this section we'll look at five essential operating principles that world-class teams in any sport possess. Don't expect a quick fix. This requires setting up a plan that will take your team to the limits of its ability.

Principle 1: World-Class Teams Know the Only Mechanism to Improve, Adjust, and Win Is to Lean Into Truth

Normal bowlers on normal teams are slightly delusional. They will believe that they are training harder, longer, and with more consistency, than they actually are. They see themselves as acting in line with their dreams and goals, not seeing the deviations from the training success principles that are essential for success. They won't particularly notice the shots and frames they take off, nor the other life management activities that help or hurt their

---

*Some source material in this section drawn from Siebold, S. 2014. *177 mental toughness secrets of the world class*. www.mentaltoughnesssecrets.com.

advancement. Normal bowlers kid themselves a bit. It may be just a touch, but there are typically some delusions on board.

World-class bowlers on world-class teams are compassionately honest with themselves. Their mirrors are clear. They have the courage and self-awareness to know the truth of their training practices, the effort they brought to competition, and why things turned out as they did…good or bad. If they err, it's on the side of being irresponsibly responsible for everything that occurs in their results. Sometimes their preparation looks insanely overdone to the average player. It's not so much that they train to get things right. They want to be so prepared that they can scarcely get things wrong.

Training step: Commit yourself and your team to a peek into a crystal clear looking glass. With true conviction you must ask whether the way you are training, the way you take in feedback, and the way you take ownership of your bowling results (and your life) will take you to the top of the mountain.

Principle 2: World-Class Results Must Reflect What You Think and Who You Think You Are

In order to excel at anything some part of you has to love what you are doing. If you went to the bowling center today because you love how you feel when you bowl—physically and emotionally; because of how it feels to be in the center and with your teammates; or how it feels to learn, grow, and master the game, then you are actually living the game.

If you went to the bowling center because you have a host of "shoulds" running you, then you are not truly owning your identity as a champion cali-ber team. Champions embrace the idea that improvement takes effort and is hard sometimes. And in the end, they still have a love of the game. The attitude that team members have about training and learning determines a great deal of your team's success.

The average to above-average bowler who is looking to improve might naturally see that gathering information about how to bowl properly and how to play the lanes will be what it takes to get better and to win. Although there's truth to this approach to getting better, and it will not be enough to win consistently. Certainly you will get better, though it's more true for below-average to slightly above average bowlers.

The best bowlers usually have a good grasp of ball dynamics, lane play, and physical game, but they know this isn't enough to be a world champion. They know there's a comfort zone associated with success and achievement that average players simply don't have.

Every player and every team has an internal barometer for success. It's as if they consciously and unconsciously know right about where they will land in any field of competitors. Players will find the level to which they think their boat can float. And within a range, will somehow make it happen.

Competitors will sometimes explain their results referring to bad breaks and circumstances that kept them from success. Somewhat better bowlers will occasionally talk about how the play of other bowlers landed them in their final place in line.

World-class bowlers think in entirely different terms. In money terms, they feel that at the deepest level they deserve to be rich. Relatedly, world-class teams have two essential qualities: They love to do the things that make them better, and their comfort zone dictates that their "normal" is to belong among the greats.

Training step: Once again, the mirror of truth has to be invoked. The team must ask from a place of real honesty and curiosity: What is our thermostat setting for bowling success? At the poverty level, you're content to be donators, paying fees, and entering tournaments, hoping for your lucky day. At the middle-class level, you're comfortable being in the thick of the field, but you have a subconscious speed bump that makes you choke, make mistakes, or do something stupid when you get too close to real success. At the world-class level, your team constantly transforms its thinking about who and what you are and what you really deserve. Virtually all of your team's self-talk and other behaviors reflect this.

Principle 3: World-Class Team Players Can Play Within the First Two Concentric Circles of Attention

Literally, true champions keep their eye on the ball. Whether it's a shot, a game, or any aspect of training, champions focus their attention, energy, and efforts only on their present action. Average bowlers will allow their minds to wander off track. They will often lose the urgency of staying on purpose and plan as they train and compete.

World-class teams have athletes who treat the pursuit of goals as a direction point on the compass, a course to be maintained with near obsession. They know where they're going and what they'll do to get there. When you're flying world class, every day is New Year's Day, You see and pursue your goals and resolutions, except the resolutions don't tend to change very much. Your commitments are like daily hygiene, you wouldn't think to ignore or go around them.

When you're average you think that you are the victim or beneficiary of fate or luck. That is actually a disempowering stance. Occasionally someone can ride the wave of chance to some success, but over the long haul in life there is only one principle that prevails: Those who can marshal their attention and energy to shots, immediate learning and recovery, and dogged commitment to their compass points become world-class bowlers.

Training step: The team, or individual players, can write down a physical game, mental game, and long-term achievement goal. Then list specific measureable actions that will be put into motion to ensure these goals are achieved. A goal can be as basic as improving shot execution under pressure, or as dedicated as winning tournaments at a high level.

Principle 4: World-Class Teams Have Players Motivated by Internal Fire

The world runs backwards. It thinks that the way to get people to perform better is to pay them more, whether it be in money or awards. That can work for a little while, but the external things are generally not enough to keep an athlete's drive at a peak level.

Champions find the juice for achievement inside their own dreams, passions, and hearts. Rewards that come from the outside are very brief. Rings and titles are like scout badges—nice to show off, but they won't give you energy or happiness. Even money runs out, and won't keep you going in the long run.

The only inexhaustible source of drive is the one that you were born with as a child. The part of you that loves to play, have fun, and dance to the thrill of rolling phenomenal shots comes from the inside of champions. There are several amazingly talented players in college and out on the professional tour who lack this internal flame. Sure, they've won money, titles, and other merit badges. But if their motivation comes from without instead of within, we'll never know how much they could have accomplished. You have to play with a true love of the game to walk amongst the greatest.

Training step: Determine the source and intensity of your internal fire by answering these four questions:

1. What makes it worth me training through the roadblocks of boredom, frustration, fatigue, and periodic disappointment?
2. What in playing this game is most important to me? Is it about money, awards, and recognition? Or is it about being my best, maxing out my abilities, and contributing to my team?
3. Training and competing are difficult. What is my target? Where am I going in bowling? There is a lot to go through. What goal do I have that will make it all worth it?
4. What are the three most important things, other than scoring, that make me happy when I train and compete?

Principle 5: World-Class Competitors Separate What They Prefer to See From Reality

This last principle is a little odd. Are believing what you are seeing, and clear perception, and fact the same thing? Of course they're not, but your average bowler tends to think that perception and fact are stacked right on top of one another. World-class champions know otherwise. We all have perceptions of how we act, think, and play the game. Since our subconscious can't separate truth from perception, we tend to believe our own perceptions of how we bowl, how we play as a team, and how we play the game of life.

Virtually everyone has blind spots. World-class players know this. Champions know that their arm swings, feet, and deliveries don't always coincide with their perceptions. They know that the way they manage their mental and emotional game might seem one way to them but appear very different from the outside. And similarly, we all have blind spots in how we are as teammates.

For average players and average people, perception equals truth. World-class players are willing to face the discomfort of being wrong, or off about how they might be executing shots, about what is happening with the lanes, or about how they are matching up with their balls. Since the subconscious mind can't distinguish perceptions from truth, for most players truth exposure is like an icy shower to the ego.

Training step: Decide 3 to 5 aspects of your game that you believe to be facts. These might involve your arm swing, your position at the line, your release, your coachability, your emotional reactions to shots, or any other aspects of your physical or mental game.

Now consider whether you really *know* your perceptions are true, or if you merely hope they're true. The acid test, of course, is to check with a coach or teammate who has the courage to tell you the truth, even if you don't like what you'll hear. Find a teammate who can deliver accurate feedback without hurting your feelings. Every now and then we get a surprise. Yet everything you learn will help you to be better.

You now have effective guidelines for practice, coaching, and championship team commitment. Take a long look at the training steps and resources. At the end of the day, the thing that separates the big dogs from the rest of the field are the steps that champion teams actually take. Not the view from the porch. Unless you're willing to be the lead dog, the view never changes. So when it's your team's turn to bowl for the title, make sure you're already world class.

TOP STRATEGIES FOR IMPROVED TEAMWORK AND COMMUNICATION

**The strength of the team is each individual member.
The strength of each member is the team.**

Phil Jackson, coach of 11 NBA champion teams

Team-building and communication skills can immensely enhance your effectiveness in competition. Mastery of these fundamentals can significantly improve your chances for success.

Success in team building is measured by accomplishments that are beyond what team members would achieve on their own. The following are cardinal features of team building, communication strategies, and consistently

■ Committing Yourself to Your Team With Gordon Vadakin

We are playing against players who are at a level higher than ever before. We have to do everything quicker, faster, better or we're not going to be in the hunt.

Gordon Vadakin, USBC Hall of Fame coach

A lot of people in the bowling industry would consider Coach Gordon Vadakin to be one of the pioneers in collegiate bowling. His Wichita State Shocker teams have won 20 national championship titles and innumerable major invitational first-place finishes. This is more than any collegiate bowling coach in history—perhaps more titles than any coach in any sport.

When asked about these historic achievements, Coach Vadakin is a bit unsure of the numbers and lists of accomplishments. He doesn't care to languish in these things. "That's kind of irrelevant to me." It's the *now* and the *what's next* that interest him. His amnesia for records and recognizable feats is genuine. He seems almost puzzled that I would ask about his past successes.

Gordon Vadakin (right)

Courtesy of the United States Bowling Congress.

Coach Vadakin states that he has no magic to offer related to coaching champion teams and champion athletes. This is despite all the national titles, the current (at the time of this interview) number one ranking of his women's team, and the host of PBA titles, international titles, and Hall of Fame appointments by current and former Shocker bowlers. Then, without appearing to know it, he offers the magic.

I called to talk about bowling. Yet the feat that he gets excited about is the fact that 18 of his players had grade-point averages of 3.5 or better last semester. It's practically formulaic. In Coach Vadakin's words: "That's what it's all about. Let them be successful at whatever. All the time. If they improve as people, their bowling improves by osmosis. It's automatic. Let them be successful at whatever, all the time, with whatever they touch. It's doing it so much that you expect to be successful (at everything). If you can learn these things, then bowling ends up being part of that equation."

If you do all things at a championship level, this mindset transfers to the lanes. Coach Vadakin is clear that when he recruits athletes, and for those who bowl for him, they must have core values and ethics. "We wanted to attract students who wanted to improve, to work, to learn, to be loyal. If they have those things, they can succeed at anything."

The principles of team play illustrated in this chapter are no stranger to Coach Vadakin. In fact, we've had the opportunity to work together over the years to implement these. He teaches the toolbox standards of visualization, self-talk, repetition, and relaxation. He gives his team reading assignments on everything from leadership to

(continued)

Gordon Vadakin *(continued)*

lane play to the mental game. "We make it (actually rolling shots) simple. It's not a lot of thinking; it's the opposite of that."

Above all things, Coach Vadakin is relationally oriented. "It's a bigger mission than being selfish." He encourages his players to do things together outside of bowling. He wants them to be friends, "You need that glue to get through the tough times."

I asked Coach Vadakin what he would advise if an individual or a program wanted to change their self-image, from an also-ran to that of a champion. He had some solid suggestions. And I know by observation that he lives by them. "You have to have a willingness to fail and try something new. People get hung up on failure; I don't like failing, but we keep what we think works, and even that changes. People think we have a boiler plate; I don't look at it that way at all."

Perhaps Coach Vadakin's most vital piece of direction for team play involves commitment. "We never had a team that had success that didn't go all in—it's a decision. 'I'm going to give it every thing I've got.' Players commit. Others get it, feel it, buy in. Then you feel like there's nothing you can't do. It sounds simplistic. But it's not magic. It's their commitment to each other. They only get things done when they commit to each other. They have to see that it's not about the program; it's not about the coaches. It is as it always will be. It's about each other. If they make that commitment to each other, success is what tends to happen."

Coach Vadakin was adamant that no one, no matter how decorated, can coast. "It's not about being successful. It's trying to figure out how to stay ahead, to reach further. We have to do every program facet better than we did the year before. We will be irrelevant real quick if we don't continue to evolve and stay relevant."

Author's note: Coach Vadakin credits Wichita State Coach Mark Lewis for cocreating their bowling program's success. He credits Coach Fred Borden for giving him the opportunity to coach Team USA. He also highlighted the excellence of several other collegiate programs throughout his interview.

successful teams. Use this section as a checklist for your team's path to championship play (Dudiy 2002).

1. **Everyone must have the same sheet music for where the team is going, what they think is possible, and what they are willing to do to get there.** This has to be crystal clear, and thoroughly understood by each member of the team. At a team meeting early in the season, make sure every player is on the same page.

Be sure that everyone on the team is in alignment with the goals for any particular tournament and for the season. In addition to this you should have a vision of the team's character, competition attitude, and overall mental toughness. Your vision might include team cohesion, a fighting attitude, an ability to be playful with each other at the right times, or any other qualities you value.

Every team member must agree with and accept the goals, mission, and vision. If you asked any team member what the team's stance is on any of the aforementioned goals, you should get universal agreement on what they are. Once your direction is established, players can be held accountable for whether their training habits, life habits, and personal behaviors are aligned with the team's mission and vision.

Establishing goals, mission, and vision is picking a direction for the team, like being in Boston and aiming for San Francisco. Once everyone is on board for the trip, virtually every step a team member takes can be seen to be in line with the declared journey or not.

2. **It must be made clear that everyone is responsible for the team's results, whether they are actively rolling balls in a game or not.** It may that someone is always in the lead-off spot, or anchor, or managing logistics, or any of the innumerable tasks related to managing a team. It may be around making sure that everyone is attentive, supportive, or involved in problem solving. Everyone must know how they are expected to contribute. Just as important, team members should understand that virtually everything they do either furthers the team on its mission or creates drag on the engine. There are few throw-away decisions or behaviors.

3. **Involve as many team members as possible in decisions around practice planning, other aspects of training, and tournament play.** It's important that each team member experience ownership in some of the decisions and outcomes that affect the team.

Decisions, such as lineups, practice protocol, and discipline, remain with the coaching staff. But other decisions along the journey should involve all team members. This is a big part of the buy-in. When team members fail to take ownership of a team's values and performance, the team will fail to get the maximum out of itself as a unit.

4. **Stay vigilant for any possible blocks in the lines of communication.** Teammates must be fully aware of strategies for lane play, equipment usage, and even travel details. Emphasize mutual responsibility for everyone knowing about plans, agendas, and changes. If there's ever a lapse in the transfer of essential information, a nonjudgmental review of where the breakdown occurred is needed.

5. **The coach, team captain, or other designated team member should periodically check with individual team members about how they are doing.** Be loyal. Be very cautious in talking negatively about team members. Anything you do or say is sure to be repeated and copied. Don't say anything to a team member that you're not willing to have published for all team members to see.

6. **Players meld as teammates when they have opportunities for team members to develop trust and to connect with each other.** This can be done through team-building games or such activities as group lunches. Contact is like superglue. Separation is a breeding ground for distrust, blame, and false assumptions. But, as mentioned earlier, beware of one-shot team-building interventions. Watch for small opportunities. Usually anything that requires mutual participation for task completion is a good chance for connection building.

7. **Address any interpersonal issues among team members, such as conflicts or romantic involvements.** Like a pebble in a shoe, you know when an issue is there. If you try to ignore it, it only turns worse.

Make a distinction between brutal honesty and productive honesty. It's important in any kind of relationship to understand that brutal honesty is honesty without compassion or care. It rarely turns out productively. Productive honesty is honesty that includes concern for the receiver. Once this distinction is well understood, the doors open for authentic communication.

8. **Catch team members "being good."** Don't miss chances to reinforce, empower, and recognize the positive work of other team members. Most coaches and teammates pay maximum attention to bad behavior, but unexpected positive attention is a powerful reinforcer. Many coaches attend only to reinforcing athletic performance. If you're coaching, make sure you notice other actions that are in line with the team's mission, and vision.

9. **Team members should have a strong sense of belonging to the group and esprit de corps.** Teammates must experience ownership and commitment to direction, actions, and outcomes of the team. Whether a sense of belonging exists among team members depends largely on the coach's experience. If the coach has seen the value of a shared sense of belonging, she'll want to help establish this for the team. A team's DNA can generally be found in the beliefs and values of the coach. If the team lacks a strong feeling of belonging among themselves, the team is not really a team.

GAMESMANSHIP

It's how you show up at the showdown that counts.

Homer Norton, football, basketball, and baseball player and coach

Sometimes even a really good team will be involved in league or tournament play, waiting for their turn, and get thrown off of its game by something an opponent is doing. Players and teams will sometimes try to mess with your head. Perhaps an opponent takes an inordinate amount of time fiddling with thumb tape. Or maybe when someone on the other team is supposed to roll, the team holds an impromptu meeting instead. Other classic moves are players commenting on how many steps you take, or noticing some other aspect of your physical game. There are a million of them.

Sometimes opposing players will make a direct challenge to your skill level or even to your man- or womanhood. Players will run shots out across lanes with a shout or a fist pump. There are even stories on tour of players walking in front of opponents and passing gas. Whether this was an attempt to make someone laugh or get mad, I don't know.

All these examples and more fall under the heading of gamesmanship. Gamesmanship is sometimes called "the game within the game." Whether you approve of it or not, it happens with some frequency. In fact, it's not just in professional tournaments league that we observe mind games in force but in collegiate and as other tournament play as well.

There are many ways to interfere with someone else's game. This is *not* a section on how to do that. Instead we'll look at ways to defend your team against the kinds of tricks and schemes that competitors use to affect your best performance. There are three prominent strategies that competitors and opposing fans might use to get you off of your game.

Gamesmanship Mind Game 1: Distraction

Distraction techniques can take many forms. Players can fiddle with equipment in view of opponents. They can stand just back from the approach, well within your player's space, seemingly innocently awaiting their turns. Players and fans can cough, clink a glass, or even *accidentally* drop a bowling ball while putting it back in a bag.

To distract you, players might talk about good shots and bad shots, good breaks and bad breaks. They might chit chat about almost anything. If they know you like to keep the pace going, they might try to disrupt it. If they know you like to be deliberate, a distractor might be up on the approach waiting for her turn as soon as you finish your shot.

Once a distractor has gotten your attention, it often doesn't matter whether she continues the obnoxious behavior. Once you start wondering if your bowling will be affected, the damage is already done. For some players, you might as well set off firecrackers right behind them.

Gamesmanship Mind Game 2: Intimidation

This is one mental game "tactic" that can take place without the intention of the intimidating team. It's not uncommon for rookies on tour to be awed when playing with established stars. The same is true when young, inexperienced teams are up against established champions. Sometimes a collegiate team will be loaded with both national and international team members. Feelings of intimidation might occur even in league play when teams are scheduled to bowl against better players.

In such cases a bowler's focus can shift away from bowling his best to wanting to impress the other players, or perhaps to intimidate the other team. Sometimes it can be even worse, when a bowler just wishes to avoid looking stupid in front of the other players, the other team, or in front of the audience.

Any time a bowler holds another player, or another team, in awe, he risks diminishing himself and his game. Respect is fine, even honorable. But reverence or hero worship can weaken every aspect of personal power. It doesn't matter whether players are entertained by the other players' skills or mannerisms, or even disappointed by another player's quirks or behaviors. Attention outward diminishes team cohesion, purpose, focus, and effectiveness.

Players can run out shots, cross lanes, and create the biggest bowling displays of intimidation they can think of. There might be massive fist pumps, whoops, and hollers. Teams might chant and cheer louder and longer than is sportsmanlike. All of this is designed to elevate the home team and send a message to the opponent.

Gamesmanship Mind Game 3: Suggestion

Suggestion is a tricky mind game because it's often disguised as normal banter that bowlers engage in all the time. In this mind game it's common for opposing players to talk about the lane conditions, or they might let themselves be overheard talking about some aspect of play.

An example is talking about long or short oil patterns and how they should be played. Or they might speak about how the lanes have burned up, or what the TV lights are doing to the oil. They might discuss what kind of ball needs to be played, or how tacky the approaches are. A player might even take out a roughing pad and heavily scuff up a ball before playing. There might be no intention of using that ball, or even of playing the line that's used in shadow practice.

What makes this gamesmanship is that there is an intention to deceive the opponent, or to affect the opponent's game in some way. A hidden agenda is designed to get you to question something about how you'll play, or to make you think about something other than your game.

The Answers

No matter what someone else throws at you or your team, unless it's a physical object, no one can really touch you unless you give them permission to (in your mind). When you practice having control over yourself, you're free to play without anyone shrinking your game.

The first key, of course, is to play your own game. If an opponent can get into your head, they sort of own a part of you. So the first two lessons are easy. The very first is to *expect* other players and fans to do things that you don't care for. More than that, you have to know ahead of time that there's likely to be some people who actively try to unnerve you.

You might remember a player named Dennis Rodman from the NBA in the 1990s. Rodman specialized in harassing other players, often out of sight of the officials. Other players would receive technical fouls when they tried to retaliate, while Rodman snickered behind the refs' backs.

If you were going to bowl against Dennis Rodman, you would surely plan ahead. You would know that he was going to say things about your game, your mother, and your manhood. You would know that he might sneak a pinch in your side, and gloat when you missed a shot. And you know what? You would be so ready that you would expect it. The behaviors would *not* unnerve you, and you might even laugh when he cut loose with his act. In effect, you would have given yourself a gamesmanship flu shot so that nothing Rodman could do would affect you or your game.

A second key is to let your game show up in response. The best reaction to gamesmanship is a magnificent effort. If you push back in any other way, your opponents have won the gamesmanship battle. You give power to anything you have to fight back against. Don't respond with the same behaviors, whether it's talking trash, running shots out, or fist pumping.

If your team's mental game is rock solid, even a glee club singing behind you won't keep you from executing your shots. Your team must know ahead of time that they'll have the kind of attention, and intention, to block out the world when they bowl.

Even if you're playing on TV, your team must decide beforehand to focus on their targets, not on players behaving in loud, rude, or distracting ways. When someone does something on purpose, such as jingling keys, decide whose universe you choose to live in, his or yours. Don't even comment, as that might encourage him or make him think he's getting to you. Get your team into its own space and into the present moment. Decide what you're going to do, and let the rest of the world play its own games.

Dealing With Suggestion

Words are powerful. If you're not careful, words can affect you at some level of consciousness. Whenever someone is spewing information, you must decide whether you want to listen to or consider what's being said. If it's an opponent talking, you must analyze her possible motives. If you suspect someone is using suggestion as a distraction technique, treat it as such.

Opponents' words can create doubts in your strategies and other parts of your game. You must decide what seems to be the truth about the oil, the balls, and the lines of play, and then go with it wholeheartedly. As we've discussed many times in this book, your game only works to the degree that you believe completely in what you're doing.

Wrecking Someone's Game

All of this raises the question, Is it okay to mess with someone else's mental game? The answer to this is personal to you and your team's values. Some would argue that gamesmanship is part of competitive bowling, that all's fair in bowling wars. Others say that it's bad character to purposely try to wreck something that someone else is creating. That it would be like scratching someone's painting in a painting contest.

Ultimately, if you feel you need to influence someone else's game in order to win, this can detract from your own game. You can focus exclusively on your own excellence, or you can try to play with someone's head in order to win, but you can't do both. Whether it's OK to attempt to mar someone else's game is a personal, ethical decision.

Playing Your Own Game

Your bowling has to occur within your own universe. Everyone else is just a visitor. It's like keeping unwanted trick-or-treaters out of your house. Ignore the doorbell, the costumes, the threats. Decide you're going to play your own game.

STAGES OF TEAM DEVELOPMENT

**The way a team plays as a whole determines its success.
You may have the greatest bunch of individual stars in the world,
but if they don't play together, the club won't be worth a dime.**

Babe Ruth

People often remark that bowling is an individual sport. They ask how important team building really is. Much like gymnastics, diving, golf, and other sports with no defense, it would seem that all one has to do is send a bunch of individuals out there, add scores together, and call it a day.

But it is not that simple—not by a long shot. If it were, the most talented bowlers would pretty much win all the time. They don't. There are so many factors that determine the focus of individual players, whether they feel safe and supported, and whether the intelligence of the group can benefit them. Team play is huge for these, and other, effectiveness issues.

Back in 1965, a psychologist named Bruce Tuckman described a model of team development that really seems to hold true for athletic teams. He would say that teams must successfully negotiate these stages in order to perform at the highest levels.

Many teams start anew each and every year. This is certainly true for high school and collegiate teams, many international teams, and other traveling teams as well. No one can expect a team to perform at peak efficiency right off the bat. It speeds up the process of excellence if you can put a frame around what great teams must go through.

• **Stage 1: Forming.** When teams are newly assembled there are a variety of characteristics that are normal. These include excitement and gratitude about being part of the group, private fears about their spot in the group, and some feeling that they need to prove their skill and worth to the group.

At this stage, the coach, or other team leadership, sets agendas, training schedules, and takes a very dominant role in the actual coaching of the physical and mental game. The team itself is too young, and probably too eager to avoid a conflict, to do this on their own.

• **Stage 2: Storming.** The next natural stage of groups is the discovery of individual differences and needs. Take caution here. Many groups fail to negotiate this step well. At this stage, athletes are confronted with differences in personality, training habits, and in how they respond to coaching and rules. After the early honeymoon period, irritations and different need requirements can manifest themselves.

• **Stage 3: Norming.** Once the team has had some time to really experience one another, to risk revealing differing needs, and perhaps to bump into a bit of conflict, developing their own thumbprint as a group can occur. Players figure out how to find common ground between them. In spite of annoyances, at this stage players recognize the positive attributes that teammates bring to the team, make room for one another's idiosyncrasies, and clearly respect the direction of the coach and team captains.

At this stage, teammates become more available to give and receive feedback. Their efforts to support the team's mission becomes evident, and the team genuinely enjoys hanging out with one another on and off the lanes.

It's important to note that as the team moves from brushing up against one another to hitting their stride in defining their selves as teammates, that it is not a perfectly unidirectional shift. Teams can wobble a bit back and forth between stages, particularly as they face different challenges throughout the year.

• **Stage 4: Performing.** This is when things get really reinforcing. You and the team get to enjoy the payoffs for your hard work. You trust that the issues that inevitably come up between teammates are workable. Proving to your teammates that you can play is no longer an issue. There is freedom to execute shots without fear of judgment or rejection

At this stage every team member understands that they have a leadership role. They know that everybody contributes in some way. There is room to co-coach one another, and to give and take direction reciprocally. You can make line-up changes and substitutions without overly disrupting the team.

• **Stage 5: Saying good-bye.** At some point, the year, or the team's life, is over. It's important to guard against simply allowing things to disband. Players will have feelings about ending and leaving. The way the team attends to saying good-bye will help frame their overall experience with you and the group. The way the team adjourns is also a key element in the lasting construction of the values and culture that a coach hopes to impart in his or her program.

Good ending processes and rituals leave players with a contextual memory for the season they just had. An absence of positive transition rituals can actually have a deflation effect on how players recall the season.

Hopefully, knowing this sequence associated with high-performance teams will help you feel comfortable with the rough stages of team development. You can direct your team-building experiences to match particular stages of team development.

The coach's tasks are as follows for each stage:

- **Stage 1: New team, new season.** Set expectations and role requirements. Establish goals. Teammates tend to be nice right off the bat. Get to know one another.
- **Stage 2: A little bump, a little grind. Work out individual differences.** Build trust and develop relationships. Teach ways to resolve conflict. Consider explaining this whole stage model to the team so they can see what they're moving through.
- **Stage 3: Cohering.** At this stage, players have a sense of familiarity with each other and the coaches. Everybody is now held accountable for all that has been set up and agreed on.
- **Stage 4: Delivering their best efforts.** Teammates should now have a sense of ownership for all aspects of training and performing to a far greater degree. The coach gets to enjoy the increased assumption of responsibility for team members. He can work more individually with players as needed
- **Stage 5: Saying "so long."** Review and celebrate the highlights. Say good-bye in an authentic manner. Whether it is in a team meeting or a banquet, recognizing achievements and contributions is an important part of the termination process. Skipping this step can leave the team with a sense of unfinished business and no real sense of closure. Not every team wins, yet ending things properly can leave team members with a solid sense of team affiliation and achievement.

Building a team is an organic experience. The team is like a biological organism that needs attention to the growth, maintenance, and repair functions that lead to optimal functioning in superior athletes. One of the hardest things to do in sports is to run faster when you are in front. Follow these team training principles. You can advance to the top in the honored company of those with whom you get to roll.

CHAPTER 9

Coaching and Raising a Champion

If you don't make a total commitment to whatever you're doing, then you start looking to bail out the first time the boat starts leaking. It's tough enough getting that boat to shore with everybody rowing, let alone when a guy [the coach] stands up and starts putting his jacket on.

Lou Holtz, football coach

A primary goal of nearly every competitive bowler is, quite simply, to win. An equivalent mission for coaches is to help them win. The bowling world has both coaches and college programs to whom everyone tips their hats when referenced. The list of esteemed, productive bowling coaches is long and generally agreed on. Elements of exceptional coaching always show up in the winner's circle. No one achieves greatness on his or her own.

Coaching comes in many forms: personal mentors, team leaders, even your own spouse. The best coaches are identified experts who can teach the game, highlight blind spots, and inspire individuals and teams. World-class coaching hones your physical game, strengthens your mental game, and teaches you to play well with teammates.

They say that a doctor who treats himself has a fool for a patient. I don't know if a bowler who relies only on self-coaching has a fool for a student, but I do know that no bowler can spot all the holes in his physical, mental, and team game. In this chapter we'll examine some of the prime elements of successful coaching, as well as effective parenting, of the championship athlete.

When looking at recent collegiate, PBA, national, and international championship individuals and teams, the backbone of great coaching is easily seen under the jersey. Similarly, the other potent source of successful versus unsuccessful player development starts early, and sometimes extends through the competitive life cycle. This, of course, is parenting.

Although the power and influence of a parent is most salient for youth bowlers, what a parent or mentor does in relationship with their player does not end when that child grows up. Whether it's through direct continued contact, or simply remaining present in the player's mind, the impact of parent and player interactions can't be overstated.

As we move through the chapter, virtually every reference to a coach can be translated into parent-child dynamics as well. For the most part, I'll leave the extension of language from "coach" to "parent" up to you.

CREDIBLE VERSUS INTIMIDATING COACHING

**A coach is someone who can give correction
without causing resentment.**

John Wooden, NCAA Championship basketball coach

In the old days, the predominant image of the coach was an intimidating, ranting, military sergeant. The belief was that if enough fear was generated, athletes would focus better. Indeed, in some parts of the world, this is still a prevalent coaching ethic. At times, the international community witnesses coaching that might be labeled abusive.

As coaching has evolved, it's become clear that athletes respond best to coaches who run on their credibility, not their whips. Today's athlete wants a coach who can communicate, relate, teach, and be trusted. Yes, it's possible to teach, and to win, without having all the aspects discussed next. But the most consistently effective coaching is based on these standards.

Seven Principles of Stellar Coaching (Janssen and Dale 2006)*

1. **Great coaches walk the walk.** In bicycle-racing terms, no one wants to draft someone who's slower than themselves. When you have a coach, she need not be able to bowl better than you, but she should have the ethics and integrity that makes you willing to trust and follow her.

When you're with a coach who has characteristics of integrity, commitment, and standards of conduct, you tend to believe what they're attempting to teach. There's also a professionalism and pride in presentation that trickles

*Source material for the seven principles was drawn from *The Seven Secrets of Successful Coaches*. Jeff Janssen helps coaches and athletes develop the team chemistry, mental toughness, and leadership skills necessary to win championships. www.jeffjanssen.com

down to the bowler and influences how she competes and carries herself. Coaches like this teach essential character development qualities that work everywhere, on and off the lanes.

Coaching tip 1:
**A lot of our success . . . has to do with character.
And at the heart of character is honesty and integrity.**

Mike Krzyzewski, basketball coach, U.S. national team and Duke

2. **Great coaches know the technical aspects of the inner game.** It goes almost without saying that great coaches know about footwork, swing fundamentals, releases, lane-play strategies, and ball dynamics. However, as any student of the game knows, there's a lot here to master! In most professions, individuals are required to practice continuing education as part of their professional licensure. Coaches and parents probably should do that, too. The other aspect of being a professional is in knowing the extents and limits of one's knowledge of the game.

At one of the USBC coaching conferences I drew a big square on the flipchart paper and asked the following question, "If this square represents all there is to know about bowling, how much would you color in?" I heard various answers about shading in portions of the square, until one wise soul said, "There's not a dot small enough to show how much more there is to know about this game." Unfortunately, many coaches think that because they were bowlers, or because they have achieved an advanced certification, they have it knocked. But that is no place to stop developing. Masters of anything are always seeking to deepen their understanding of their craft.

Coaching tip 2:
**Sometimes the most important listening you do
is the listening that comes after you've reached the top,
after you've gotten very good and could be susceptible
to the idea that you know everything. Even though
you're having a lot of success, you still have to be open.**

Dan Gable, former wrestling coach, University of Iowa

3. **Great coaches consistently demonstrate their commitment to their athletes.** A committed coach has thought about you. They have a vision of what you and your team might become. They have a compass and a map for how to get you where you are going. What they are doing is more than a job, they have passion for the whole package, including players, championship training, and for the crucible of the competition arena.

In chapter 8, on team building, we discussed this aspect extensively. Even if you're coaching only one athlete, the two of you are a team. Read this chapter, and the entire team-building chapter, from that perspective.

The coach must have the internal resources to handle whatever challenges and adversity might show up for an individual or team. Internal resources can mean many things, including emotional IQ, confidence, trust, and commitment. The coach must be able to stare at virtually any shot, any event, any pothole in the road, and say, "No worries, we've got this. I've been here before." Players will be instilled with confidence that they can handle anything that comes up in competition or training sessions.

Coaching tip 3:
I've been fortunate that my commitment almost demands
that the players have the same type of commitment. . . .
I think the commitment I give them sort of asks
for them to give that back without me saying anything.

Roy Williams, basketball coach, University of North Carolina

4. **Great coaches care about their athletes in very real and personal way.** As a player, you know whether how you feel, and who you are, matters to your coach. When you know that about your coach, it helps you to get past fatigue, disappointment, and frustration. It is like having someone who walks with you through the dark places. There is nothing like it

A coach is not required to be her bowler's counselor or caretaker. However, particularly for high-level players, it quickly becomes apparent whether a coach is in it for her own ego or to take care of her bowler(s). This is particularly true for coaches of high-profile and famous players. They can certainly enjoy their players' successes, but the success belongs to the players. The coach's part in it is mostly private.

Coaching tip 4:
I know if somebody really cares about me
and is really fighting for me, I'll go through a wall for them.
The same works in reverse. If somebody knows you don't care
about him and aren't really fighting for him,
then he won't go through the wall for you.

Mike Shanahan, football coach, Washington Redskins

5. **Great coaches are confidence generators.** This does not mean that they are cheerleaders. Rather a coach must have a vision of a player that's both realistic but perhaps higher than the player has for himself. Simply put, the coach must believe in the player even when the player loses faith in himself.

When a great coach works with bowlers, the bowlers tend to feel good about their capabilities and their chances when competing. They appreciate the probability that they'll achieve their short- and long-term goals. This is a tricky bit of business for coaches. On the one hand, they must challenge their players to go beyond their present skill set; on the other hand, they must convey the absolute belief in their players' abilities to get where they say they want to go.

There's a theory of learning that claims individuals learn by being stretched just beyond their current capability. If they reach too far, they fall. If they reach too little, they lose interest. It's the coach's job to encourage his bowlers, to assist in designing their "stretches," and to help them understand that the learning, growth, and competition process is a rising, jagged slope on a graph. Eventually the low points are higher than the high points once were. Learning, like coaching, is a process (Feldman 2014).

Coaching tip 5:
When people realize that someone has faith in them,
productivity usually increases. We have a natural desire
to not want to disappoint those who believe in us and trust us.

Tom Osborne, legendary football coach, University of Nebraska

6. **Great coaches are masterful at practical communication.** Whether it is through language, modeling, demonstration, or experiential exercises, great coaches know how to land their teaching points. These days, particularly with the coaching training programs now available, it's more common for coaches to have an ever-increasing sophistication about the game. But a common mistake among coaches is to rely on a very limited set of verbal and demonstrative communication skills.

Everyone learns differently. Most spoken communication gets distorted, at least slightly. Great coaches watch to see the impact of their coaching interventions; then they make adjustments in what, and how, they communicate in order to be most effective with their players.

Different situations demand shifts in coaching messages, coaching intensity, and coaching style. Whether a player is winning, losing, tiring, or becoming overexcited, responsive coaching is called for. As a coach gains depth in knowing her players, she should gain commensurate depth in knowing how best to communicate with them.

Many coaches stick to a limited range of communication styles and strategies. There's no one right way to talk or intervene. Just like learning to play different parts of the lane, a coach must learn different modes of interacting with her athletes. Like players, coaches must have more than a house shot.

Coaching tip 6:
You have to listen to develop meaningful relationships with people . . .
you can't do that by talking. You do that by listening.

Pat Summitt, legendary women's basketball coach, University of Tennessee

7. **Great coaches stand for standards of training, conduct, and competition composure.** A coach must be clear about practicing and training, competitive attitudes and gamesmanship, and application of team rules. Coaches should be prepared to address breaches in training schedule, poor sportsmanship, and infractions involving alcohol and drug use.

There are many situations, pressures, and tensions that might cause a coach to lose his grasp of training and competition needs. The coach must know what he stands for ahead of time. Players need to be able to count on a coach having an even keel during the ups, downs, and heat of matches. There's an old saying that all battle plans change once you engage the fray. But great coaches make the necessary adjustments without surrendering who they are. This sort of consistency builds trust, confidence, and a sense of security among players.

Coaching tip 7:
If your actions inspire others to dream more,
learn more, do more and become more, you are a leader.

John Quincy Adams

IF IT'S TO BE, IT'S UP TO ME

It's not just the coach who's responsible for adhering to the seven principles discussed previously. If you're reading this as a parent, or as a player, let these principles be your compass points. If you really want to reach for the stars, review the principles and ask yourself how you can improve in your integration and execution of any of them. Every coach, parent, and player who wants to be truly great must be individually responsible.

Every time you read this book, pretend it's New Year 's Eve and you're making next year's resolutions. If you're willing to declare a resolution that stretches your current abilities, adopt the strengthening of each of these seven principles for yourself. If you coach others, adopt them for those who rely on you.

No one's perfect in all of these measures. But if you look at the best team programs, you'll see these coaching principles at work in full force. The same is true for the top bowlers. These principles apply everywhere. No one ever plays worse when they're in effect. Stars are waiting to be born every day. These coaching standards are the cradle within which they happen.

MAGIC COACHING

Science you don't know looks like magic.

Christopher Moore, author

This chapter is about getting better. Whether you're coaching or being coached, you're reading this chapter, so this probably fits well with your personal agenda. Improving one's bowling is a tricky process. Helping someone else to improve their bowling goes beyond tricky . . . it's like magic.

There is a technology to the coaching side of change. But few break it down. Every coach wants to help his players be great, but it's a rare and special thing when both a coach and an athlete are willing to do what it takes for the player to become exceptional. More rare still is the existence of a coach–athlete relationship that allows the athlete to reach maximum potential.

Players want to get better. The coach wants his players to get better. So, if everyone wants to get better, how come so few players are willing to change . . . anything? And if we really look, the same question may be asked of us coaches as well.

One-Shot Coaching

In the mythology of coaching, if you can just give enough information, the bowler should get better. If this were true, all anyone would have to do is read one of the excellent coaching books available or attend one of the workshops at USBC's coaching convention.

You could set up some sessions with one of the master coaches in your area. That's a good bet. The upside of this is that you're quite likely to get some tips, feedback, and teaching that will improve your game. The downside is that no single tip or piece of coaching generally lasts for long. One-shot coaching can help for sure, but true transformation as a bowler takes time, repetition, and often an ongoing coaching relationship. Good coaches know the game. Great coaches can spot nuances that lead them to suggest improvements in bowlers' approaches and deliveries.

"Magic coaches" do something exceptional. They not only know the game, and know what they are seeing in their bowlers, but they pave the way for real improvement. It's said that everyone wants to get better, but no one really wants to have to change to do it. Magic coaching is a relationship and a set of training practices that produces lasting change.

Throughout this book we've looked at aspects of what makes the great bowlers great. In this chapter we'll do the same for great coaches.

> **Each person holds so much power within themselves
> that needs to be let out. Sometimes they just need a little nudge,
> a little direction, a little support, a little coaching,
> and the greatest things can happen.**
>
> Pete Carroll, football coach

Why Bowlers Don't Change

With decades of refinement in coaching training, levels of coaching advancement, and access to camps and clinics, one would think that bowlers would be getting better in a big way. But if you talk to experts in the field, the general consensus is that scores are going up because of lane conditions and power balls, not because players are getting any better.

So, there's no shortage of information available on how to change and improve. Why don't players just learn and do the right things?

Well, let's examine that. I don't want to be moralistic, but look at the following:

- If you go to any local gym on January 3rd, of any year, it looks like a fitness party has been started; the place is packed. Two months later, if you go, it's like you own the place. Where did everybody go?
- Almost every person you ever met says he would have gotten better grades in school if he would have studied or tried harder. Most of them knew at the time this would have worked. They just didn't do it.
- Despite the suffering that comes with marginal results and personal limitations on bowling execution, many players fall back into their habitual styles of play and technique, even after investing in camps, coaching, and other instruction.

Do people really change? Sometimes. Can bowlers change with coaching? Yes. Will they? Believe it or not, this often depends on the coach as much as the player. In order to have maximum effectiveness, a magic coach needs to understand five pillars of transformation:

1. **First and foremost, athletes who state clearly that they are motivated to improve physically and mentally have a better shot at doing what it takes to make changes.** Otherwise stated, if an athlete isn't asking for coaching help, she isn't going to take it.

2. **Second, an athlete passively agreeing that coaching would be helpful, or even paying a coach, is not as predictive of long-term success as declaring they are driven to improve.** You have to listen to what they say, and whether they have a thrust of credibility in their speaking. The bowler's changes and adjustments must be more important to her than they are to the coach.

3. **Change and growth are natural processes.** It happens all the time if conditions are right. Coaches can orient back to the most basic laws of learning—there are only two signals that get through to the brain: comfort and discomfort (or pain and pleasure).

Coaches must work with this law of human behavior. If an athlete isn't integrating coaching suggestions, there's a reason—something else is more comfortable or important than doing what you said to do. Or something the coach offered is markedly uncomfortable for the athlete. These are the house rules. Athletes will change and grow when they see and feel the payoffs.

4. **Athletes are influenced to change not just through receiving information but by the relationship with their coach.** Athletes' human factors come into play way more than many coaches realize. When athletes feel or fear judgment or criticism, especially from the one person they are supposed to trust the most, they lock up. In essence, they choke. Athletes must feel they can trust their coach.

Almost universally, if an athlete respects his coach, he'll want the acceptance and approval of that coach. If there's any thought that there could be ridicule, the athlete won't take the risks to develop new skills.

More to the point, athletes will go farther, train longer, endure more frustration, and trust the changes they need to make, if they feel they're in a connected relationship with their coach. Left to their own devices, most people will revert to what's familiar, safe, and comfortable, as soon as they get tired or don't see immediate results.

5. **Coaches can coach far more effectively, and athletes will positively surrender to the coaching, if the athlete feels that the coach knows what she feels like from the inside.** This one is a magic bullet. If an athlete thinks her coach gets what it feels like to be her—physically, mentally, and emotionally—she'll accept coaching far more easily. She'll also follow her coach to heck and back—this is the power of perceived empathy. In short, empathy effects change, and gives a coach's interventions credibility.

The single best predictor of lasting change is confidence, on the part of the athlete and the coach, that the athlete will incorporate the needed changes. For athletes, confidence comes and goes. Confidence needs to last far longer and greater for coaches than it does for athletes.

When a magic coach teaches skills, he must truly believe that the athlete is capable of incorporating these skills. When the athlete learns a new skill or way of competing she will periodically get frustrated, tired, or discouraged. Moreover, she'll subconsciously test her coach to see if he'll go along with that frustration or discouragement. The coach shouldn't take the bait. If the coach wants to be magic, he must hold onto the ideal of what the athlete can do.

The word *confidence* comes from the Latin *confidare*, which literally means "with faith." Athletes lose faith in themselves sometimes, but coaches should never lose faith in their athletes. When a coach loses faith, it's like the captain of the ship putting on a life jacket and jumping overboard. Who's left to get it done? Coaches should strive to be magic. It's their job to keep the faith in their athletes until the athletes regain faith in their own capabilities.

> **Magic is believing in yourself;**
> **if you can do that, you can make anything happen.**
>
> **Goethe**

Confrontation and Humiliation Do Not Work!

Here's a news flash: Making athletes feel bad doesn't help them learn new skills, make changes under pressure, or play better. Despite this, coaches often chastise players for failing to integrate new skills fast enough, for forgetting what they've learned, or for making mistakes as they're working on their learning curve.

If you think the old-school approach is the way to go, and that bowlers should be able to handle a little guff, let's consider something that's even older school—human behavior. The normal response to confrontation, humiliation, or disrespect is to feel stressed in a number of ways.

When an athlete feels disrespected, she must do something inside of herself to reestablish self-respect. So what does she do with her coach, either aloud or in her head? The athlete who feels disrespected or put down by her coach must either defend herself, discount her coach's words, or think the coach is a jerk. What follows is a host of negative results. The athlete withdraws from training, withdraws from her coach, stops paying attention, and gives no credibility to what the coach is trying to teach.

The Four Steps to Magic Transformations*

Any sufficiently advanced technology is indistinguishable from magic.

Arthur C. Clarke

Let's operationalize these transformation pillars. Make sure that you have these next four steps in order. When you execute magic coaching properly, it is amazing how athletes respond.

1. **Connect.** It seems so obvious, but every coach needs to know the following: His ability to understand his bowler(s) is one of the best predictors of lasting positive outcomes.

Magic begins with understanding what makes bowling so important to a particular athlete, understanding what would make the frustration of learning new skills worth it, and understanding what it physically feels like to bowl both the old way and the new way. This is truly connecting with an athlete.

2. **Focus on the specific change to be made, to the exclusion of everything else.** This can be surprisingly hard to do. Whether it's hand position, steps, release, targeting, or whatever, "only the thing is the thing." The coach breaks the skill down nonjudgmentally and isolates what he's teaching. Then he builds the new skill into the bigger picture. In these moments, the skill changes have to be more important than pin-fall, or looking good.

3. **Determine if the athlete can distinguish the old way from the new way.** The magic comes when the athlete can feel the changes, identify the benefits of what the coach is coaching her to do, and feels more comfortable with the new way than with the old way.

---

*Some source material for this section drawn from Miller WR, Rollnick S. *Motivational Interviewing.* London: Guilford Press, 1991

4. **Elicit a real commitment to work on, and execute, the skills being taught.** Many clinics, and much coaching, are based on hit-and-run attacks. But all integrated change occurs through follow-up and practice. One-hit interventions might seem to make solid impact, but it's the follow-up practice behaviors that determine what takes hold in the long run.

Think about it. You could give the greatest Spanish lesson in the world. Right afterward your student could speak several phrases. But if that student did not immerse himself in continued practice, he would go back to using English exclusively, and most of the Spanish would be lost. The same is true of bowling instruction. Commitments, plans, and structured follow-up practices are vital.

Everyone wants to get better. Almost no one wants to change. But there are exceptions. If a coach knows how to make magic, she can create the space that allows for real transformation.

These are simple steps that work like the laws of nature. Perhaps there are ceilings on what individuals can learn and do, but most bowlers are far from reaching that ceiling. This is no trick. You *can* create magic.

It's still magic even if you know how it's done.

Terry Pratchett, author, *A Hat Full of Sky*

ADVANCED COACHING CONCEPTS

In this section we'll look at advanced coaching interventions. Like the rest of the chapter, this section is aimed at coaches but pertains to parenting an athlete as well. Let's start with four questions.

1. What is the most important aspect of teaching and coaching?
2. What would you have to learn and develop to be paid $200 an hour two years from now, and to have your athletes comment that you were well worth that kind of fee?
3. Have you seen your bowlers get more joy and enjoyment out of the game; how are the joy meters running?
4. Are your bowlers better able to coach themselves, or are they better at the process of training and learning?

In this section I'll take a stab at answering these four questions.

Here's the typical coaching curriculum: Coaches teach how to develop more power, how to shoot spares, and other specific skills and techniques; they assess bowlers, spot faults, and try to fix them; they teach the fundamentals of the game. In all these pursuits, they use technology to aid them.

There are some major problems with this traditional approach. First, assuming your bowlers want to get better, so they can both win competitions and enjoy the game more, the traditional approach will often not get this done.

Second, the most important aspects of teaching and coaching are left out of this approach.

So, what are the most important aspects of teaching and coaching? There are at least four: enhancing performance, reinvigorating enjoyment, teaching the bowler to self-coach, and strengthening the mental game.

1. **Enhancing performance.** Coaches, of course, coach both the physical and mental game. The coach sees and knows things that are outside of the player's awareness. As a matter of course, you will eventually share everything that you can see. The trick is to offer skill enhancement that stretches a player, but is not so far above his capability that failure to execute creates too much frustration. Most important, see if the player's perception of what she's doing matches what you see her doing.

2. **Rediscovering the love of the game.** If you ask most bowlers what they enjoy about the game, by the time they're in high school they'll answer "striking" or "scoring." Neither of these is actually bowling. They are the results of bowling. It's math. It's best to love the game of bowling not just for the results but for the simple joy that free motion can bring.

Many bowlers have forgotten the simple joy in the movements involved in rolling a ball: the perfect timing of the push-away, the pause at the top of the backswing, a clean thumb release, the balanced posting of the shot, to name a few.

To truly love the game, you must love how the game feels when you play it. At the 2015 World Series of bowling I asked PBA champion Lonnie Waliczek what motivated him. His response, "It's not competition. I just love the feeling of throwing great shots. It's what turns half-hour practice sessions into three-hour ones."

3. **Teaching the bowler to self-coach.** Coaches want their players to be like self-cleaning ovens, able to diagnose and adjust themselves. Players should learn to keep their minds clear and open immediately after rolling the ball. They should be able to detect what changes must be made in terms of lane play, physical action, and their mental game. This involves both education and awareness. If they don't learn to self-monitor, bowlers can become overly dependent on their coach.

Along these lines, it seems that the classic primary medium of exchange in coaching bowling is "the tip". I'm generally skeptical about tips. Perhaps one good tip is to cut down on tips. Sure, tips sell magazines and lessons, but they foster dependency on the coach and interfere with the bowler's ability to self-monitor and transform herself. Also, no tip, in and of itself, lasts as a cure-all for anyone's bowling. Just like keeping a car in tune, the critical feature is to notice what is out of alignment, so you can adjust it.

4. **Strengthening the mental game.** The purpose of the mental game is to be free, focused, and forwarding. Think of the three Fs. To be free means

to be unencumbered by thoughts of the past and the future, doubts and fears. To be focused is to hold attention in the present moment on whatever seems most useful at the time. To be forwarding means to be present and aware of what's happening, to learn with each shot, and to make the required changes and adjustments. All of this can, and should, be coached. (A focus and attention exercise later in the chapter facilitates coaching the mental game.)

COACHING AS A PROCESS

Test fast, fail fast, adjust fast.

Tom Peters, writer on business management practices

Real coaching involves learning on the part of the bowler, leading ultimately to self-coaching. How do you know when bowlers have really learned something? You know it when they don't need positive self-talk to accomplish what they want to do.

It requires no self-talk to raise your spoon to your mouth, yet you can repeat this "shot" flawlessly. You don't have to self-talk to walk to the car, get in, and start it up. The reason for this is that you have overlearned these "moves" to the degree that self-guidance is not necessary. And if you trip, or slip, or stumble, you self-correct immediately. One's bowling can come near to this, and it should during competition.

THE BEST TIP

Here's how most tips work:

1. First, you're given a swing or timing tip that seems to work.
2. There's a feeling of relief, maybe even joy that you found a key to the game. Life is good.
3. You might feel like you have unlocked your game.
4. You stay with the thought, but it starts to lose its magic.
5. Your old game starts to come back.
6. You cling more tightly to the tip thought.
7. Anger, fear, or frustration seep in.
8. You're back to where you started, or nearly so.

This process is like getting a tip on car care. Say that someone tells you to keep your car's tire pressure at a certain number. It's a good tip. The car drives well. You're ready to travel. There are, of course, all kinds of other things you could be attentive to as you drive, but you count on that tire pressure. The windshield gets dirty. The car needs gas. Perhaps there's a ping in the engine. But tire pressure? A-OK!

The point is, if you maintain awareness of whatever might be wrong as you travel, the trip will go well. The car needs gas; you get gas. You hear a ping in the engine; you buy a higher grade of gas. But if your attention is locked in on the tire pressure, a lot can go wrong before you even notice it.

It works the same with bowling. Getting a tip on a perfect push-away, and hence better timing, is wonderful, but if you think this will unlock and "fix" your game, then of course you're mistaken. The vehicle that is called an athlete needs constant attention and tuning. Tips don't work nearly as well as your own self-awareness.

The primary source of failure of most bowling instruction ("tips") is that people attempt to fix, teach, and improve things that the athlete himself has not experienced. Awareness is curative. Think of it this way—if you gave a player a shot of Novocain in the hand, and then tried to work on thumb release, you would fail. Players must be able to feel the things they're trying to adjust.

The best coaching tip is this: Attempting to change things a bowler is not experiencing ensures that the changes won't stick. This is where careful attention, video, and any other coaching tools to increase player awareness come in. The point is for the bowler to catch herself in the process of doing whatever she's doing. What we're aware of, we can change. If we're not aware of something, if we can't feel ourselves doing it, for better or for worse we are stuck with it.

Self-Awareness Goals

Players will improve most quickly and effectively when they can identify and feel what is going on inside of them. A coach can give the greatest gift by instructing bowlers how to self-assess in the following areas:

1. How to spot the critically important aspects of their games that aren't present on their radar screens but which need attention.

2. How to experience (feel) the variations in those blind spots and how they affect delivery.

3. How to bridge the gap between what they think is happening and what's really happening—matching internal reality to external reality.

FOCUS AND ATTENTION EXERCISE

One of the most important mental skills for bowlers to learn is to focus their attention. There's a really good exercise that facilitates this process. This exercise is one way to both fill in blind spots and to learn relaxed concentration.

1. First, pick a point of attention before rolling a shot. This point can be external, such as a spot on the lane. It can be physical, such as your elbow, shoulder, or hand, or your step cadence. It can also be almost

metaphysical, such as focusing on your overall relaxation or freedom of motion.

2. Note exactly where your attention is right before rolling your shot. The most important thing is to keep your attention right there.

3. Determine where your attention is one second after your stroke is completed.

4. Assess whether your focus remained entirely on the identified point, or if it shifted either during your approach or right after your release. The objective is to be present to your point of focus from beginning to end.

What usually happens is this. A player's intention is either vague, or in a number of places at once. True commitment doesn't occur. The player's attention moves to several points throughout her approach and delivery. And, finally, her thoughts and reactions after her shot are really a judgmental review of what happened. They tend to be more concerned with making a good or bad shot than with maintaining focus on the declared intention.

Almost all players shift their attention, usually to check the results of their shot, even when they're trying to learn a new skill. If you've been bowling for 10 years, you've likely thrown somewhere in the neighborhood of 50,000 shots. You have probably not maintained focused attention on only one aspect of your shot on any one of them. Many bowlers have told me that performing this exercise is the first time they've been fully present, without judgment, for a shot from beginning to end.

Relaxed concentration is the ability to be present to the point of your attention for as long as you intend. This requires curiosity about what you observe, a genuine interest in what you're doing, and the will-power to let go of every other concern.

Great bowlers are like cats watching birds in a feeder. They are alert, awake, and fascinated. They watch everyone's ball reactions, not because they are supposed to, but because the game is so interesting to them. Too them what is happening on the lanes is so important that they cannot look away.

If you can keep your attention on one aspect of either the lanes, your body, or the freedom of your execution throughout the entirety of the shot, three vital things occur. First, you learn a lot about the object of your focus. Second, there's no room for doubt or interference to enter your mind. Last, anything else that might be important has space to easily enter your field of awareness. Probably the most important time for learning is right after your release. Much of the feedback you need is most available at that moment.

Great moments in bowling will occur most often when you can maintain your focus in a relaxed state. Good things happen less often when you're agitated, or thinking of multiple things at once.

TEACHING THE LOVE OF THE GAME

**Somewhere behind the athlete you've become
and the hours of practice and the coaches who have pushed you
is a little girl who fell in love with the game
and never looked back . . . play for her.**

Mia Hamm, Olympic soccer star

There are many aspects of the bowling experience that originally engaged players but got lost in the process of trying to score, win, and get better. Players love to strike, score, and win of course, but that is really all mathematics. The game itself, like a gymnastics event, feels awesome. Balance, timing, mastery of movement, power, and flow all feel amazing. But we forget to focus on those feelings as a primary target.

For instance, if you ask a youth gymnast what she loves about gymnastics, you might get answers such as how fun it is to flip, how good it feels to re-grip the bar after a release move, or the pleasurable feeling of balance with a stuck dismount. Note that these remarks involve how good the activity itself feels—they're not based on score.

Similarly, bowling is really a gymnastic event. It involves balance, movement, timing, and execution. For most bowlers, it feels good to bowl well. They just forget to focus on that. The possible sources of enjoyment in bowling are many:

- The assured comfort of a balanced starting position
- The intuitive sense of well-being in good timing
- The weightless hang of the ball at the top of the backswing
- A clean release
- The joy of the tug of the fingers at the bottom of the swing

Focusing on the parts of the game that are inherently physically enjoyable serves several purposes. As mentioned earlier, it clears distracting thoughts and provides a single point of attention. It gets bowlers involved in the process of bowling instead of results-oriented thinking. And focusing on the most enjoyable parts of one's approach and release is an amazing pressure-release valve during competition.

A good coach can reinvigorate the love of bowling for his bowlers. If a coach doesn't know which part of his players' games are their favorites, he has something essential to learn. It's important for coaches to be successful in getting players to recognize and remember the pleasures involved in the sport. Players will then understand that feeling great while bowling can be one of the biggest contributors to scoring and winning.

There are two kinds of coaches: those who see their athletes as different from themselves, and those who are willing to walk the walk. Players will mirror and mimic their coach's commitment, enthusiasm, and faith in their progress. In this game stars often come from stars. If you are a coach, thank you for making a difference.

SUMMARY CHECKLIST FOR COACHING THE CHAMPION BOWLER

Most would wish that they had made that spare.
I wish that I would have reacted better to it.

Lonnie Waliczek, commenting on a missed washout spare that cost him a PBA title

Every bowler who shows up on the field of play brings himself, equipment, and his "team" to every competition. The "self" is comprised of an individual's training, ability, and psychology. Equipment is self-explanatory. "Team" is an athlete's experience of his support network, including coaches, teammates, friends, and family.

No matter what level of competition, families that support each other properly have the best experiences, and often the best results. The same is true for the student–coach relationship. Whether a coach is present for an event, or present in an athlete's mind, virtually every youth player carries a sense of his coaches, his parents, and all that comes with that, to every game. The following is a set of guidelines and principles designed to maximize the support, growth, and freedom to play of every bowler.

The Principles

1. **Your bowler can see, feel, and sense your facial expression before, during, and after shots.** You unconditionally support and appreciate your athlete's participation in the contest. They should never feel that your encouragement, liking, or love is based on performance.

2. **You are the pilot—remain calm under all circumstances.** Your bowler is like a passenger on your airplane. Flight crews and passengers take a read on the pilot's response to turbulence and the demands of travel. They then respond to the pilot's attitude. Similarly, your reactions to shots, lane conditions, and fair or unfair results will steer your bowler's responses and effectiveness in the competition environment.

3. **Although you're "wired" to mentally, physically, or emotionally react to your bowler's game, learn to develop distance from immediate events.** For instance, parents react to any significant event in their child's life (e.g., the first bicycle ride with training wheels; falling over on that bike; in bowling, a made or missed spare). Your ability to create some psychological and emotional distance from the immediacy of competition will build a supportive environment, as well as teach your bowler to respond more effectively when competing.

4. **Refrain from too much coaching input during competition.** By and large, some of the input you give during a tournament can be experienced by your bowler as judgment and pressure. This can be exceptionally difficult to reel in when you can see what's happening on the lanes. The exceptions to this are if the relationship you have allows for this level of input during competition, or if your bowler is actively asking for help.

5. **Wait for a period of time following any event to give your analysis or feedback.** When emotion is running high, there's little room to absorb information. If things did not go well, your feedback will be taken as criticism. Give some time and space.

6. **Emphasize the importance of your bowlers' reactions to their shots and game well beyond the importance of results.** Great shots and great results come and go. The only thing that lasts is character, attitude, and resiliency. You must be consistent in the behaviors and values that work in the long run. Learning to be poised before and after shots builds confidence and mental toughness.

7. **When results are great, ask if anything could have been done better. When results are disappointing, focus on what was done well.** In either case, allow for some time and emotional settling to occur.

8. **Share in goal setting, mental game preparation, and behavioral expectations.** Before league play or a tournament, discuss sportsmanship, employing good mental game principles, and how to react to shots. If you or your bowlers wait until the competition lights are on to do this, it's too late. They should have a plan for physical execution, demeanor, reactions, and sportsmanship.

9. **Combat "choking" by emphasizing that the most valuable and courageous quality is the willingness to train, prepare, and put one's self on the field of play, not on makes and misses.** Few people have the commitment and fortitude to train like champions and to risk entering competitions. If pride is appropriately placed on these character qualities, it depressurizes performance shots.

10. **Make a plan ahead of time for the nature of coaching contact during the competition.** Discuss whether there will be contact, connection, feedback, or even encouragement during competition. Bowlers are prone to overinterpret the meaning of everything a coach or parent does. Discuss ahead of time the meaning of being quiet, leaving to get food, or anything else. Bowlers are prone to assuming that everything you do is related to how they're performing.

**I've never felt my job was to win basketball games—
rather, that the essence of my job as a coach
was to do everything I could to give my players
the background necessary to succeed in life.**

Bobby Knight, basketball coach

SPECIAL CONSIDERATIONS IN PARENTING YOUTH BOWLERS

At the end of the day, the most overwhelming key to a child's success is the positive involvement of parents.

Jane D. Hull, politician

There are two special considerations that come up fairly frequently in parenting the youth bowler. The first has to do with balance in life; the second concerns potential conflicts between parents and coaches.

Balancing Bowling with Life

Parents' interest and investment in a child's athletic success can be a bonding experience for both parties. However, problems can ensue when the focus is on bowling rather than balancing attention with other significant life concerns. It has been said that successful lives are based on fulfilling play, fulfilling love, and fulfilling work. Successful parenting trains and teaches to all three of these vital aspects.

Few individuals on the planet are making a living solely at bowling. Many of the game's superstars can boast successful college careers. Many high-achieving bowlers have careers that occur simultaneously with, or immediately after, their professional bowling lives.

Most children and adolescents are supremely geared to responding to stimuli that feel good or bad, things that pay off or don't, in the immediate moment. So it has always been the parent's job to ensure a balanced approach to school, health, and social development. These are the things that have long-term consequences, but aren't clearly felt in the moment by many youth players.

Not only does attending to school, attitude, and solid self-care have the obvious benefits of preparing your child for the larger game of life, but the more balanced the life of the individual player, the less pressured and stressful the competitive bowling experience will be. Quite simply, when people know who and what they are, that's far greater than any particular shot or tournament. That player is free to execute shots without fearing he'll fall from grace because of a bowling stumble.

The Parent as Coach

Another parenting quandary that can occur is when a parent who has, or doesn't have, bowling experience attempts to coach a son or daughter. The child has two competing drives. One is to enjoy the love and acceptance of their parent. The other is to individuate, literally to become a separate individual.

Any time a parent coaches her own child, the two roles of coach and parent are both present, and can be easily confused. It's critical that the parent clearly delineate which hat she's wearing during training and competition.

■ Making Parents Your Allies With Jeri Edwards

If you can help these kids in excellence to reach and strive, they'll just do that all the time.

Jeri Edwards, Bowling Coaches Hall of Fame

Jeri Edwards has coached bowling in more countries than most people will visit in a lifetime. The former Team USA head coach and current head coach of the Puerto Rican national team has seen the good, the bad, and the ugly with respect to parents, coaches, and kids. She has had phenomenal success in leading young athletes to medals, scholarships, and professional careers on and off the lanes. Jeri knows how to win, and she knows what parents and coaches can do to facilitate championship play.

Courtesy of the United States Bowling Congress

Jeri recognizes what it means for parents to have to step back from the competition floor when their child is playing. She advises that coaches communicate with parents early on. "From a coaching perspective, it's very valuable to have an opportunity to meet with the parents, and to be clear about ground rules as a coach."

"Not all coaches handle it the same. If I'm the head coach, the buck stops with me. I'm the one making the decisions here. And it just has to be clear. It's hard when you have a child who is playing, and you as a parent have also coached that child all these years. It's hard to let go, and give a child permission to work with teammates and the coach, and change first points of contact."

To make sure that a child is not put in the middle, there must be a clear delineation of coaching versus parenting responsibilities. "It's not easy, but some guidelines and parameters need to be set. Everyone has to be on the same page. Lines of communication need to be clear."

Years ago, there was this child, Amanda Burgoyne (now Amanda Vermilyea), smallish in stature, upbeat, with an unceasing work ethic. It might not have appeared that this young girl was going to become one of the best youth bowlers in the United States, helping her Nebraska team win an NCAA championship and becoming a stalwart for Team USA, but she did.

Most people, in analyzing the rising slope of success for this young player, would have focused on only the athlete herself. Coach Edwards saw a bigger picture. In breaking down the path to success for Amanda, Jeri repeatedly cited the family system. About the parents (Jeff and Jane Burgoyne), she noted, "They had a tremendous amount of acceptance. They were great, supportive parents. They knew a lot about Amanda's game, and they also let her play. I never saw a disappointed face or heard a negative word."

On the other end of the continuum, Coach Edwards comments on the kind of parenting that can stifle a child's love of the game. "It's feeling like there is a lot of judgment and not a lot of acceptance, not looking for anything solution related. The parents ask unanswerable questions, like, "Why aren't you bowling better? Why aren't you striking? Especially if it's a parent who doesn't bowl a lot, and the child is playing on something that isn't a house pattern, and they don't understand why their kid isn't scoring highly."

"I think sometimes there have been parents who have been living through their kids. There are a couple of places where they are questioning the kid's abilities, motives, and raising doubt. 'Why aren't you bowling better?' Creating doubt and fear in an athlete who's already struggling. It snowballs. It turns into a fireworks show that is not pretty."

"When you're out there, when you're on the stage, you're putting yourself out there. It requires confidence and poise to pull that off. You need to know that someone's got your back and that they are there for you."

Parents can turn this around with some self-awareness. "It doesn't take much, but it's important to own it. To see yourself, that there are times you know you looked down or rolled your eyes."

"Some parents don't understand that the (oil) pattern is more difficult and their kids are not going to average 200. I've seen parents have a look of sternness, or a look of disgust. I have seen the bad faces, the rolling of the eyes, the turning and walking away. That stuff is hard on an athlete."

"The bottom line is that kids want their parents to be proud of them. If you think that you're a disappointment, that's a really bad feeling. Kids then either get depressed or angry."

Coach Edwards highlights how attuned kids are to their parents' body language and facial expressions. "We are all geared to take cues from what someone's face is doing, particularly if things don't turn out. You're not always going to win. Perhaps you just missed that last scholarship spot, or you're not selected for the team, or you don't start. You have an opportunity as a parent to model how to handle it. Encourage the child to hang in there, and to support teammates."

Coach Edwards is clear about the treasure that youth bowling can be for a family. It's a briefly lived time that should be valued. "I think if someone is reading this book, they have an athlete that has some talent. It's a blessing that a family gets to experience this together. It builds things that the kids remember years from now."

"You are in the present with your child now. There are no guarantees in life. It's a blessing for a child to recall that they spent Saturdays with their parents behind them. Not everybody has that wonderful opportunity as a family."

In building an alliance with parents, coaches can do some things that promote family cohesion. "One of the things that I want the kids to understand is that it's a commitment from the parents to support them. It takes money and time. I think sometimes when you are young and bullet proof you don't really think about that so much."

"The parents appreciate being appreciated. The coach can best do that, especially if the coach is close to the family. The coach is a connected bystander. They can do some things that the parent can't do. If an athlete has a strong connection with the coach, they look to the coach for guidance. He or she can help them think about their family differently."

Coach Edwards says that bowling, ideally, is an opportunity for parents to teach and instruct about many things in life. "You need an adult who celebrates making a great shot, or who helps you work on solutions. Then you're teaching empowerment, instead of teaching being a victim."

"That takes discipline from a parenting or coaching standpoint. You want to focus on a gold medal effort. The majority won't be pros, but they can learn to give gold

(continued)

You must know that as much as you might think you're operating in coach mode, your child always has his radar on you as a parent. This means that teaching, suggestions, and feedback that seem neutral to you are often translated as criticism, or suppression of self, to the young player.

A person can certainly coach her own child. But it's the parent's responsibility to train and restrain her emotional reactions to what's happening on the field of play. And she must make sure she doesn't withdraw or withhold love, acceptance, and encouragement when, inevitably, her child has a bad shot or bad day on the lanes. The coach must believe that her child's attitude and demeanor while they compete is more important than any shot or result. This is life training that will never hurt performance, in any arena.

There's a mantra for parents coaching their own children: "Watch them play." If you live by these three words, you're going to be in good shape with your child.

1. When the competition starts you're there to watch, to appreciate, and to enjoy the game and your bowler.
2. At that time it is all about him (or her).
3. At the end of the day, bowling is play.

Your son or daughter should feel these sentiments coming from you.

The Coach, Parent, Player Dynamic

Sometimes just as challenging as coaching your own child is the drive to stay relevant, involved, and influential when your child has a coach other than you. There are multiple issues here. First, if you see some aspect of coaching that you disagree with, decide whether you can live with what you're observing. If you can, great—carry it off with grace and silence. This is often your best move.

But if you simply can't tolerate a coach's behavior or technical instruction, decide whether direct inquiry about coaching style or decisions will be helpful. You must assess whether direct contact with the coach will adversely affect how the coach behaves with your child, or whether the embarrassment of your young bowler overrides your need to express your viewpoint.

The exception to this is when anything akin to physical, emotional, or verbal abuse has occurred. In this case, an intervention of some kind is important, even if it's uncomfortable for your child.

You can imagine it like this. Your young player has a hand on two power poles; one is the coach, and the other is you. The less electrical current you send between those poles, through the player, the better.

Forcing a child to choose whose technical advice, lane-play strategies, and philosophies to observe creates tension and stress, and can have all kinds of emotional and athletic consequences. It might be tempting to bond with your child against a coach, but be cautious; the desire to stay connected and relevant makes sense, but in this relationship triangle there can be many unintended consequences.

In the end, help your child find what works best for him or her. No matter what she or he chooses, maintaining a certain respect for the position and authority of the coach has value, irrespective of whether there's agreement on coaching style and technical instruction.

CHAPTER 10

Putting It All Together to Play Boldly

There's an old story about a Cherokee Indian chief who was teaching his grandchild about succeeding in life.

> "A fight often goes on inside people," he said to the boy. "It is a terrible fight and it is between two wolves."
>
> "One wolf is evil—he represents fear, doubt, anger, envy, sorrow, regret, greed, arrogance, self-pity, guilt, resentment, inferiority, lies, false pride, superiority, self-doubt, and ego."
>
> "The other wolf represents good—he is confidence, self-assurance, joy, peace, love, hope, serenity, humility, kindness, benevolence, empathy, generosity, truth, compassion, and faith."
>
> "This same fight is going on inside you, and inside every other person, too."
>
> The grandson thought about it for a moment, and then asked his grandfather, "Which wolf will win?"
>
> The old chief simply replied, "The one you feed."

This is the essential question for all of us: Which wolf will we feed?

The bowling landscape is littered with the names of bowlers, some unknown, some famous, who never reached their potential as players or competitors. People might say, "Yeah, she was talented, but she just couldn't make it in international competition." Or "Sure, he has fifteen titles, but imagine how many he could have had if . . .."

This chapter is about putting it all together so that people (and yourself) aren't saying similar things about you one day. The next sections are an aggregate collection of guiding directional arrows, an application of some of the key constructs found in the book.

The goal is for you to be able to play with all you've got, with no disappointments or regrets. Also, I want you to become even more of what you really are. I'll start with some of the poison darts that take players down, and then move to the essential tools in a champion bowler's toolbox.

PLAY BOLDLY, WITH NO DOUBTS

You're not born with doubt in your ability to do anything. Doubt, like fear, is learned. In fact, because kids are so convinced they can learn or pull off anything, we're constantly monitoring children to make sure they don't do things that put them in danger. What child hasn't believed he could jump off the roof with an umbrella and float safely to earth?

We begin life believing we can do just about anything. Then life gives us feedback. Real-world feedback, like gravity, helps us to function effectively. But other feedback, such as being laughed at for falling down, criticized for spilling a drink, or yelled at for making mistakes, creates a different kind of result. We learn shame, embarrassment, and the need to self-protect.

Self-protection shows up in the nervousness and apprehension that bowlers feel when they compete. No one wants to blow it or fall short when they strive for great things. There's a chasm between our genuine desire to reach for the highest heights, and the fear of falling down in one way or another. What we fear, deep down, is the judgment that might come from ourselves or others if we fail.

In this book you have been encouraged to put 100 percent focused effort and intention into everything you do. All successful athletic feats have one element in common: faith. Your natural faith in yourself doesn't have to be learned; it has to be remembered. When you lose, or forget, faith and try too hard to control the outcomes of your shots, you die a little each time.

If you want to bowl out of your mind, you must make a decisive read on where to play and what to do, and then be done with it. Anything short of this equates to doing cautious research and development on the way to the line.

Here's an illustration of the problem. Everyone has heard of the differences in right-brain versus left-brain thinking. What follows is not scientifically accurate, but for our illustrative purposes, let's go with this. The left brain knows what you're supposed to do. The right brain gets a picture of what it intuitively knows. The right brain's impressions are based on information obtained through observation and feel. The left brain's impressions are based on what you're supposed to do given your understanding of the situation.

The intuitive part of you will generally have more say in steering your steps, your line, and your ball speed. But your left brain still has plenty of votes. The essence of second-guessing yourself boils down to being of two minds. If you could bowl with a single mind, all one consciousness, you could then bowl out of your mind.

We say it all the time, but here's the lesson we must learn first in life, and then relearn over the years, and then probably finally understand when we're on our death beds: Intention and commitment are everything. You must let go of overconcern with the outcome of anything you do, including rolling a bowling ball. You must train yourself to bowl with an undivided mind.

The universe has so much power to intervene, in the form of shifts in lane oil, pin-rack variation, approach surface, and so on, that the best you can do is to make a decisive read, go through your setup routine, and do what you have done thousands of times before. Gradually, you must learn to care less about whether a shot carries, and to care far more about whether

- you play whole-heartedly, be it in sports, business, or relationships;
- you are great sometimes;
- you have a full understanding that sometimes you'll fall hard on the field of play;
- you can forgive silly little moments of absentmindedness, or tension, or distraction, or any number of common human experiences; and
- you have the character to come back and try to do better.

PLAYING IN THE ZONE

**It's a very strange feeling. It's as if time slows down
and you see everything so clearly. You just know
that everything about your technique is spot on.
It just feels so effortless. . . . Every muscle, every fibre,
every sinew is working in complete harmony.**

Mark Richardson, sprinter, on running in the zone

There's a scene in the baseball movie *For the Love of the Game* in which the pitcher asks the catcher, "Has anyone gotten a hit yet?" It's late in the game, and a no-hitter is being pitched by the visitors in Yankee stadium. "No, Chappy," says the catcher. "No one has gotten a hit yet!" The pitcher, unaware, is simply pitching the best game of his life.

This scene is a beautiful illustration of the phenomenon that all athletes dream of achieving during competition: to play in flow, or "in the zone." In terms of a mental or emotional state, the zone is the holy grail of competitive mindsets. When you're bowling in the zone, everything happens effortlessly. Your intuition about lane transitions feels completely trustworthy. You feel as if you're bowling in your own space, with no intrusion by other bowlers, fans, or observers. Time seems to revolve around you instead of the other way around.

When you're playing in the zone, you feel good inside; you experience an almost indescribably positive emotional state. You don't think about the mechanics of how to bowl. Your focus is outward on what you intend to do.

And in the moments of play you have no real concern for how things are going to turn out.

This is an ideal state of mind for an athlete. If we could bottle it and sell it, we'd never have to work again. Although bottling, buying, or bartering for zone consciousness isn't an option, there are ways to approach the game that can enhance your chances of playing in this free and focused state. In this section we'll look at ways to maximize stepping into the river of *flow*, and letting your natural game take over.

Your Gut Feelings

First and foremost, the zone can't be reached analytically. When you're playing in the zone, your instincts run the show. There are two elements to this. Number one is complete trust in your feelings about how to move, how to play, and how to adjust, from shot to shot.

The second element, of course, is action. Playing with trust means you execute actions without questioning the gut feeling you have about your shots, your execution, and your strategy. Playing in the zone involves complete surrender to your intuition.

A Sunny Disposition

Most people play better in a positive state of mind. Negativity saps both creativity and your sense of empowerment. By contrast, when you're in a positive state of mind, your belief in yourself is much higher, your creativity and intuition are free to function fully, and your flexibility and blood flow are conducive to optimal athleticism.

There are many ways to sustain a positive frame of mind. I'll describe two of the most creative. You can recall any great shot, great performance, or great feeling you have had, in your mind's eye. Let the picture that appears in your memory generate the associated feelings of warmth, competence, and confidence. Everything should loosen up when you do this.

Another strategy is to focus on an internal thought or memory of your loved ones. Something about the sense of connection with those who are most meaningful to us opens up the channels of flow that allow us to perform freely. (Mindsport Ltd., 2007).

Look Out, Not In

During competition, your focus of attention should be different from when you're practicing. When you're learning techniques, addressing your footwork, or attending to any other aspect of changing your game, you have an inward focus. You have to. This is how you become aware of your physical adjustments. But in the heat of competition, your focus should be much more outward than inward (Mindsport Ltd., 2007). Think about it. When you teach a child how to open a car door, you might instruct her to curl her fingers and pull at the right time. The first time or two, the child must do this consciously (inwardly). But very quickly the child need not think about how to open the door anymore; she can do it outwardly, without thinking.

Of course bowling is more complex than opening a car door, but the principles are the same. When you're thinking outwardly, you're far more focused on what you intend to do with the ball, and what you'll accomplish on the lanes, because you already know you can execute the shot. Your execution is as automatic as opening a car door.

Endgame

There's an old story about a great teacher instructing her students on how to live the best possible life. At one point, one of the students raised a hand and asked a question.

> "Great Master. You have given us so many lessons on what to do in order to live a full and successful life. Can you boil it all down to make it simpler to remember?"
>
> "Absolutely," said the teacher. "Simply do all the things that you're going to do on the day before you die."
>
> "The day before you die?" asked the student. "How would anyone know when that is?"
>
> "Exactly!" smiled the instructor." One never knows. So you must live as if it's your last day of life."

If you knew that this was it, that you would not be here tomorrow, would you be able to play with no fear of your results (Mindsport Ltd., 2007)? Try it. Next time, before you begin bowling, take a moment to get into the mindset that this will be the last time you ever bowl. You're free. This is the last opportunity to show yourself, and anyone else, what there is inside of you. This strategy doesn't work for everyone, but if you feel exhilarated when you employ this technique, then stick with it. Like all strategies, if it doesn't work for you, drop it.

Don't Try Harder

If someone told you to try harder, what would you do? Most likely you would use more muscle, tense up, and get increasingly concerned about your results. Does anyone ever tell you to try more gracefully, or more fluidly? Pretty much as a rule, anything that is done with *hardness* in bowling doesn't turn out too well.

In fact, trying too hard is a half-step from desperation. Any time you attempt to make up for bad play or to force a result, you'll fly right out of the zone. Yes, you must bring effort and intention. Look for the middle ground between relaxing too much and trying too hard (Mindsport Ltd., 2007). Discover the flow, grace, and essential energy of your game. Do this without squeezing any part of your brain or body harder.

No Time

When you play with an outward focus, or in those too rare times when you slip into the zone, you enter a kind of timeless dimension. Afterward you usually have the sense that time didn't just fly—it didn't seem to exist at all. While bowling, practice becoming still in your mind, slowing everything down. If you can do this for just a moment, then you know that with training you can do it for longer. With practice, you can eventually, through your own will, control your sense of clearing everything out. One way to achieve this is to focus on enjoyment of any aspect of the moment. Revel in the opportunity to reach for the stars. Love the feel of executing movements. Enjoy the slowing down of time.

Keep Your Act Together

Every time you compete there will be pressures and distractions. Other players might be loud, or they might go out of turn. If you're bowling well, you might draw a crowd. Internally, you could experience some of the old messages about how you're supposed to perform or succeed. Any of this is enough to pull you out of the zone.

When distractions occur, you need an inoculation strategy. You must know upfront that you will keep your composure no matter happens around you. There's a harbor you can always return to in your mind. Find an aspect of your game that feels like home. Whether it's your stance, the power in your legs, the freedom of your arm swing, you should know, *This is how it feels to bowl like the real me.*

You can't enter the zone by force of will. It happens when you're completely absorbed in the moment. What fills these moments are the key physical motions that make for great shots. When you continually refocus on the enjoyment of key physical motions, you can glide right back into the zone. It's no coincidence that your performance elevates at these times as well.

Go Bowl!

For most athletes, including bowlers, playing in the zone is the most pleasurable way to play. For some it's almost a spiritual experience. Plus, when you're in the zone, you're generally playing to the highest level of your training and ability. But playing in the zone is rare. Some bowlers never get there. By reading this book, and reflecting on what you've read, the zone should become more accessible to you. You should be more likely to bowl in a frame of mind that's conducive to the zone. Try it. See what happens. Go bowling.

The more you bowl in the mindset I have described, the better your chances for experiencing flow

THE SPIRIT OF BOLD PLAY

**The spirit, the will to win, and the will to excel
are the things that endure.
These qualities are so much more important
than the events that occur.**

Vince Lombardi, Hall of Fame NFL coach

Similar to the quest of playing in the zone, the search for the Holy Grail in bowling is never-ending. Players continually seek to find the ultimate solutions to flaws in their games and in their performances. They try to find the magic swing thought, the magic ball, or the magic coach. Month after month in the sports journals, articles are written about how to handle stress, pressure, and performance demands.

The problem is that sometimes, when handling the strains and excitement of competition, this search for the right magic is like raking the lawn by climbing into the trees. The real task is to get down to the ground level and handle things at the roots. When you can run your athletic experiences from the deepest part of you, you can be untouchable in terms of competition stress.

The deepest part is the truest part. You can call it the real self, the core self, or even the soul. A challenge arises when exploring this area of the mental game. As soon as we start looking at connecting at this deeper level, it's like stepping into forbidden territory. Generally, no one talks about this in sports.

When we think about bowling, with all of the grit involved, like leverage, sweat and effort, and getting your hand in and out of the ball correctly, there's no mention of anything called "soul." Images of college competitors shouting, players running shots out, and high fives being slapped all around leave little evidence for a higher part of the self on the lanes.

Depending on the way you frame it, there's a definite, powerful, and subtle aspect of spirit in bowling, as in any art or sport. We have other words for the experience of our spirit. As we've seen, athletes sometimes use the word "flow" or "the zone" to describe an exquisite feeling when bowling at their best. At the highest level of your bowling is that feeling of being completely connected, empty of needing to focus on extensive swing thoughts, and knowing that you're releasing maximum energy into the ball. In a sense, this might be considered a spiritual moment. For many athletes, the search for this experience is the reason they engage in sports.

Bolder Play

Before we go any further, I better define my terms. First, when people hear the word "spiritual," all kinds of images can come forth. Let me be clear.

While some religions might arguably be more spiritual than others, spirituality need have nothing to do with religion. When I propose that bowling, like most activities, can include an element of spirituality, please don't think I'm saying anything about religion or the ways in which anyone should worship. More on spirituality later.

When I say "bold play," you can take that to mean any of the following:

- Bowling with connection
- Bowling with flow or in the zone
- Bowling with trust
- Bowling with truth
- Bowling with well-being
- Bowling with freedom
- Bowling with exhilaration or joy

If you're at all competitive, you probably have a deep desire to feel open, free, strong, and aligned when you bowl. On their best days many champions have reported being completely absorbed in their shots and game. The awareness of others being present, the concern over what others might think, and the worry about the outcome of the match all fade into the background. This is the complete expression of yourself—some might say an expression of your soul.

To be completely absorbed in the moment of any endeavor can be a spiritual experience—or not. Plenty of people get involved in video games, TV, and beer without a trace of active connectedness. It all depends on the way you go about it.

I'm talking about the active involvement that comes with applying one's full concentration and mental efforts. When you're challenged, awake, alive, and creative while you bowl, you have a better chance to get into flow (though of course there's no guarantee). Once you hit this gear you gain a sense of mastery and control over your mind and body; you almost feel that you can *will* the outcome of your shots.

When you're in flow, the mental garbage pit of worry, desire, and chatter is absent. Instead you often feel limitless energy and a positive, sometimes joyful, mood state, a definite peace of mind.

So what makes this experience spiritual? Some might say that spirituality is the experience of ultimate truth. Whether you believe in a higher power, or simply in physics, there are some ultimate truths that can be embraced. One truth is that there's energy in the universe. Some energy is outside of you. Some energy is inside of you. There's energy in the earth. We live in a gravitational field. Now get this: No matter what force you believe in, if you want to bowl with greatness you must be one with this force.

Let's look at this from an energy management point of view. At the most elementary level of bowling, your job is to start the bowling ball in motion.

You actually appear to initiate the energy chain. If you're completely free, connected, and open, the ball falls to the end of your arm, rises behind you as you move forward in your approach, and then drops to join the earth. The ball then hits your hand and fingers, and to the degree to which the channel is clear, energy is transmitted into the ball.

If you're one with the force (of physics), for instance with your balance and unimpeded arm swing, then all of the stored energy in your body—which you acquired from the universe in form of oxygen, food, and sunlight—is transmitted into the bowling ball. The results can be spectacular, even cosmic.

Many athletes, including bowlers, believe in some kind of higher power, be it God, the unified quantum energy field, or some other energy source outside of themselves. If an athlete has this belief, the chain of energy starts earlier than just described (with our bowler) and ends later. The athlete feels a sense of connection, inspiration, and support from the source of creative energy, for some players, literally, "the creator." This inspiration essentially breathes life and energy into the physical action sequence of the bowling approach and delivery.

Within this framework, the bowler never feels cut off, alone, or empty. Also, following particularly well-executed shots, she might feel a sense of gratitude for the gifts and opportunities that allow for the experience. Bowling as a spiritual experience? Yes, it can happen. But use whatever language you like.

The Zone Revisited

As we've discussed, bowlers will often talk about being in "the zone"—those wonderful moments when everything clicks. When you talk to bowlers who have shot extremely high series, they'll often report that "it just happened." These bowlers moved to a higher level of performance, even for them. Even experienced champions might view their accomplishments as astounding.

In special circumstances, at certain times, everything is simple. The act of bowling, in every sense, is natural. It feels perfect. Time slows so that you play completely in your own rhythm. There is flawless anticipation of how to move, balance, and deploy shots. You're in a world all your own, like bowling with the mute button on. When it's over, it might feel as if you have emerged from a dream back into the real world. Someone has clicked the mute button back off.

If you're open to transcendent experiences, you can find them more easily in bowling than in most other places in life. Jobs, school, relationships, and all the demands of daily living seem to summon our life energy and drain it away. We are hit by meteor showers of sensory stimuli. The lights, noise, smells, and changing scores in the bowling center require immense amounts of energy to deal with. To manage all of this, many players simply have a beer and check out.

PLUGGING ENERGY HOLES

The energy of the mind is the essence of life.

Aristotle

It's no secret that bowlers stress about competition, results, money, and performing under pressure. When we use up energy dealing with these ego-based concerns, we have less energy available to focus, clear our heads, and detach from the pressures of trying to be impressive.

In religious and spiritual practices the great masters often recommend meditation to still the mind and open it to higher mental and emotional states. When an athlete can become still, she can get clear and clean from the normal strivings of competitive life. To attain a spiritual experience on the lanes you must first plug the holes that drain your sense of connection.

Here are three particular holes that drain energy out of yourself and the ball, and result in weaker bowling.

1. **Thinking too much.** Any time you're processing information, you are potentially taking energy flow away from the essence of your free self. The thought activity that you engage in is often chatter about technique, consequences of made or missed shots, and other life or bowling concerns. As you learn to truly arrive at one point of concentration and focus, this mental noise naturally eases off and away. The result is the peace and fulfillment associated with being in the zone.

2. **Dealing with other people.** When it comes to people, the bowling center is an energy-management ecosystem. Think of each interaction with other bowlers, coaches, family members, waitresses, and spectators as having a positive or negative impact on the battery of your psyche. You're responsible for knowing who are the givers and who are the vampires in your environment. You must give yourself permission to create your own space, especially in the moments before your shots.

3. **Overtensed muscles.** When coaches focus on mental relaxation, they often ask bowlers to calm down the wrong thing. The point is to relax the body, not necessarily the mind. This seems so counterintuitive to players and coaches that it deserves a couple of looks. You can grind as hard as you like on any part of your mental game. You can pick a spot on the lanes; you can crank up your mental intensity. It really doesn't matter. In order to have energy flow through your body, the body must be relaxed. So try not worrying too much about whatever your mind wants to do. Have it grind on something if you like. Just make sure the body is fluid.

In light of the principles outlined here, bowling has as much claim to expression of spirit as virtually anything you might do. You really do have to be one with the force. However you identify that force is up to you. Put it all together, and sparks will fly through your fingertips.

THE SEVEN DEADLY SINS OF BOWLING

**Being the best that you can be
is possible only if your desire to be a champion
is greater than your fear of failure.**

Sammy Lee

If we're going to discuss the zone, which is basically bowling heaven, for balance we should also look at bowling hell. These are the mental game hindrances—the deadly sins, if you will—that account for more pressure, more choking, and more competition wreckage than could probably ever be realized. Here we'll look at seven of the worst of them, along with ways to bolster your defenses against these pitfalls.

1. Approval Seeking

The need or desire to impress anyone besides yourself can cripple your bowling. Whether it's your coach, your teammates, your significant other, or your parents, you surrender your power when you feel you need to impress someone. This sin probably accounts for more league, tournament, or TV choking than any other single factor.

As soon as a bowler is bowling to impress someone else, he chips away at bowling from his true self, his true center. Many bowlers can still bowl with the backpack of approval-needs on their shoulders, but it never feels as free. They tend to tighten their muscles. And the fun and life of the game has had its plug pulled.

For a bowler to compete just one game without reflecting on the appreciation, approval, and acceptance of anyone else is to compete freely. Most bowlers have never played one whole tournament that way in their entire careers.

2. Perfectionism

There are three kinds of sin here. Everyone uses the term "perfectionism," but seldom is the three-headed monster that comprises this beast identified. First is the kind of perfectionism that most people think about: demanding that you execute perfectly. Arm swing, target, and footwork are all *supposed* to look a certain way. And, of course, your results are supposed to be amazing—perfect—as well.

The second ugly head of perfectionism is a team killer. Whether you're a coach or a teammate, demanding perfect execution and results from others can truly hurt your team's development. We've all heard, "I'm only demanding from them what I ask of myself." The problem is that what you ask of yourself borders on crazy, not to mention impossible, so you're asking others to be crazy, too.

The third head of perfectionism is the bowler's belief that others are demanding perfect bowling from them. Under such circumstances, the body cramps and tightens up, the mind swirls with mental noise, and decent bowling—much less perfect bowling—becomes a real challenge.

Perfectionism leads to stressing over making any kind of mistake. This causes anxiety, lowered confidence, and repetitive thinking about mistakes and failing. It's difficult to focus, concentrate, and enjoy the game with this going on. Remember angels can fly because they take themselves lightly! Make them your role models.

3. Being Unprepared for the Good, the Bad, and the Ugly

Most players are not really prepared for anything out of the ordinary, no matter how good or bad. In one outing, PBA star Michael Haugen Jr. shot 300-279-300 in a three-game series. What's striking about this is the amount of prosperity he was prepared to endure without sabotaging this spectacular set.

Not many bowlers can achieve such a feat mentally, independent of their physical skill. Many players will sandwich a 300 game between other pretty good games. Or, similarly, fit in a four or five bagger with a spare in the middle, and then continue striking.

There's a whole lot of clenching that occurs in the 10th frame when a perfect game is on the line. The same thing is true for the last several frames before an 800 series. Bowling extremely well brings its own kind of stressors and internal noise—*How am I doing this? Can I keep it up?* You must be ready to be great and not be thrown off when greatness occurs.

Frequently, bowlers will come back on the approach shaking their heads because a ball didn't strike, or because a sleeper pin continued to sleep on a spare shot. The expectation is that if you do all the right things, the pins will respond appropriately. But the truth is that good drivers get T-boned in intersections, good people get ripped off by con artists, and great bowlers do not carry the rack sometimes. If you expect life to behave differently, brace yourself.

Finally, worse yet, sometimes you don't feel good when you play. Sometimes you miss badly. Sometimes you just can't handle the lane condition. This is "the ugly."

You must prepare yourself for all of it—the good, the bad, the ugly—because if you bowl long enough, it's all going to happen.

4. Distraction: Voices Inside Your Head and Noises Outside

Whether it's doubt, negative self-talk, irritation, or fear, there's a lot of vibration that can prevent bowlers from focusing on what they do best—bowl. Outside noise might be other players stepping up on the approach, cheers for or against you, people talking on cell phones, or general chatter among spectators. Most bowlers have a personal pet peeve that bothers them more than other annoyances.

Counterintuitively, an attempt to control a mind that wants to roam leads to even more distraction. This is why you shouldn't try to push distractions away. Bowlers flirt with bowling hell when engaged in destructive self-talk, when they focus on what's going wrong, or when they try to attend to anything out of their control.

Rather, learn to attend to your inner self, and to direct your attention to empowering thoughts and feelings. You can then direct thoughts to actions you *can* take that will be effective.

You know that you can push away at the right time as you begin your steps. You know that you can let the ball begin its descent by itself. You know that you can summon up feelings that smack of courage, empowerment, and assertiveness. Teach yourself to control your decisions. You know what's important to focus on in order to make your best shot.

5. Getting Psyched-Out Before the Game

Painfully, players and teams who don't succeed have often scripted their results ahead of time. On the good side, the same is often true for those who triumph. In the average street fight, both combatants probably have a sense for who's going to win ahead of time.

Before a tournament or a PBA telecast, if you ask bowlers where they think they'll finish, their predictions will likely be close to accurate—based on self-belief, not skill! If you could get a *real* read on players' hearts and minds before playing someone with a big reputation, playing on TV, or facing a stout competitor in the finals, you would have an advanced preview of who had a chance to play to win. You would see who was playing on hope instead of conviction.

You must play with conviction. It doesn't matter who you're facing. Goliath was a 40-point favorite over David. All you need is a slingshot and the conviction to use it to your utmost ability.

6. Playing Not to Lose Instead of Playing to Win

Defensive driving works on the freeway, not on the bowling lanes. Playing defensively might help you stay on the lanes. It might even ensure that your ball gets to the pocket. But you'll generally get mowed down by other players who are playing to win.

Playing not to lose is a common mindset for self-protection. It's a form of taking all the deadly sins of bowling and converting them into a bad news competitive attitude. You might not look stupid playing this way. You might even stay relatively clean with respect to strikes and spares. But you'll also find yourself dissatisfied with pin carry, the constricted feeling in your muscles, and the joylessness with which you end up playing.

7. Focusing on Winning

**A gold medal is a wonderful thing,
but if you're not enough without it,
you'll never be enough with it.**

Irv Blitzer (John Candy) in *Cool Runnings*

This can be a confusing one. But think about it. Focusing on winning can be a fine motivator in practice. But it can be a confusing, stressful hindrance during competition. Focusing on winning before or during a competition has three accompanying problems:

1. If you're attached to having to win in order to be okay, you put your very *self* at stake. You might as well bowl with a gun to your head. Your bowling performance has nothing to do with your *self*.

2. Second, focusing on winning is like focusing on having a perfect game, or concentrating on getting a double—before you throw the first one! There's nothing really there to focus on.

3. Third, focusing on winning doesn't give you any cues or clues for effective ways of getting it done. Better that you should focus on aspects of the lanes, your body, or your competitive spirit. Focusing on winning is consuming empty mental calories.

Feed the Right Wolf

We've just looked at seven of the deadliest sins of competitive bowling. We're all human; hence we all err. Expecting to avoid all seven sins all the time is like expecting perfection, of which we've seen the dangers. Instead, always encourage yourself simply to do your very best every time. This constant reminder—100 times a day, if necessary—will contribute significantly to your well-being. It's always your choice: Do you feed the good wolf or the bad wolf?

FOURTEEN PRINCIPLES
OF BOMB-PROOF BOWLING

**Whether I fail or succeed shall be no man's doing
but my own. *I am the force*; I can clear any obstacle before me
or I can be lost in the maze. My choice; my responsibility;
win or lose, only I hold the keys to my destiny.**

Elaine Maxwell, author

Every athlete in the world wants to know that given the opportunity he or she will bring the very best of what they have trained for during competition. This has become a sort of Holy Grail of the mental game. In short, bowlers seek to establish the three Fs—to be free, to be focused, and to be forwarding (that is, to learn with each shot).

One of the goals of this chapter is help you become "bomb proof." This means that nothing that happens in the competition arena can destroy you, shake you, or undo you. Curiously enough, this tends to come easily to children. They focus on a goal, say tricycle riding, and really go after it. Even though they wipe out along the way, they remain undeterred. When they're really into it, nothing distracts them. They don't give up. A few falls don't keep them from achieving success.

Progressively over time we can only seek to become like children again, convinced of our invulnerability, knowing that we'll achieve whatever we set out to do, and ignoring the naysayers who suggest that we can't do something.

What follows is a set of practices, principles, and thoughts to assist you in developing a bomb-proof mindset. As in all things human, some transformations can be accomplished in the blink of an eye. Others require the mental grooving involved in any other kind of muscle memory.

   • **Bomb Proof Principle 1: Champions don't spend a lot of time and energy trying to make their feelings go away. They redirect and channel nervous energy into action.** The more attention you give to something, the more you give it power. Don't fight your mind. You only elevate the thoughts and fears with which you do combat. Take a cleansing breath, feel the freedom of being in a place that no one can touch you. Convert your energy into free-flowing power, and go.

   • **Bomb Proof Principle 2: Champions learn how to focus under virtually any circumstances.** A key to victory is to shrink the playing field to your immediate area. Think about what you would have to do if you were bowling on the green belt between two roads. You would need to have a narrow and select area of attention and commit to living there until your match was over.

      Don't expect people to be courteous, quiet, or even respectful. The world will behave however it chooses. You have the freedom to live entirely in your own space when you bowl.

   • **Bomb Proof Principle 3: Champions bring themselves into the zone by willing themselves to play with their hearts wide open.** Most bowlers have never played a tournament, top to bottom, in which they felt free the entire time. The decision to play wide open happens before one plunks down an entry fee. It's part of a visualized rehearsal that's part of daily life. It must be part of your intention as you lace up your shoes.

      Every part of your practice, your imagination, and your competition attitude should have this at the top of the priority list. No matter how much skill you develop, without this quality you will not consistently play in a manner you're capable of. Moreover, even when you win, you won't feel the satisfying boldness that champions get to enjoy.

   • **Bomb Proof Principle 4: Champion bowlers shake off errant shots and come right back with focused peak performance efforts.** Bowling is full of stories about bowlers who came back from bad shots, bad frames, and unfortunate tournaments. Nothing negative that happens in bowling should stick with you. In fact, many champions will tell you that great feats have been born of falls and temporary setbacks. Once the learning is over, everything else is "no thing." A shot is like a business deal. Once it's done, it's done. Now set up your next one.

   • **Bomb Proof Principle 5: Champions write their own stories in any given moment.** Great champions, great leaders, and great teammates are not bound by previous results, reputations, or the agreement or approval of others. To compete at the highest levels, the only authority you need is your own. Far too often players are bound by whatever happened before in their lives and the way that they previously defined themselves. In bowling, if you can take it, it's yours. The truth is based on results.

   • **Bomb Proof Principle 6: To make great shots and achieve maximum results over time, give up control over what happens after you deliver the shot.** There's probably no principle of play that we have to reteach and relearn more than this one. It's like a relationship. You can't make someone date you. All you can do is send really good love notes. Bowling is the same. It's a vulnerable enterprise. All you can do is deliver your best effort. Then live with it. This is perhaps the first lesson we should all learn as bowlers—and it's generally the last one we really understand.

   • **Bomb Proof Principle 7: Champions visualize the future.** In virtually every sport the great ones predict and prepare for what's going to happen. There are three places you can put the time machine of your mind: the lanes and ball, your body, and your attitude.

   If you were a competitive skier, you wouldn't just slouch into the starting gates, launch onto the course, and casually slide and turn through a race. You would know what it feels like to be completely centered, balanced, and focused. You would know where you want your attention to be, and you would know just how you like your hands to feel on the ski poles. You would spend time imagining crucial portions of the race, as well as the victory scenario. If you were really into it, you would probably do this even as you were lying in bed the night before the competition.

   Bowling is the same. You can imagine the ball path. You can project how you want your body to feel, from feet, to torso, to balance. See yourself shooting spares under the gun. Visualize any competition scenario you can imagine. Then live it before it occurs. After that, anything wonderful that happens you've already seen.

- **Bomb Proof Principle 8: Know what you intend to feel like at the line.** This principle involves feel more than visualization, though the objectives are similar to those of visualization. If you know what you intend to feel in your body when you're at the shot delivery position, your subconscious can go to work for you. You'll also perform the necessary adjustments on the way to the line. Last, if you do this step, and then add in a good post-shot analysis, you can be a great self-correcting bowler as you compete.

- **Bomb Proof Principle 9: The post-shot routine sets up all learning, adjusting, and improvement in your game.** This principle is so critical that it can't be overstated. Everyone talks about the preshot routine, which is extremely important, of course. But in the end, knowing what to adjust, correct, or recover from, comes from what you're immediately aware of after a shot, game, or tournament. Post-shot awareness is the first step in your preshot routine. Become disciplined in maintaining instantaneous awareness after a ball leaves your hand.

    The key here is to hold on to a clear, nonjudgmental hologram of the shot that just occurred. For just a moment, observe the ball roll, the lane reaction, the way the ball went through the pins, and what your body felt like. The keys to every adjustment you might make are in that snapshot.

- **Bomb Proof Principle 10: Have a "go" signal in your mind.** Every sport that self-starts, from gymnastics to golf to bowling, requires athletes to find their magic moment to begin. Whether you use a word such as *go, yes, or now*, or simply an intuitive feeling, find your perfect moment to initiate your approach. Take a breath, feel the right moment, and push. Don't ever initiate your motion if it doesn't feel like the right time for you.

- **Bomb Proof Principle 11: You create what you fear. There is nothing to be afraid of in bowling, anywhere or ever!** At some time in your career you'll have to discover this truth, or you'll never consistently bowl to your potential. Whatever we focus on enlarges and begins to dominate our mental field.

    If you have thoughts that tighten you up, do what baseball pitchers do. When they receive a sign from a catcher for a pitch they don't want to throw, the pitcher shakes the sign off until he gets one he likes. You can do the same thing with your thoughts and fears. Shake off any negative thoughts that enter your mind. Do this until you're able to replace the thoughts with positive, forward-thinking successful imagery about what you intend to do.

- **Bomb Proof Principle 12: No matter what else you do, commit to unconditional poise and execute with grace.** You win with grace. You miss with grace. A commitment to grace, poise, and unconditional self-acceptance will spear fear right through the heart. No fooling yourself by faking it here. It must be bone marrow deep, genuine acceptance of you and your results upfront, and after the shot or game is over.

- **Bomb Proof Principle 13: You must ask the right questions.** There are really only two essential questions you need to ask. The first is simply, *Am I present?* If you have your mind elsewhere, you'll immediately see that. The act of checking in with this question is that it automatically puts you back to the only moment in time that you should live in—this one!

The second question is, *What is called for here?* Other versions of this are, *What am I doing?* or *What do I need to know?* Whichever one you use, this is another orienting question. It brings you into the moment and provides an opportunity to get all parts of you pulling the wagon in the same direction.

What do I need to know? As mentioned earlier, this was Kari Schwager's silent question before each shot on the final day of the Mini-Eliminator. Kari is the only woman to win a Las Vegas Megabucks bowling tournament.

Now there are a number of questions that bowlers privately ask themselves that send them into a tizzy, including these:

Wrong list:	**Right list:**
What if . . .	Am I here?
I choke?	What is called for here?
I miss this spare?	What is my target?
I make a fool of myself?	How am I going to play this shot?
I don't make the cut?	What do I need to do to win this frame, game, match, or tournament?
I don't shoot the number?	What should I focus on?
I don't carry?	
I grab one?	
I don't get my exemption?	
This guy beats me?	
I just wasted my entry or bracket money?	

Remember that your mind can't help but answer what is asked of it. You'll find one way or another to resolve the question. Just make sure you ask the right ones!

- **Bomb Proof Principle 14: Issue one or two general orders, and that's all.** Typically, what works best is to have one physical key and one heart key. Your physical key, if you choose to have one, will change from time to time with your awareness of how you're bowling. Having one point of attention serves to coordinate your whole body, whether it's focusing your eyes, keeping your balance, maintaining soft hands, your third step, or whatever.

Your heart key is simply one of surrender to full commitment to the shot, as discussed earlier. Then, *get moving!* Believe that you know how to walk and bowl. Trust and faith are all or nothing processes, not to be measured on a 1 to 10 scale.

To be bomb proof is a way of living. It's what you were before life put doubts and fears into your mental game backpack. Beyond techniques, beyond luck, and beyond any circumstances, being bomb proof is knowing that you'll execute to the best of your ability. As for the previous list, practice what looks right for you. Like a buffet, take what tastes the best, sample the rest, and trust yourself to transform into the champion you were always meant to be.

YOUR COMPETITION TOOLBOX

Bowlers who advance in tournaments have mental game bags of tricks as familiar to them as their physical tools. Terms like *visualization, self-talk, championship attitude,* and *trust* are part of the vocabulary of many tournament players. Yet, during crunch time, many really great players can't remember how to employ these strategies in order to win.

This section is designed as a further preparation for bold play. In readying yourself for competition, you should assemble a competition toolbox—a summary of methods and techniques that work for many champions. It's handy to have a ready-made plan. This is a self-coaching tool you can throw into your bag for use as needed.

Five Techniques to Take Boldly With You

1. **Visualization.** This was discussed in the last section. The number one gold standard technique that has been used by athletes throughout the ages is visualization. Could you do it in a pinch right now? Could you do it for a national title? Let's hope so. It's one of the easiest, most effective tools you can pack in your bag.

Visualization keeps getting highlighted in the mental game. What makes this technique so important? Here's your answer: The mind and the nervous system can't make a distinction between a real event and one that's vividly imagined (Mindsport Ltd. 2007). As far as your brain is concerned, executing a shot perfectly in your mind's eye is almost like throwing the shot with the body. Your muscles actually get stimulated by your mind's eye.

Here's a brief training summary. Close your eyes and see your favorite bowling ball in your mind's eye. There, you just started. Now imagine, see, or sense yourself rolling your best shot. Boom! You just did it again. Now imagine a rolled ball along a line to your breakpoint; see the ball find friction and turn to the pocket. There you have it—you have taken your first steps toward visualization mastery.

You can play with this skill in a number of ways, too. You can think about how the ball feels in your hands. You can imagine feelings of happiness, thoughts of confidence, and the great feeling of great timing. You can even picture and hear the crack of the pins being blown around.

2. **Internal dialogue.** It's no secret that bowlers talk to themselves before, during, and after they roll their shots. Yet for something that has so much critical impact on how they perform under pressure, it's often surprising how little training or discipline players have in controlling their internal dialogue.

Bowlers engage in four primary kinds of self-talk:

1. **Positive:** *You can do this. Nice shot! This is your chance. Be great.*

2. **Negative:** *You stink. I always choke under pressure. What if I mess up?*

3. **Instructional:** *Keep your head down through the shot. Soft hands, Push, posture, post* (mantra of the 2004 U.S.B.C. Singles Champion John Janawicz who shot 858 for three games).

4. **Random:** *I wonder what we're doing tonight. If the Giants win, they'll be in first place. That girl bowling on lane three is hot.*

Your first move is to simply pay attention to what you actually do. Note that it's rare that beating yourself up verbally will help you in any way. Usually negative self-talk just bumps up self-loathing, anger, frustration, and doubt.

Positive self-talk can be a con job, so be careful. Whatever you use to bolster yourself has to be based in truth. You can remind yourself of the great things you've done before, the shots you have delivered, the assurance that you'll bring your best game, and the knowledge that you can play. Here's a key note: What you know with certainty in your mind will be reflected in your athletic actions.

3. **Cooling the engine.** The ability to calm yourself down, to relax, at least a little bit, while you play is very important to any bowler looking for peak performance. If you can keep yourself in an optimal state of activation while you compete, you can greatly reduce mental interference, such as doubt and worry. You can also prevent physical interference, such as nausea and shaking. Ultimately, your concentration and performance shoot up.

By far the easiest technique to learn and to practice is breath work. Try practicing any one of the following techniques for three seconds to two minutes. Once you become proficient at this, simply initiating breath work will signal your brain that it's time to relax. Note that you're never hyperventilating, picking up speed, or even having to stay with any technique past a breath or two.

- Focus on the rise and fall of your chest as you breathe. Make an internal note about how calm and steady your breathing is.

- Breathe down the *back* of your throat a couple of times. Notice how you take in extra air when you do this. This signals the brain that everything is safe and under control.

- Take one breath, and then take a second breath in before you exhale. You'll take in extra oxygen this way.

- Practice breath work once or twice every time you stop at a red light or get off of your cell phone. And always practice this during your preshot routine, and even after your shot. It might well change your life.

4. **Add an anchor.** A technique called *anchoring* can push reset in your brain and help create confidence as you bowl. On your exhales from any of the breathing techniques just listed, add a focusing or cueing word that sets up your desired state of being.

Examples of great cue words are *relax, smooth, laser, clean, one (won)*. Really, any simple word or short phrase can work to orient you to your best play.

An especially good time to add your anchor word is after a particularly sweet shot. See if a word appears. One probably will. Much like with imagery, this is when you mine the gold for future excellence. These anchor words work on exhales and as centering words for your self-talk before shots. So when you pull your anchor word out as part of your preshot routine, your brain and body gets into the appropriate gear for the moment.

5. **Flow to go.** Let's add one more word on relaxation; from a purely physical perspective, it might not really matter if you get your mind quiet. What matters is that you can relax the parts of your body that are important for shot delivery.

As mentioned earlier, there's a technique called progressive muscle relaxation. In this method, all you do is take four to six seconds to slightly overtighten the area of the body that you wish to relax. For soft hands, make a fist. To relax your brain (sort of), knit your eyebrows together and purse your lips (make sure you're off camera for this one). To settle your midsection down, do a half-curl with the arms along with a standing sit-up motion.

As with any physical motion, be respectful of your body. Don't do anything to the point of pain. Do not overtighten or tighten for too long. Check with your physician if you have a question about whether, or how, to do any of these exercises.

If all of this is too much for you, then do the absolutely simplest body relaxation move there is—wiggle your toes before you push the ball away. This will do two things. First, it helps you to balance correctly on your feet. Second, no one can stay tense when they're wiggling their toes!

They say that it's a poor workman who goes to the job site without his tools. The mental game tools in this section are as basic and essential as a hammer and a saw. Armed with this equipment in your personal arsenal, you're prepared to do battle anywhere, anytime. No opponent, no tournament, no TV finals could be too big. The world can be won with one determined warrior with the right arrows in her quiver—and now you have yours!

Ten Mental Game Tips That Build Careers

Beyond every other section in *Bowling Psychology*, this final section is a pure treat. In addition to the player profiles in each of the chapters in this book, there are secrets that some of the other top players and coaches in the world have mastered as well.

Many of these secrets apply particularly to playing under fire. In this chapter you get a peek into the mental game processes of some of the finest in the game. In some cases, one player or coach offers something that seems contrary to what another suggests. That's perfect because, just like the execution of the physical parts of the game, you need to see which tips match your personality and playing style. Simply take what works for you.

Tip 1: Bob Learn Jr.

Nicknamed "Mr. 300"—five PBA titles, including the 1999 U.S. Open, nearly 120 300 games, over 120 800 series.

"The dominant thought for me is not the relaxed mind, but more the aggressive attitude. In my mind when I am aggressive all fear goes away. When I am in attack mode that works best for me."

When asked how he feels when he has the first 9 or 10 strikes, nervous or at ease, Bob says, "You've got good ball reaction. You've got everything going for you. This is what you are here for. There's nothing to be afraid of. Everything is aligned for you. There is no better feeling than to get to throw three when it really matters. That's what you practice for."

Tip 2: Amleto Monacelli

20 PBA titles, 1989 and 1990 PBA Player of the Year, first international player to be awarded Player of the Year, PBA Hall of Famer

"When I need a strike to win a match or tournament, I don't think about the result. I keep myself in the present here and now. I think about how to make the best shot possible. When I didn't think about the future, that's when the results have been positive. If I think about something (distracting thoughts), I just focus on my breathing; I listen to the sound of my inhale or exhale. The sound gets me in the here and now without thinking about it, without having any expectation whatsoever."

Amleto has another strategy for pressure shots, especially in the finals. "When I am bowling on TV, or I am waiting for my shot, I am focused on the floor, and just thinking about that. Not thinking about making a result, or a strike or anything like that. But if I think about that, or look at someone else, I don't make a good shot. I already know what I need to do on the lanes. If I look at my opponent I get more anxious."

Tip 3: Diandra Asbaty

Over 60 international medals as member of Team USA, 2012 Queens winner, 2 PBA Women's series titles, two-time United States Amateur champion

Diandra's advice is similar to Amleto's: "Me just being me. Allowing myself to just be." She's clear that you can't force a result to occur. "Allow it to happen. Don't try to make it happen." This is probably the first thing that a player must learn, and sometimes the last thing we really understand.

(continued)

Ten Mental Game Tips That Build Careers *(continued)*

Tip 4: Fred Borden

Former Team USA head coach and advisor namesake for the Fred Borden USBC Gold Coach, USBC Hall of Fame

"Train your brain to improve your game. You have to have a training program that allows you to have a very clear picture in your brain of what you intend to do. Your brain can simulate 600 muscle movements simultaneously. The training program equals winning."

"The great ones have had the mindset of training hard, working hard, prepared to win. They have a precise clear plan. In your mind's eye, see your own perfect delivery. See the lanes played at the highest level without having to think about it, with a quiet mind. Just let it guide you around, and go ahead and do it."

"When you have a perfect picture, it will be free. A mixed picture is out of focus. It gives you a fuzzy picture and a bad shot. If there is one very important thing, it's the mental process and the mental picture. If you can design that for every aspect of your game, including the delivery and the lanes, then you can calm your mind."

"The more confidence you gain, the better you perform. That is the difference between winning and losing, and being a champion or not. All the great ones have this. They develop poise. They play in a dignified manner. The self-talk is 'I am a poised world-class athlete.' You must be ready for that test. The toughest time is when you are in the heat of the battle. Draw a line in the sand, and say, 'I will do this. I'm going to enjoy this ride.' If I can commit to that, and go through my routine, I have a pretty good chance of winning. You simply must have the proper attitude."

"Practice three times mentally and two times physically. If you're not ready to win, you're not going to win. You have to be able to say, 'I'm a world-class player, and I'm ready to win.' It is a journey, and you have to prepare."

"Don't make losing an issue. Make the good things an issue and remembrance, not all the bad things. I see a lot of people dwelling on the bad, not on the good, even right before the telecast. You have to say, 'I'm going to go play. Only two things can happen. I'm going to win or I'm going to lose. I'm going to enjoy the journey. I'm going to put my heart and soul into it.' And in the end you will win or not. That is all that there is."

Tip 5: Del Warren

USBC Gold coach, two-time PBA titleist, coach of national collegiate champion Webber International University

Del's comments on effective team play apply to individual competition as well. He keys on the importance of playing your own game, and removing both your ego and your fears from the field of play.

"You can't have a tug of war if no one is on the other end of the rope. You see teams have a letdown. The team then has to emotionally push. Then the other team thinks it has to push back. It does not have to be like that, really. In reality, if the other team pushes, and there is no one holding on to the other end of the rope, they are wasting their efforts playing someone who is focused only on their own bowling."

It's similar to individual match play. "When we play our best, we are sort of oblivious to our opponents. And they go to push, and there is nothing there, because we are so focused on what we are doing that we don't give a s**t what they're doing.

We are so focused and engaged and enjoying each other that we couldn't be less concerned that another team is looking at us. We're just bowling. There is no battle. We are not battling. We are just bowling. If the other team is having a tug of war, they'll fall on their butt. If we have an open, the next guy thinks he has to bowl better. Forget that. We just bowl. We cruise at 80 miles per hour (mph). The mistake is thinking that you have to go 90 mph. You don't. If you do that, it goes badly. There's no need. I'd rather have them dial down to 70 miles per hour and just be the best version of themselves."

"If you start saying, 'Oh we are bowling so and so.' That's the wrong attitude to have. I always believe that if we are at our best, we can win."

Tip 6: Leanne Hulsenberg

26 PWBA titles, two-time PWBA Player of the Year, USBC Hall of Fame

Leanne emphasizes understanding that in the competitive environment there are so many sights, sounds, and human behaviors, that any attempts to control them

Leanne Hulsenberg, USBC Hall of Fame bowler.

only lead to upset and frustration. "You have to know that virtually everything that is happening in the competition environment is supposed to be happening. Take the nerves, put them in your pocket. Know that they are there, and let them go."

Leanne's approach to excitement is a stabilizing approach. "Nerves are normal. Your heart gets pumping. There are all kinds of nerves." And she takes an empowered stance with respect to being amped up. Instead of feeling like a victim of her feelings, she takes the mental game driver's seat. "You have to know that you are where you want to be."

"You have to feel it come off of your fingers. You're not supposed to be thinking about your timing, or anything like that. You should be focused on the lanes. Everyone is different in terms of what they like to focus on. Maybe for some it's the push-away. Maybe someone else likes to feel it at the bottom of the swing. It was actually something that I learned working with [Dr. Dean Hinitz]. [Dr. Hinitz] told me to key on one thing only."

And, finally, like every great champion who ever played the game, Leanne extolls, "I never gave up, even when I was out of it. Some of my best tournaments were when I was behind. I had inner confidence that as soon as I got my feel and things came together, I would be okay."

Tip 7: Del Ballard Jr.

PBA Hall of Famer, USBC Hall of Famer, 13 PBA titles, including four major championships (The ABC Masters, the U.S. Open twice, and the Firestone Tournament of Champions)

Del extolls the vital process-versus-results message that's essential for managing your game, and for your ultimate success. "You can't make it happen; you have to let it happen. I see people who want it so bad that they can't execute. I see it in their eyes. I see it in their bodies. It's all about the process; it's not about the result. If you don't have the process, you're not going to get the result."

(continued)

Ten Mental Game Tips That Build Careers *(continued)*

When Del was on the pro tour, he had a technique for maintaining his rhythm and his orientation to the present moment. He used music to regulate his emotions and his physical game. This is something that anyone with an ear for music can practice. "I always had a song in my head. It got me in the right frame of mind. If I was throwing it hard, I had a hard rock song. If I was throwing it slow, I had a ballad in my mind. When I won the Tournament of Champions, I had 'Wanted Dead or Alive' by Bon Jovi going in my head. When I won the Masters, it was 'Wrap It Up I'll Take it' by The Fabulous Thunderbirds. I used 'Barracuda' by Heart when I needed to throw it hard. When I had to throw it soft, I used 'Still Loving You' by the Scorpions for the ballad."

Tip 8: Rod Ross

USBC Gold coach, head coach for Team USA and the International Training and Research Center (ITRC) at USBC headquarters, U.S. Olympic Committee Coach of the Year

Coach Ross' teams and athletes have won innumerable international and professional titles. He dispels some of the reverence sports psychologists sometimes have for self-talk (and I agree with his point of view). He feels that talking to yourself about what you're doing is counterproductive for smooth, flowing, trained athletic action. "I believe that you should not carry on a conversation with yourself while you're stepping up onto the approach. Words are to communicate with other people. But that's not how our body communicates."

"Sights, sounds, smells, and feelings are how we experience things. You have to shut down the analytical part of the brain, and open up the feelings. Sometimes you help a player focus on one part of the body. Other players visualize, and see themselves performing from outside. Even in training we have bowlers play in their mind five or six times and then throw it once. Instead of just rolling a ball."

"There are two problems with self-talk. One is that it can be lying to yourself. Your body and your mind know reality. If you're telling yourself things you don't believe, you know the truth. And, second, words require too much translation into the body. It's better to see yourself doing what you do. Turn thoughts into physical feelings. Get past the point of just seeing it, until you can feel it."

Tip 9: Tommy Jones Jr.

PBA Rookie of the Year, PBA Player of the Year, fastest to win 10 PBA titles after first win, 16 professional titles, U.S. Open champion, winner of Tournament of Champions, highest professional television win percentage

Tommy discussed the evolution in his thinking that allowed him to go from winless in his early years on the professional tour to having the best win percentage all time on television. The key for Tommy was to learn to manage his attention, his concentration, and the rate of speed of his thought processes. "My first couple of shows I bowled okay. But there was always those one or two shots that weren't so good. My mind would get ahead of the moment. I'd think about winning."

"When you compete, you try to improve the number of quality shots you make. When you're young, you think about winning. That doesn't work for you while you're competing. You have to stay 100 percent in the moment on TV. It goes by so fast. The biggest thing is slowing everything down."

A key for Tommy is emotion management. He balances his highs and his lows in order to keep himself in the most effective playing zone. "Don't get too excited on one lane because you're going to go to the next one. Not letting emotions carry you away is very important to me."

I was a big fan of the sport my whole life. As much as my job was to make money, that was not what things were about for me. It was always about winning a title in a PBA tournament. It was so easy to get ahead of it. Whether you are bowling for a PBA title, or even in league, you have to slow it down."

Tommy uses one of the all-time standard game management techniques. "One of the biggest things is to have a preshot routine. It needs to be the same every time. Control your breathing."

Tommy is not afraid of his feelings. Instead he encourages embracing the competition experience. "Being nervous is part of the fun of it. You're doing what you are trained to do and what you love. My first two shots on TV, even now, I have to slow the whole process down. I am amped up, but that's when it's the most fun. I get closer to normal, maybe 30 percent above normal. Then my shots are repeatable."

"Last, it helps to play for something more than me—for example, if I'm with a team. Some people are different. Some play better when they are mad or worked up. You have to know yourself; you have to know what makes you go."

Tip 10: Jason Couch

PBA Hall of Fame, 16 PBA titles, winner of four major championships, including three consecutive Tournament of Champions titles

A poster printed years ago said the following: "The Tournament of Champions, where players go to lose to Jason Couch." When you win three major championships in a row, people wonder what you eat for breakfast. I asked Jason about the magic, and it turned out that his answers were far more human than magician. "Honestly, the best thing I did was keep everything in the rear-view mirror. I never thought about defending my title, or winning three in a row. It was just another major."

For Jason, training and preparation are key. You don't coast into spectacular success. "I prepared ahead of time physically. The majors are more demanding, physically and mentally. You have to take full advantage of practice sessions. I used to see guys who would go down for 10 minutes during a practice session, get lined up, and leave. I acted like I was competing the whole time—lots of preparation. Richard Shockley (USBC Gold coach) would work with me so hard in my practice sessions. Then he would tell me, 'Don't forget to shut off your brain when you play.'"

It wasn't just pressing reset each time for Jason. "To be honest with you, Doc, it was three different cities, three different formats (each Tournament of Champions). I approached every major as a new event to conquer. Majors mean more to players. I approached every one as a brand new event. You knew at the end of the week that you would be exhausted. I won the tour players championship in 1993. In 1999 and 2000, I bowled for the title at every major. I seemed to take full advantage of it at every opportunity. These events are so demanding, I don't consider second a major loss. Any top 10 is a success."

Jason learned the value of maintaining your poise and a sense of confidence no matter what the circumstances. "I got a really great piece of advice from a Hall of Famer. For years I roomed with Parker Bohn. I was losing a lot on TV. Parker asked me why I thought that was happening. I said to Parker, 'I don't want to let my fans down.'

(continued)

Ten Mental Game Tips That Build Careers *(continued)*

He said, 'You're crazy, you don't want to approach it like that. Act like you know you are going to win, and show them why you are the best bowler that week.' I bowled with determination after that. It's amazing what confidence can do. You have to prepare yourself for different formats, TV, etc. Every single time you have to experience every part of it. It becomes second nature to you. It doesn't become TV, it's just your job."

Once again, Jason cites one thing you can pack with you and take anywhere you travel to play. "You have to have a great preshot routine. Your body takes over without you thinking about it. There were shows that I would bowl that I would have to look over to see what frame I was in. Sometimes it would be the fourth frame, sometimes it would be the eighth. I would just get up and do my preshot and roll. Just get up there and do your job.

Jason visualizes his outcomes upfront. "I concentrate on one particular spot on the lanes. I will visualize how I want my ball to go through the target. Then I commit fully to what I'm doing. If you have any doubt about what you're doing before you get up on the approach, then don't get up on the approach. I go up there and have more fun now. I truly relish the times I get to get up there on the lanes."

THE LAST WORD ON PLAYING BOLDLY

**Do you want to be safe and good,
or do you want to take a chance and be great?**

Jimmy Johnson, football coach of 1992 and 1993 Super Bowl champion Dallas Cowboys

Wrapping up what it takes to play this game with courage is a final listing of cues to stuff into your bowling bag. The word *courage* is derived from Latin. It means to tell the story of who you are with your whole heart. If you do this, then you have a shot at the same greatness that any Olympian has ever had—just in a different venue.

Here are 10 essential championship principles. By now, you already know them all, but here they are in one place. Make sure you understand them well. Then coach them. Practice with them. Play with them. These principles are the basic nutrients that will lead you to championship bowling.

1. **In any competition, at any level, you must be committed to bowl greatly. Do not play the game to avoid playing badly.** Commit to the spirit of your game. One way to get fooled in competition is to think that if you're simply bowling with proper execution that you're playing championship ball. Playing to avoid bowling badly will tighten you up, get you into aiming mode, and freeze your moves on the lanes.

2. **Whether it's practice or competition, you must love the challenge that the day presents to you.** It's common for bowlers to complain about all kinds of problems. We hear things about lane conditions, approach surfaces,

equipment problems, and physical game aspects being out of tune. Anything that appears as a challenge becomes a factor that makes the game interesting for you. You must really appreciate the fun and opportunity of encountering, facing, and ultimately overcoming challenges. Just like in life.

3. **Stop sweating your results and get completely involved in the process of enjoying the feel of your best stroke.** You have to love how it feels to execute a great shot. The game itself has to feel better than the score. You're an athlete—enjoy feeling like one.

4. **You have to know upfront that virtually nothing that happens during the course of play can make you lose your cool.** If people, pins, and performance must turn out a certain way for you to be OK, you've made yourself a hostage to the universe. Nothing in a performance arena should own you. You must be very clear long before the competition that this is true for you. Prepare to handle anything, and you will.

5. **In the moments of shot execution, bowling is the most important thing you do. However, you must know that before and after your shot, in the grand scheme of your life, that it's not.** When you know that the next 10, 30, or 50 frames are simply the middle frames of the million or so tournament frames you'll bowl over your lifetime, it takes the heat off. You can care. You can make things matter. You can prepare for the important moments in your competition career. The thing to watch out for is that care does not turn into worry.

6. **You must believe completely in the game you play, the game you brought, and your ability to execute the game in your way.** You have to know what you do, what your physical keys are, and then you must believe, not hope, that what you're going to do will work. This is probably more important for spare shots than for your initial shot.

7. **You should be using visualization on every single shot.** The most well-recognized form of visualization is to see the ball path on the lanes. But despite its name, visualization is not always visual.

You can also use visualization to get your mind right for ball speed, ball rotation, and even skid, flip, and roll. You need not tell your body what to do to achieve this. If these skills are in your arsenal, you simply have to see them happening in your mind's eye. Visualize perhaps one physical key that creates the ball motion, and then trust yourself to execute what you have seen.

A third kind of visualization involves your body. You can know the feeling ahead of time of a perfect push-away, steady and smooth approach, and leveraged release. You can pick any feeling in the body, use your mind as a time machine, and let yourself unfold with the physical part of your visualized experience.

8. **Roll every shot with mental and physical authority.** Decide where you're going to play the lanes, including on your spare shots, and then shelve any doubts you have about whether your decision was a good one.

Clarity about what you intend to do, commitment to follow through with it, and the willingness to adjust ball, line, or body based on what you learn, is the essence of this principle. All things stem from this decision-making command post. What you're certain will happen will tend to happen. What you're uncertain about will cause distortion in your execution.

9. **Be the best partner a bowler like you could have.** Your self-talk must be self-supporting. If you're a self-punisher, you risk creating the kind of long-term pressure that produces choking. Two other consequences for self-punishment are a seriously delayed learning curve and losing sight of the inherent joy in athletic endeavors.

10. **Fall in love with the physical feel of your game.** In any sport, the physical joy of performing the movement is both a reason to do the sport, as well as what you fall back on under pressure. Few bowlers can tell you off the top of their heads what they enjoy about their game. Yet remembering what you enjoy about your setup, approach, swing, and release clears blind spots in the swing, prevents and cures burnout, and opens the way to reach for greatness under all circumstances.

There you have it. As the old saying goes, "You play like you practice." Practice winning by following these 10 principles. By putting them into play, you'll wring the most out of your game. One reason players tighten up in competition is the unfamiliarity of playing with their whole heart. If you practice using these principles, the finals will feel remarkably similar to the way you live your life.

MAKE A BOLD PROMISE

You are never given a wish without also
being given the power to make it come true.
You may have to work for it, however.

Richard Bach, writer

Finally, make a bold promise to yourself. The only thing that ever made anything great happen is pure commitment. Here are five commitments worthy of a champion:

1. I'll keep my composure on each and every shot. I'll be mentally tough no matter what happens.
2. I'll have the discipline to believe in myself, my game, and my ability to figure it out, no matter what happens.
3. I'll view every shot as an opportunity to meet a challenge.
4. I'll view virtually everything that occurs in the bowling center as part of my learning and improvement process.
5. I'll have a phenomenal time playing this game!

Give your word to these five, if you dare. Your bowling, your very life itself, will turn out roughly to the degree that you keep your word. The world is about a quart low on people willingly to play boldly. We could use a few more like you.

Bibliography

Arbinger Institute, The. 2010. *Leadership and self-deception: Getting out of the box.* San Francisco, CA: Berrett-Koehler Publishers, Inc.

Canfield, Jack. 2005. *The success principles.* New York: HarperCollins.

Coop, Richard. 1993. *Mind over golf.* New York: Wiley Publishing Co.

Davis, Martha, Elizabeth Robbins Eshelman, and Matthew McKay. 1995. *The relaxation and stress reduction workbook.* New York: MJF Books.

Douglas, Cherry. 2016. Overcoming self-doubt. http://www.how-to-change-careers.com/overcoming-self-doubt.html.

Dudiy, Sergey. 2002. www.time-management-guide.com.

Feldman, R., 2014. *Understanding psychology.* 12th edition. New York: McGraw-Hill.

Goldberg, Alan. 2015. The mental side of athletic injuries. https://www.competitivedge.com/rebounding-injuries-0

Gould, Daniel. 1986. Goal setting for peak performance. In *Applied sport psychology* by Jean Williams (ed.). Palo Alto, CA: Mayfield Publishing Co.

Gould, Daniel, Kristen Dieffenbach, Aaron Moffett. 2002. Psychological characteristics and their development in Olympic champions. *Journal of applied sport psychology*, 14(3): 172–204(33).

Hinitz, Dean. 2013. Laser focus. *Bowling this month.* 20(1).

Hinitz, Dean. 2012. Steel mind. *Bowling this month.* 19(11).

Hinitz, Dean. 2011. Tough enough. *Bowling this month.* 18(1): 35-37.

Hinitz, Dean. 2007. The answer. *Bowling this month.* 14(4).

Hinitz, Dean. 2005. Visualizing your success. *Bowling this month.* 12(6).

Hinitz, Dean. 2002. Bowling dangerously. *Bowling this month.* 9(12).

Janssen, Jeff and Greg Dale. 2006. *The seven secrets of successful coaches: How to unlock and unleash your team's full potential.* Cary, NC: Winning the Mental Game.

Klemmer, Brian. 2004. *If how-to's were enough we would all be skinny, rich, and happy.* Tulsa, OK: Insight Publishing Group.

Kubistant, Tom. 1986. *Performing your best.* Champaign, IL: Life Enhancement Publications.

May, Jerry R., and Michael J. Asken (eds.). 1987. *Sport psychology: The psychological health of the athlete.* New York: PMA Publishing.

McDougall, Christopher. 2009. *Born to Run: A Hidden Tribe, Superathletes, and the Greatest Race the World Has Never Seen.* New York: Vintage.

Millman, Dan. 1984. *Way of the peaceful warrior.* Berkeley, CA: Publishers' Group West.

Millman, Dan. 1999. *Body mind mastery.* Novato, CA: New World Library.

Mindsport Ltd. 2007. http://mindsportlive.com/Articles/Article/?articleId=236, Get in the Zone.

Murphy, Shane. 1996. *The achievement zone.* New York: Putnam.

Nideffer, Robert. 1985. *Athletes' guide to mental training.* Champaign, IL: Human Kinetics.

Orlick, Terry. 2008. *In pursuit of excellence.* 4th edition. Champaign, IL: Human Kinetics.

Parent, Joseph. 2002. *Zen golf.* New York: Doubleday.

Porter, Kay, and Judy Foster. 1986. *The mental athlete.* Dubuque, IA: William C. Brown.

Proctor, Bob. 2010. *You were born rich.* Scottsdale, AZ: LifeSuccess Productions.

Rotella, Bob. 2001. *Putting out of your mind.* New York: Simon & Schuster.

Shoemaker, Fred, and Jo Hardy. 2006. *Extraordinary putting.* New York: Perigee.

Siebold, Steve. 2014. 177 Mental Toughness Secrets of the World Class. www.mental-toughnesssecrets.com.

Team Builders Plus. 2015. *Team building lessons we can learn from geese.* http://teambuild-ersplus.com/articles/team-building-lessons-we-can-learn-from-geese

Tracy, Brian. 2002. *Focal point.* New York: AMACOM Books.

Tuckman, Bruce W. 1965. Developmental sequence in small groups. *Psychological bulletin,* 63(6): 384–399.

Valiante, Gio. 2013. *Golf flow.* Champaign, IL: Human Kinetics.

Vealey, Robin. 1986. Imagery training for performance enhancement. In *Applied sport psychology* by Jean Williams (ed.). Palo Alto, CA: Mayfield Publishing Co.

Vernacchia, Ralph, Rick McGuire, and David Cook. 1996. *Coaching mental excellence.* Portola Valley, CA: Warde Publishers.

Vint, B. 2008. *The Windy City Bowling News.* East Troy, WI. Sept. 2008.

Vint, B. 2015. *Memphis' Gary Faulkner Jr. Wins First Title in Rolltech PBA World Championship.* December 17, 2015. www.news.PBA.com.

Wagner, Christopher C. 2011. Motivational interviewing: resources for clinicians, researchers, and trainers. http://www.motivationalinterview.net

Waitzkin, Josh. 2007. *The art of learning.* New York: Free Press.

Walton, Shannon. November 2009. Dealing with defeat. http://sportspsychologyconsultant.blogspot.com/2009/11/dealing-with-defeat.html.

Weinberg, Robert, & Gould, Dan. 2015. *Foundations of sport and exercise psychology,* 6th edition. Champaign, IL: Human Kinetics.

Worthington, Valerie. 2015. Developing self-awareness: a messy, ugly, five-step process. http://breakingmuscle.com/sports-psychology/developing-self-awareness-a-messy-ugly-five-step-process.

Index

Note: Page references followed by an italicized *f* or *t* indicate information contained in figures and tables, respectively.

A

acceptance 84-85
action plans 13-17, 14*f*, 16*f*
adversity, dealing with 84, 135-139, 146-150, 205
alcohol and drugs 144-145
Allen, Patrick 95
all-or-nothing thinking 126
anchoring 214
anticipation 52-53
anxiety 41
approval seeking 140-141, 204
arousal 51-53
arrows, marking cross 96
Asbaty, Diandra 62-64, 215
authority, bowl with 221
autographing your shot 75-76
awareness 56-57

B

Ballard, Del, Jr. 123, 217-218
ball path and speed visualization 111, 114
Barnes, Chris xii, 29, 94-95, 122
Belmonte, Jason vi-ix, 9, 24-26, 62
blaming 121
Bohn, Parker 219-220
bold play 195-196, 200-202, 215, 220-223
bomb-proof bowling 207-212
Borden, Fred 162, 216
boredom 147-148
bowling performance evaluation logs 12, 13*f*
breaks, from bowling 123, 145
breathing skills 64-66, 213-214

burnout
    about 140-141
    curing 145-146
    preventing 142-145, 143*f*
    signs and symptoms 141-142

C

care *vs.* worry 78
catastrophizing 126-127
champion thinking 138-139
change and growth 178
choking 55, 57, 188
Ciminelli, Ryan 49
clearing and recovery (shot cycle) 59-60, 61
coaching 121, 123, 154, 170
    about 171-172
    advanced concepts 181-183
    bowlers' resistance to change 177-179
    checklist for championship 187-188
    confrontation and humiliation in 179-180
    focus and attention exercise 184-185
    four steps to magic 180-181
    one-shot coaching 177
    parent as 189-192
    principles of 172-176
    as a process 183
    self-awareness goals 184
    teaching love of the game 186-187
    tips approach 183-184
collegiate bowling xiv
comfort zone, outside of 86-87
commitment 33, 36*f*, 101-102, 120, 162, 173-174, 181, 220

communication
    coaching and 175
    on teams 153, 160-164
competition cycle, mastering
    about 54
    clearing and recovery 59-60, 61
    execution and commitment 55-56, 61
    observation without judgment 56-57, 61
    planning and intention 54-55, 60-61
    reaction and emotion 58-59, 61
competition environments 38, 80, 114, 216, 220-221
competition outcome goals 9, 10
competition toolbox 212-214
concentration 37, 72, 73, 87-90
    mindfulness and 87-90
concentric circles of attention 154-155, 154*f*
confidence 37, 72, 73, 96, 128, 174-175, 216, 217, 220, 221
consistency 47
control 37
Couch, Jason xv, 219-220
courage 220
criticism 130, 131

D
deep practice 3
Delaware State University 20
DeVaney, Mike 29
distractions 79, 83, 165, 199, 206, 215
Dorin-Ballard, Carolyn xii, 21, 39-40, 62, 138
doubles bowling xiv
doubts 195-196
drive, internal 159
Duke, Norm xii, 4, 77

E
Edwards, Jeri xiv, 62, 190-192
emotions
    emotional pain 147
    management of 219
    mindfulness and 87-90
    recognition and awareness of 51-53

    redirecting 208
    in shot cycle 58-59, 61
    and slumps 119-120
    when losing 137
energy holes, plugging 203-204
excellence thinking 132-133, 134*t*
excitement 51-53
    regulating 61-69
execution and commitment (shot cycle) 55-56, 61
exercise 144-145
experience, championship 28-29

F
Fagan, Mike xiv, 121, 122-123
family 154, 189-193
fatigue xii
Faulkner, Gary, Jr. 49
fear 52-53, 210, 216
fear busting 77-79
feedback
    on goals 12-13, 13*f*
    during slumps 130-132
    on your perceptions 160
feel 44, 98
feelings 208. *See also* emotions
fight-or-flight response 52-53, 65
flow 61, 65, 66, 81, 101, 196-202, 214
focus 214
    of champions 208
    commitment to 103
    as essential xii, 33, 36*f*
    focus and attention exercise 184-185
    for mental toughness 79-83
    in preshot routine 42-43
    through silence 4
    on winning 207
Focused for Bowliing (Hinitz) xi, xiii, 50
forehead, tension in 66-67
fourth-arrow system, for spares 106-108, 108*f*

G
gamesmanship, for teams 164-168
goal setting
    about 1-2

goal setting *(continued)*

 action plans 13-17, 14*f*, 16*f*

 bowling goal achievement journal 15, 16*f*

 bowling performance evaluation logs 12, 13*f*

 burnout and 141

 and championship mindset 27, 33, 36*f*

 competition outcome goals 9, 10

 evaluating results 12-13, 13*f*, 17-18

 five steps to excellence 17-18

 integrity in 10-12

 Kim Kearney on 7-8

 nine secrets of goal attainment 2-5

 personal performance goals 6, 8-9

 self-assessment 184

 setting clear vision 5-10

 for teams 152, 162-163

Gomez, Andres 32

go signals 97, 210

grace and poise 210

H

Hall, Bill 111

Haugen, Michael, Jr. 94-95, 205

Healy, Patrick, Jr. xiv, 95

heart keys 98, 212

Hoffman, Bill 111

Holman, Marshall 32

honesty 164

hoping 6, 101-102, 206

Hulsenberg, Leanne (Barrette) 74-75, 217

I

imagery, positive 67-68, 78

injury, dealing with 91-93, 135-136, 147

instincts 197

instructional self-talk 213

integrity 10-12, 172

intention 101-102, 133

internal drive 159

International Art of Bowling 62

intimidation 165-166

J

Janawicz, John 43

jaws, tension in 66-67

Johnson, A.J. 29

Johnson, Liz 122

Jones, Tommy, Jr. 29, 122, 218-219

Jurek, Jack 122

K

kaizan 17

Kearney, Kim xii, 7-8, 20-21

Koivuniemi, Mika 95

Kulick, Kelly xii, 60, 62

L

labeling 127

lane conditions 38, 41, 42

 adapting to 4

Larsen, Martin 29

laziness 3

leadership 155

Learn, Bob, Jr. 215

Lewis, Mark 162

lights 38, 41

limiting beliefs 148-149, 206

long-term goals 11

losing, dealing with 136-137

love of the game, teaching 186-187

M

mastery, nature of 3

mechanism, spare-shooting 102-103

mental game checklist 131*f*

mental game tips from pros 215-220

mental laziness 82

mental toughness

 about 70-71

 accept unchangeable conditions 84-85

 autographing your shot 75-76

 in championship mindset 33, 36*f*

 fear busting 77-79

 five steps to 85-86

 focus for 79-83

 inventory for 71-74

mindfulness and concentration for 87-90
   outside comfort zone 86-87
   Samurai game 76-77
mindfulness 87-90
mind games, team 164-168
mindset, championship
   about 20-21
   adversity and 31
   experience fallacy and 28-29
   Jason Belmonte on 24-26
   process of 27
   self-assessment and 23-27
   self-concept and 21-22
   street fighting 30-31
   traits of 32-35, 36*f*
   will 22
Minshew, Susie xiv, 104-108
Monacelli, Amleto xv, 112, 215
motivation 33, 36*f*, 72, 73-74, 141, 159
muscle memory 30
muscle relaxation, progressive 66-67, 203-204, 214

N
negative thoughts 23-27, 25, 81-82, 124-127, 137, 206, 213
nerves or nervousness 50, 52-53
noise 38, 41
Norton, Scott 49, 51
notebook, bowling 11
nutrition 141, 144-145

O
observation without judgment (shot cycle) 56-57, 61
O'Neill, Bill xiv, 112-113
opponents 38
optimism 33, 36*f*
overanalyzing 113, 203
overconfidence 22
overgeneralizing 126

P
Page, Rhino 24, 44
pain 147

Palermaa, Osku vi, vii
panic 41
parenting youth bowlers 189-193
peak performance 101
perfectionism 33, 36*f*, 127, 132-133, 134*t*, 140, 204-205
personal performance goals 6, 8-9
pessimism 125
physical game checklist 131*f*
physical keys 98, 211-212
planning and intention (shot cycle) 54-55, 60-61, 65
playing modes 26-27
playing not to lose 206-207
poise and grace 210
polyester balls 105
positive expectations 33, 36*f*, 197
post-shot routine 210
potential, achieving maximum xii
practice
   deep practice 3
   focus and concentration during 3
   practice habits 2-3, 4
prediction and control 38-41
presence 44-45, 54, 100-101, 199, 211, 215, 218
preshot routine
   about 37
   Bill O'Neill 112-113
   breathing routine 65-66
   Carolyn Dorin-Ballard on 39-40
   creating 42-43
   cues 43
   doubts and failure 45-46
   internal self-direction 38
   mental toughness and 83
   orienting questions 45-47, 211
   prediction and control 38-41, 42
   presence 44-45
   setting up 41-42
   for spare-making 101
   three Cs 47-48
   triggering the zone or feel 44
pressure situations 10, 71, 73, 199
process improvement path 50, 217-218

progressive muscle relaxation (PMR) 66-67, 214
pscyhed out 206

Q

quiet mind 33, 36*f*
quitting bowling 146-149

R

reaction and emotion (shot cycle) 58-59, 61, 188
reading, about bowling 3, 6
Reid, Trisha 21
relaxation, regulating 61-69, 213-214
resiliency 71, 73
responsibility, taking 120, 133
rest 142-144
Rodriguez, Maria Jose 60
Ross, Rod 218
Roth, Mark 32
Russell, Ronni 112

S

Samurai game 76-77
scapegoating 121
Schwager, Kari 44
self-assessment 12-14, 13*f*, 23-27, 28, 184, 210
self-coaching 182
self-doubt 23, 126-127
self-talk, positive 213, 218, 222
    of Carolyn Dorin-Ballard 40
    for confidence 68-69
    facing fear with 78
    with imagery 68, 69
    not needing 183
    in preshot routine 44
    in slumps 128-130
seven deadly sins of bowling 204-207
short-term goals 11
shot cycle
    about 49-51
    being in sync 50, 51
    breathing skills 64-66
    imagery, positive 67-68

    managing excitement 53-54
    mastering competition cycle 54-60
    muscle relaxation, progressive 66-67
    recognition and self-awareness 51-53
    review of 60-61
    self-talk 68-69
shots, mastering variety of 5
silence 4
Sill, Aleta 39
sleep 141, 142-144
slumps
    changing thinking 128-130
    excellence *vs.* perfectionist thinking 132-133, 134*t*
    faulty belief systems 118
    feedback 130-132
    markers of 117-119
    mental traps 124-125
    Mike Fagan on 122-123
    perfectionist thinking 132-133, 134*t*
    taking action 119-124
    thinking disorders 125-127
Snell, Brad 91
soul 200-202
spare balls 103
spares, making
    about 94-95
    commitment 103-104
    finishing 104
    formula for 99-104
    Minshew's system for 104-108, 107*f*, 108*f*
    O'Neill's approach to 112-113
    same-side shooting 108-109
    system for 104-108, 107*f*
    tips for 95-98
    visualization 109-111, 114
spiritual play 200-202
sport intelligence 34, 36*f*
staying in the present. *See* presence
Steelsmith, Rick 91-93
stress, dealing with 34, 36*f*
succeeding, dealing with 137-139
suggestion 166, 167
support people 26

ιc, being in 50, 51

T
Tackett, E.J. 49
teams, bowling
  about 151
  components of best 152-156, 154f
  gamesmanship 164-168
  stages of team development 168-170
  team building and communication 160-164
  training principles of 156-160
Team USA xiv, 20
thinking distortions 125-127
toughness, mental. *See* mental toughness
Traber, Dave 77
training
  commitment to 5
transformation 178-179
Tuckman, Bruce 168

V
Vadakin, Gordon xiv, 161-162
Vermilyea, Amanda (Burgoyne) 190
victim attitude 85, 120, 158

video recordings 130
vision, setting a clear 5-10
visualization 63, 212-213, 216, 220, 221
  champions' mindset 209
  for making spares 97, 98, 109-111, 114
  in preshot routine 43

W
Waliczek, Lonnie 182
wanting 101-102
Warren, Del 123, 216-217
Weber, Pete 29, 122
Williams, Walter Ray, Jr. 29, 112, 122, 138
winning, focusing on 207
Wiseman, Danny 122
wishing 101-102
women's bowling xiv
work ethic 2-3

Y
youth bowlers, parenting 189-193

Z
zone, in the 44, 81, 196-202, 209, 214, 219

About
the Author

Dean Hinitz, PhD, has been practicing sport psychology for more than 30 years. He is the sport psychologist for the U.S. bowling team, with facilities at the International Training and Research Center at USBC headquarters in Arlington, Texas, previously training at the United States Olympic Training Center in Colorado Springs. He is the lead mental game consultant in revising the curriculum for the United States Bowling Congress Gold Coaching Program.

Hinitz has been the consulting sport psychologist for esteemed bowling programs at Wichita State University, University of Maryland Eastern Shore, Robert Morris University, and Webber International University—all of which have won national championships. He is the consulting psychologist for the Trevino Golf Institute and has consulted to the gymnastics team at the University of Minnesota as well as to the men's basketball and baseball teams and the women's volleyball and basketball teams at the University of Maryland Eastern Shore. He is also a consultant to the athletic department at Georgetown University in Washington, DC.

Hinitz has worked with numerous champions on the men's and women's pro bowling tours as well as with many amateur champions. For more than 10 years, he was a staff writer for *Bowling This Month*. He is considered by many to be the leading authority worldwide on the mental game of bowling.

Hinitz earned his PhD in psychology from the University of Nevada at Reno, where he is an adjunct professor. He is a former governor's appointee to the Nevada State Board of Psychological Examiners and was previously the chief of psychology at West Hills Hospital in Reno. Hinitz maintains a private practice in Reno.